# Political Theory, Modernity and Postmodernity

οὔκουν ἐμόν γε περὶ αὐτῶν ἔστι σύγγραμμα οὐδὲ μή ποτε
γένηται· ῥητὸν γὰρ οὐδαμῶς ἐστιν ὡς ἄλλα μαθήματα, ἀλλ᾽ἐκ
πολλῆς συνουσίας γιγνομένης περὶ τὸ πρᾶγμα αὐτὸ καὶ τοῦ
συζῆν ἐξαίφνης, οἷον ἀπο πυρὸς πηδήσαντος ἐξαφθὲν φῶς,
ἐν τῇ ψυχῇ γενόμενον αὐτὸ ἑαυτὸ ἤδη τρέφει.

Plato, Seventh Letter 341d

# Political Theory, Modernity and Postmodernity

## Beyond Enlightenment and Critique

### N. J. Rengger

BLACKWELL
Oxford UK & Cambridge USA

First published 1995

Blackwell Publishers, the publishing imprint of
Basil Blackwell Ltd
108 Cowley Road
Oxford OX4 1JF

Basil Blackwell Inc.
238 Main Street
Cambridge, Massachusetts 02142
USA

*British Library Cataloguing in Publication Data*

A CIP catalogue record for this book is available from the British Library.

*Library of Congress Cataloging-in-Publication Data*
Rengger, N. J. (Nicholas J.)
  Political theory, modernity, and postmodernity : beyond enlightenment and critique / N. J. Rengger.
      p.    cm.
  Includes bibliographical references and index.
  ISBN 0-631-19158-5. – ISBN 0-631-19159-3 (pbk.)
    1. Political science – History.  2. Modernism.  3. Postmodernism.  I. Title.
JA83.R468  1995
320 – dc20

94-46741
CIP

Typeset on 11/13pt Sabon
by Best-set Typesetter Ltd., Hong Kong

Printed in Great Britain by Hartnolls Limited, Bodmin, Cornwall

This book is printed on acid-free paper.

# CONTENTS

*Acknowledgements*                                                     vi

*Preface*                                                              xi

*Introduction: Political Theory Agonistes*                              1

**Part I: The Modernity Debate**                                       37

1  Two Senses of Modernity                                             39
2  Defenders of the Faith, Disturbers of the Peace                     77

**Part II: Living With/in Modernities**                               127

3  An Ethico-Political Imperative?                                    129
4  Towards a *Political* Theory                                       199

*Select Bibliography*                                                 234

*Index*                                                               243

# ACKNOWLEDGEMENTS

I have been living with the themes explored in this book for rather longer than is comfortable. Their origins can be found in my doctoral thesis awarded in 1987, a shocking six years ago. Since then I have turned my attention to various other areas of contemporary political theory but the thesis and its themes remained central to my thought and work, squatting on my bookshelf like an impatient Goblin, always beckoning me back into its lair. During the last six years I have discarded draft after draft of a book based, however loosely, on the thesis, fearing that the book I felt that I wanted to write would be too heavy to lift, still less read. Finally, however, I hit on a theme which seemed to unify both some of the material in the original thesis as well as some of the assumptions I now make about the character of political theory. Thus with some regret (but with a sigh of relief that I suspect the reader will share) I jettisoned the bulk of the manuscript as it had developed and worked on a much slimmer and, I hope, more focused argument, abstracting from the historical sections of the thesis and concentrating on the problems inherent in contemporary political theory as I see them.

During such a protracted process I have, of course, incurred a wide range of intellectual and personal debts. It is one of the great pleasures of finally presenting this work that I can, at last, acknowledge them. To begin at the beginning, Professor Alan Milne of the University of Durham was the eventual supervisor of the original dissertation. Anyone who knows him will know also his kindness, humour and enthusiasm for scholarly life and debate and these – as well as many other qualities (I remember especially his extremely potent home-brew beer) – were liberally bestowed upon me. He is, indeed, a liberal in both the classical and modern senses of that much-abused word. Moreover, since both Professor Milne and Durham came to my rescue at a particularly dispiriting moment, I am more grateful than I can say to both scholar and scholarly institution. Alan, in particular, performed many heroic acts of supererogation supervising both thesis and its wayward author. He was, as an individual of whom we are both great admirers might have put it, the very model of a modern research supervisor.

I was also an undergraduate at Durham and my undergraduate tutors, in politics, philosophy and classics, must also take some of the blame for what follows. It was they who first introduced me to many of the authors and ideas discussed herein and who inspired me to think that I could have no better life than that of a teacher and scholar in a university. I am enormously grateful for both their scholarship and their example. To three in particular, I must give special thanks. Henry Tudor, whose knowledge of the history of political thought I have yet to see exceeded and whose capacity for the sagacious well-timed remark is justly legendary. Bob Dyson, whose kindness, thoroughness and deep understanding of ancient and medieval thought was always at my disposal. Last, but never least, I must mention Paddy Fitzpatrick. If there was a Nobel prize for academic lectures, he would unquestionably have won it every time he cared to enter. A man who is capable of reducing first-year logic students to helpless fits of laughter while conveying difficult and abstract logical questions, methods and answers with ease and elegance, while also inspiring the same students with a genuine love of ancient philosophy – sometimes all in the same lecture – is a rare thing indeed. It is of no credit whatever to the contemporary system of what is laughably called quality assessment in universities, that such a scholar would have had virtually no chance today of developing the knowledge and style that made his teaching so memorable.

In the writing of this book I have been greatly helped by discussions with theorists spread across many universities and in at least three countries. The annual meetings of the Oxford Political Thought Conference are an especial joy and I say a special thank you to all of those who helped inaugurate that remarkable event some twenty-three years ago, and also to those who regularly turn up to sample its unique combination of excellent papers, atmospheric and animated discussions and cold bacon and eggs. A full description of all I owe to the political theorists who have been so generous with their time and energy in discussing themes from the book, commenting on draft chapters, inviting me to present papers at their own institutions and so on would take up at least a chapter, so I shall simply say a collective thank you, for all their kindnesses, to Brian Barry, Richard Bellamy, David Boucher, Chris Brown, Dario Castiglione, John Charvet, Janet Coleman, Bill Connolly, Fred Dallmayr, James Der Derian, Michael Donelan, Maurizio Passerein d'Entreves, Ian Forbes, Murray Forsyth, Bruce Haddock, Iain Hampsher-Monk, Mark Hoffman, Martin Hollis, Bonnie Honig, Jeremy Jennings, Maurice Keens-Soper, Paul Kelly, Onora O'Neill, Quentin Skinner, Paul Smart, Andy Vincent, Rob Walker and Robby Wokler.

The production of any book of course depends greatly on the environment of the writer. Since 1988, my environment has been the department of politics at the University of Bristol. I could not have asked for a better one. My colleagues in the 'theory group', Terrell Carver and Judith Squires, have both discussed the themes of this book with me (and, indeed, continue to do so) and made our joint teaching of political theory always stimulating and enjoyable with just the right element of constructive lunacy! Among the other members of the deparment I owe a great deal to both Vernon Hewitt and Mark Wickham-Jones, whose very considerable scepticism about my theoretical positions always makes me improve them (though they seem to be equally sceptical about the results), and to Eric Herring, whose hard-headed (not to say granite-like) positivism brings me down to earth – at least every once in a while. Outside the department, in the wider university community, I owe much also to Chris Bertram and Keith Graham, whose philosophical rigour and acuteness always remind me of how annoyingly good analytical philosophy at its best can be, and Catherine Edwards, David Feldman and Derek Duncan, whose initiative in setting up the Critical Theory Group has provided me and many others with a consistant source of good ideas, good companionship and good wine!

For a book, however, just as important as a good environment is a good publisher. Simon Prosser of Blackwell seemed to know I was writing this book even before I did and his letter suggesting that I might write it for Blackwell provided the final spur necessary to get me to (eventually) finish it. He has been supportive and understanding throughout the process, and his judicious mixture of good lunches and gentle reminders of shrinking (or exceeded) deadlines has been much appreciated. Moreover, the staff at Blackwell have been wonderfully efficient throughout the process of production. I must especially thank Cameron Laux, whose Herculean efforts in copy-editing the book can only be properly appreciated by its author.

Two parts of this book have been published elsewhere. Parts of the introductory chapter appeared (in a rather different form) as 'Trust, Prudence and History: John Dunn and the Tasks of Political Theory', in *History of Political Thought*, winter 1995. Parts of chapter 2 appeared as 'No Time Like The Present: Postmodernism and Political Theory', in *Political Studies*, vol. 40, no. 3, September 1992. I am grateful to the editors and publishers of these journals for their permission to reprint.

No book – indeed, no scholarship – makes much sense without a sense of perspective. Vanessa Robinson laboured – I think not too painfully – to give me that throughout the whole period that this book was being written. She succeeded so well I decided that there was no option but to marry her! I hope she thinks that the final manuscript proves that I was actually doing something all those times I never made it to Zurich or to Hamburg. She also knows just how important she has been to the book – and still is to me. Finally, my parents showed me very early on the model of an ideal city, both communal and cosmopolitan. Without them and all the support they provided, material, moral and emotional, my work would have been impossible and my life much less interesting. To them, in gratitude and love, I dedicate this book.

N. J. R.

*To my Mother and Father;*
*Your book, at last.*

# PREFACE

This book is concerned to do three things. First, it attempts to outline an interpretation of the significance of the widely used (and even more widely misunderstood) notion of modernity for political theory. Secondly, and as a central part of the process, it offers an outline interpretation of what I call the 'modernity debate'; to wit the positions and arguments of some of those who have defended modernity and some of those who have attacked it. In its currently most influential form, the modernity debate – at least in modern social, political and literary theory – is largely a debate between moderns and postmoderns, and so it is with these that I will be chiefly concerned, at least to begin with.

These twin concerns exist within a wider one, however; namely to offer an account and interpretation of the task and methods appropriate to political theory as such. In the course of elaborating this concern, I shall also address some of modernity's critics, who speak from a variety of perspectives but who share a concern to show the centrality of ideas drawn from classical Greek thought for modern political theory. While I accept some of their arguments, I shall reject others, amend their shared concern in a rather different direction, and then conclude by suggesting where, as a result of this discussion, contemporary political theory is deficient and what we might do about it.

The outline interpretation of modernity and the debate over it, which is at the core of this enterprise, is the main purpose of the first section of the book. The initial definition and discussion is made in chapter 1, where I try and give some content both to the notion of modernity itself and to various uses to which it has been put, or might be put, in political theory. Obviously given the scope of the discussion, I cannot cite every theorist of modernity nor discuss even those I do cite in anything like the detail they deserve. Instead, I have adopted the strategy of giving a broad interpretation of the positions I wish to contrast, concentrating especially on the differences between what I call the modern (and postmodern) 'mood' and its socio-economic, political and cultural forms, and then high-lighting and criticizing particular arguments relevant to this distinction in more detail. This leads, or so I hope, to a better understanding of what is at stake in the debate between the 'defenders' of modernity and their 'postmodern' critics than is often the case.

The particular arguments involved in this debate are then considered in detail in chapter 2. This opens with a discussion of those postmoderns that I term 'disturbers of the peace', which suggests that there are three distinct types of 'post-modern' argument. Each of these types is then briefly discussed. I then examine two very specific modern responses to these ar-guments, defences (as it were) of the faith in the modern mood. The chapter then seeks to offer an assessment of these debates and closes by identifying three problematic areas this assess-ment has thrown up.

To render this diagnosis plausible and to give added poign-ancy to the fact that the moderns and the postmoderns *have* been so side-tracked, these arguments are preceded by a long introductory chapter which outlines an interpretation of the current state of Anglo-American political theory in general (which largely ignores the modernity debate as such) and offers a sympathetic critique of it. Very briefly put, I contend that what John Dunn has called the tasks of political theory are rendered increasingly problematic by the issues that lie at the heart of the modernity debate as I understand it, that such has been recognized by some contemporary political and social theorists, but ignored by a good deal more (to their detriment) and adequately resolved by none. The concluding part of this introductory chapter then attempts to sketch what might count as at least the beginning of a way of coping with this, assuming that we can give an interpretation of the modernity debate which sees it in the way that I then attempt to make clear in Part I.

This question having been discussed in Part I, Part II then builds on this interpretation and seeks for some alternative views of both modernity and political theory. Chapter 3 offers some readings drawn from rather different sources and suggests why they might be particularly important or useful in constructing such an alternative. Chapter 4 then opens with a discussion of where this argument leaves political theory and what, as a result, we might do that is not being done or how we should do what is being done differently. I then move on to attempt a reinterpretation of the tasks of political theory in the light of the preceding discussion. The book closes with a sketch of what, as a result of all this, political theory most pressingly needs, to wit on the one hand an account of political judgement and practical reasoning that can serve as both a way of interpreting our circumstances and a method of evaluating and guiding our actions, and on the other an account of the institutional and practical setting which can permit such a view of political judgement the most room to manœuvre. This last point is by way of sketching an agenda for contemporary political theory and (not incidentally, of course) for my own work.

It confirms, of course, that political theory, as I conceive it, is an innately wide-ranging and hybrid activity. The late Judith Shklar saw it, correctly I think, as the place where history and philosophy meet,[1] though as I shall suggest later on, I do not agree with her as to the manner of the meeting. As such it is an inevitably messy affair, a messiness made much more acute by the inevitable, though undesirable, fragmentation of the modern academy.

Thus, political theory, as I conceive it, is now often done in departments of languages and literature, in departments of history, of economics, of law, of sociology, of international relations, in a number of other departments in modern universities and, indeed, outside such institutions altogether, at least as much as in its traditional home in departments of philosophy and politics. This fragmentation has brought with it considerable methodological angst. Does political science (or sociology, or history or international relations) have a particular method or disciplinary focus? What methods are appropriate to such a focus? If so, how (if at all) does 'political theory' fit into it or them? To anyone who did his or her doctoral research in the mid-1980s as I did, the questions are all familiar ones – indeed wearyingly so. I emphasize therefore that I do not intend to discuss these topics very much in this book, though I shall touch on them very briefly at the end. Rather my principal concern is substantive, in that I am concerned to sketch a way of doing political theory that can make a contribution to the way we understand our situation, shape our institutions and even – shocking though this will no doubt appear to some – live our lives.

To do this, it is obvious that we must of necessity cast our scholarly net very wide. One of the most depressing features of academic political theory (and indeed, philosophy) until relatively recently was its division, by means of a kind of geographical apartheid, into 'Anglo-American' and 'Continental' versions. Fortunately, this always artificial division has begun to break down somewhat of late, and a number of very good books and articles are appearing which ignore such ridiculous distinctions.[2] I certainly hope and intend that this book should reinforce this development.

The main purpose of the introductory chapter, indeed, is to highlight this by showing how debates in political theory that have particular resonance in the Anglo-American world (for example, the so-called liberal–communitarian debate as well as debates over the status and character of the history of political thought) can be much better understood and conducted if we avoid the tendency to sneer at 'the latest Parisian fashions'.

There are three additional reasons for starting with these concerns, however. The first is that both of these debates, more or less willingly (and usually less willingly), are now becoming involved in aspects of the modernity debate anyway, and therefore it is especially useful to use these debates as my stalking horses to show how and why the modernity debate should be seen as a central concern of political theory.

The second reason is that, in each case, there are particularly powerful positions expressed in these debates which serve to illustrate aspects of contemporary political theory (of all sorts) at its best, and yet still fail to properly grasp the complexities of the contemporary situation, and so therefore also illustrate very well (or so I hope to show) how necessary an interpretation of the modernity debate is to perform this task.

The third reason is rather more parochial, though not, I think, any the less significant for that. In most departments of politics and almost all departments of philosophy in Britain[3] and, to a lesser extent, in the United States, it is still the 'Anglo-American' agenda that dominates the teaching and the research in political theory. I hope that this book can make a modest contribution to widening that agenda conceptually, historically and even empirically.

I would also like to say a word about my very deliberate mixing of what is often today kept pretty rigidly apart, to wit questions of and about the history of political thought and the appropriate methodology for it, and substantive 'philosophical' questions about justice, liberty, equality and so on. In the introductory chapter I try and say something about what I take the reasons and effects of this development to have been on political theory, but suffice to say that, overall, I think they have been pretty negative. While no one can sensibly doubt the range and the power of the 'new history of political thought' or the analytical skill and sophistication of 'normative [i.e. Anglo-American] political theory'[4] in its analytical mode, the extent to which the two have proceeded without reference to one another (at least very largely[5]) has impoverished both. The concerns that become clear in the modernity debate show unambiguously why this needs to change, and also (as I shall argue) provides some interesting suggestions as to how it *should* change.

A final point here concerns the relationship of political theory to politics more generally. As will be seen, I agree with John Dunn when he says that the tasks of political theory are three-fold; (1) to tell us something about where we are and how we got here; (2) where we should aim to go; (3) some suggestions, at least, as to how we might get there from here.[6] Obviously, therefore, such a task requires some interpretation of the here and now, empirically as well as theoretically. Among the more obvious lessons of the modernity debate is the need to pay a close attention to the evolving structure of modernity. That structure, I shall seek to suggest in chapter 4, requires a scrambling of aspects of politics that have traditionally been kept separate; the categories of 'domestic' and 'international' politics, for example, should be highly suspect in a world where political theory must address issues both 'above' and 'below' the level of the state[7] (and, indeed, the nation) and will, indeed, often problematize these notions and practices *in toto*.

This brings me to my final introductory remark. Seeing political theory in the way that I do, requires that the 'normative' and 'explanatory' aspects of political theory (as they are usually called) are tied much more closely together than a good deal of modern political theory will admit. In my concluding chapter, I try to offer a set of questions that political theory should try and address and which it can only address if the dualisms/oppositions that currently bedevil it (liberal/communitarian, Anglo-American/Continental, modern/postmodern, historical/contemporary) are overcome or at least moved beyond. It is the final aim of this book to at least help to set such a process in motion. To do political theory now, I strongly believe, means that we must move 'beyond Enlightenment and critique', beyond, in other words 'attacking' modernity or 'defending' it, but also beyond denying its importance as a way of thinking about our ethico-political condition. To continue to engage in this futile conflict, 'attacking' or 'defending' this or that thinker, this or that epoch, is to assume, falsely, that one 'side' or the other can 'win', that one side or the other has necessary priority; in truth neither is possible without the other. The 'modernity debate' in its current form depends upon a dichotomy that actually prevents the resolution that both sides will often claim they seek, and hides various ways out of an increasingly sterile impasse. In the last analysis, this book is designed to show that and to trace an agenda for political theory in the light of it.

### Notes

1 Judith Shklar, *Faces of Injustice* (New Haven: Yale University Press, 1990). See especially p. 16. Shklar's actual phrase is 'political theory . . . lives in the territory between history and ethics'. I shall come back to Shklar's formulation later on.
2 I should emphasize that I am not denying the very real differences in the

evolution of philosophy and political theory in Europe and America over the course of the twentieth century; only the claim that there is as a result of this evolution some kind of natural distinction between 'Anglo-American' and 'Continental' thought. For examples of work that challenges the distinction from a wide variety of perspectives see, for example, Kenneth Baynes, *The Normative Bounds of Social Criticism: Kant, Rawls, Habermas* (New York: State University of New York Press, 1992); Jean Cohen and Andrew Arato, *Civil Society and Political Theory* (Cambridge: Massachusetts Institute of Technology Press, 1992); Chantal Mouffe (ed.), *Dimensions of Radical Democracy* (London: Verso, 1992); Bonnie Honig, *Political Theory and The Displacement of Politics* (Ithaca: Cornell University Press, 1993); William E. Connolly, *Identity/Difference: Democratic Negotiations of Political Paradox* (Baltimore: Johns Hopkins University Press, 1991). I would also add, *inter alia*, the work of Charles Taylor and, in a very different way, at least some of the work of Leo Strauss and his colleagues and pupils, to both of whom I shall return. From the 'Continental' side see Ottfried Höffe, *Politische Gerechtigkeit* (Frankfurt: Suhrkamp Verlag, 1987).

3 There are exceptions, of course. The philosophy departments at the Universities of Essex and Warwick being the ones that most obviously spring to mind.

4 I discuss these in detail in chapter 1, and so shall not prefigure that discussion here.

5 There are exceptions, of course. The exchanges between James Tully (historian of political thought) and Jeremy Waldron (analytical philosopher) on Locke being a good case in point. See James Tully, *A Discourse on Property: John Locke and his Adversaries* (Cambridge: Cambridge University Press, 1980); Jeremy Waldron, 'Locke, Tully and the Regulation of Property', *Political Studies*, 31, no. 1 (1984). It is also true that the leading paladin of the new history of political thought, Quentin Skinner, has recently embarked on some interesting essays into the terrain more usually frequented by the analysts. See for example his essay 'On Justice, The Common Good and The Priority of Liberty', in Mouffe (ed.), *Dimensions of Radical Democracy*.

6 See my discussion in the introduction below. The reference is to John Dunn's *Interpreting Political Responsibility* (Cambridge: Cambridge University Press, 1990).

7 This usage I borrow from Michael Walzer; see his essay in the 150th anniversary edition of *The Economist*, 11–17 Sept. 1993.

# INTRODUCTION: POLITICAL THEORY AGONISTES

Political theory today is enormously wide-ranging. It comes in many shapes and sizes, addresses itself to many different issues, and adopts a bewildering variety of methodological approaches. Most of this is entirely to be welcomed. It is a testimony to the strength, significance and enduring appeal of political theory as a general subject area that it has generated such huge variety. However, it has disadvantages as well as advantages, and one of its most widely perceived problems is the loss of focus that such a diversity is held to have engendered.

A corollary of this is that political theory itself is becoming more and more fragmented. What is done by one set of theorists is almost entirely ignored by another; the findings or interpretations of one school sneered at or patronized by its rivals. This has been made worse by the bureaucratic and administrative expansion of the university, especially in the fields of the humanities and social sciences, and by the growing dominance of what I shall call positivistic modes of reasoning (conceived as reasoning analogous to that in the natural sciences) on the one hand and anti-foundational, relativistic and postmodern forms of understanding on the other.

It will be my argument in this book that a consideration of what I shall call the modernity debate is central to the task of addressing this multi-faceted nature of contemporary political theory in a way that will enable us to integrate and combine the insights and strengths of a variety of differing approaches in political theory. This in its turn offers us the best hope of understanding, interpreting and evaluating the evolving structures of the increasingly complex and global politico-ethical nexus in which we all live.

In Part II of this book I shall seek to explore the ramification of seeing this situation as a distinctive 'politico-ethical' question and will suggest why, in general terms, political theory must in a very important and central sense be a philosophy of 'the political'. In Part I, I shall outline the modernity debate and assess its significance. Before I can do either of these two things, however, I want to offer a brief interpretation of the current condition of political theory. I shall come on in a moment to look at some of those tendencies in European thought which are significantly influenced by questions about the character and nature (if it has one) of modernity. First, however, let me say something about two other areas of contemporary political thought. In a moment I shall say something about the debate over the character of the history of political thought, but first let me look at what is usually called 'Anglo-American' political theory and which has certainly set the agenda of much political theory of all sorts over the last thirty years.

## The Fall and Rise of 'Anglo-American' Political Theory?

It is a commonplace among 'Anglo-American'[1] political theorists to say that over the last thirty years or so political theory has undergone a 'revival' or a 'resurgence'.[2] The argument is by now a familiar one. In the 1950s and 1960s political philosophy was dead. In Peter Laslett's famous, and famously amended, judgement, it had been killed, or at least mortally wounded, by the linguistic turn in philosophy and by the rise of behaviouralism and positivism in political and social science.

However, this announcement of political theory's death proved premature, and in the late 1960s, 1970s and 1980s, spurred above all by the publication of John Rawls' *A Theory of Justice*, though also by political events such as the Vietnam War and the launch of journals such as *Philosophy and Public Affairs*, political theory experienced a welcome rebirth and exponentially increasing growth. While remaining true to 'analytical' philosophy in method and manner, it turned this theoretical rigour from meta-theoretical questions to substantive ones, subsuming much of the positivistic literature and method and turning it to its own use in the process. Indeed, one of the most powerful aspects of the 'new normative theory' was its rejection of the anti-normative claims of much political and social science of the time, while at the same time accepting, adapting and deploying parts of the methodologies that such social science had developed (such as rational choice and game theory). The result of this was that many of the participants in this 'rebirth' felt themselves self-consciously creating a literature and an approach. As Brian Barry, one of the leading champions of this rebirth has put it, in the 1950s and 1960s 'there simply wasn't a literature to which one could relate one's work. There was nothing to do but make the stuff up as one went along.'[3]

Being an inventive breed, these political theorists went at it with a vengeance and now, of course, there is an enormous literature which, as Barry says, straddles political science, philosophy, economics and even law,[4] and which has become almost omnipresent in departments of philosophy, political science and many cognate areas in the English-speaking world. The character of this rebirth has been, of course, in itself very diverse. Writers as individual and as original as Rawls, Barry, Ronald Dworkin and G. A. Cohen (to name just four especially influential writers) are certainly not all of a piece. Several schools of liberalism, various forms of Marxism, and even the occasional 'conservative' are all present within the approach. There are fierce debates within this 'revived' political theory even while, as suggested above, it has begun to present a unified area of concern where lawyers, political scientists, philosophers, economists and sociologists (and perhaps even psychologists and anthropologists too) can all work together in a similar vein.

Moreover, this rebirth of political theory built on already growing foundations in ethics. As a number of writers have pointed out,[5] there was already a growing revitalization in Britain of the utilitarian tradition in ethics in the late 1950s, 1960s, and early 1970s, represented by the work of philosophers such as J. J. C. Smart, R. M. Hare (at least to some degree) and Peter Singer (a tradition very powerfully carried on more recently by Derek Parfit).[6]

In its most recent form, Anglo-American political theory has been at its most inventive when discussing questions that lie at the heart of the character of the liberal state. Justice, equality, liberty, the welfare state, the nature of political community and, increasingly, the character and force of our obligations and responsibilities to communities outside our own.

Many of these issues are at the heart of the so-called liberal–communitarian debate that, in some form or another, has dominated Anglo-American political theory of this sort during the 1980s. In order to see more clearly the current character of this 'rebirth' of political theory, then, I want to say something about this debate. I should emphasize that I do not intend to take a position within the debate (at least not yet); and, indeed, it will be part of my argument that the participants agree at least as much as they disagree, and that the manner of this agreement is at least as significant as any differences they have.

The essentials of the debate are too well known to need anything other than a brief summary here. Essentially, the debate began with Michael Sandel's response to Rawls in his 1982 book, *Liberalism and the Limits of Justice*.[7] As Stephen Mullhall and Adam Swift have pointed out in their excellent survey of the debate,[8] this is unquestionably the book that first elicits the description 'communitarian' and thus structures the debate around that standard, even though Alisdair MacIntyre's *After Virtue* (another seminal 'communitarian' text, of course) was published the previous year.[9] Sandel was rapidly joined as 'communitarians', in the literature at least, by three other prominent writers: MacIntyre, Charles Taylor[10] and Michael Walzer.[11]

At the centre of the debate, it is said, stand two issues. Jean Cohen and Andrew Arato structure them thus:

> The first [epistemological] issue revolves around the question of whether it is possible to articulate a formal, universalistic (deontological) conception of justice without presupposing a substantive (historically and culturally specific) concept of the good. The second [political issue] revolves around the question of how freedom can be realised in the modern world. At issue here is

whether the idea of freedom should be explicated primarily from the standpoint of individual rights or of the community's shared norms. Each side comes up with a different, indeed opposed set of responses as to what constitutes the legitimating principles of a constitutional democracy. In the process, however, the very conception of liberal democracy disintegrates into its component parts.[12]

Cohen and Arato's formulation is especially useful, I think, because it makes clear the links between the epistemological and political aspects of the debate (Charles Taylor, in a different context, has suggested we call this ontological and advocacy levels,[13] to which I shall want to return later in this chapter). However, for the moment let me just focus on two aspects of the debate. The first is the problem of categorizing it as *a* debate (as opposed to several interrelated ones) at all, the second is what the participants in the 'debate' share, rather than what they are arguing about.

As a number of commentators have pointed out, both communitarians and liberals are very disparate. John Rawls, for example, is clearly a rather different kind of liberal from (say) Dworkin or Bruce Ackerman, both of whom are far more wedded to the thesis of 'liberal neutrality' than Rawls is.[14] Then there is the awkward fact that there are liberals who define themselves outside much of this debate *in toto*, for example Judith Shklar, who has advocated what she calls a liberalism of 'fear'.[15] The communitarians present an even greater contrast. Of the four most prominently cited so-called communitarians only MacIntyre is what I would call a critic of 'liberalism' *tout court* (for reasons we shall discuss in chapter 1). Both Taylor and Walzer are not exactly anti-liberal (they would suggest that liberalism both has intrinsic virtues and is a necessary first step for democracy, and would see themselves as democrats, I think); and Sandel's position, while certainly critical of what he calls 'de-ontological liberalism', is not necessarily hostile to all forms of liberalism.[16]

In part, an explanation of these differences can be found in a point to which I have already drawn attention. That is to say that involved in the liberal–communitarian debate is a complex set of issues ranging from epistemological to political issues. As

Charles Taylor has said, in the essay I cited above, the debate between liberals and communitarians is a complex, many-levelled affair.[17] It would perhaps be better to see it, then, as a *network of debates within liberalism broadly conceived*.

One of the most important of these debates is that between liberal democrats (for example, liberals of the Rawlsian stamp) and what Richard Bellamy has called, in an important recent book, 'democratic liberals'.[18] Bellamy's book tells a complicated and multi-faceted story about the evolution of modern liberalism in Western Europe and the United States. For Bellamy, modern liberals who emphasize (as Rawls, Dworkin and Ackerman all do, to at least some extent) what Rawls has called the 'priority of the right over the good' are mistakenly assuming that the premisses of what he calls 'ethical liberalism' still hold. Ethical liberalism depended (and still does, according to Bellamy) on a conjunction between a philosophical thesis and a social one. The former stemmed from the priority of increasing individual liberty; a concern which all liberals, to some extent at least, would share. The problem of how all liberties were to be made congruent, however, had two solutions. One, eschewed by ethical liberals (indeed, by virtually all liberals) depended upon a scheme for the ranking of human values and preferences, in other words on some theory that has a strong conception of the human good and what values were central to it, what values less significant and so on. The second, which was the version adopted by ethical liberalism, was to adopt a social thesis which 'assumed that society would develop in a direction which would lead to the harmonisation of life plans'.[19] According to Bellamy, this is still the move made by most liberals, most famously by Rawls, the problem being that the social thesis that underpins it is now completely implausible.

However, the appeal to a strong conception of the good is equally implausible for Bellamy, and for the same reasons, to wit its implausibility as a social thesis in contemporary politics. Thus aspects of the 'communitarian critique' are well founded, but the solution is not to return to some idealized social whole (the communitarian suggestion), but to take seriously the task of constructing democratic institutions that recognize the plural and conflictual nature of social relations, whilst retaining aspects of the liberal project, such as the emphasis on autonomy, which remain central to such a task. Thus, the 'political' aspect of the liberal–communitarian debate, as described by Cohen and Arato, must also attempt an understanding of the nature of contemporary society *tout court*.

Enough has now been said, I think, to make an assessment of what is common to the participants in the debate. Will Kymlicka, one of the most acute recent liberal contributors to the debate, has argued that all contemporary political philosophy (of the Anglo-American type, that is) 'is a matter of moral argument and moral argument is a matter of appeal to *our considered convictions*' (emphasis added).[20] Note that this understanding of our situation fits in perfectly happily with either 'liberal' or 'communitarian' views. For the latter, moral argument must, of course, be a matter of 'our' convictions, the 'our' in question being precisely the most significant question for communitarians ('our' society, or state, or even, as some seem to imply, our 'civilization or culture'). For the former, 'our' convictions can be taken to mean the convictions of those of 'us' who exist in liberal-democratic (hence plural, modern) societies. This last point is one that Bellamy would share as well.

In each case, of course, a space is made for reflection; it is our 'considered' convictions that are important. Note, however, that little attention is paid to the process of 'consideration'. Of course, Rawls has emphasized the notion of 'reflective equilibrium'[21] as a way of evaluating and re-evaluating our sense of justice against our own regulative principles once they are brought to light. However, he also uses an interesting phrase to characterize this position. It is, he says, 'a theory of moral sentiments . . . setting out the principles governing our moral powers'.[22] This quite deliberate echo of eighteenth-century thought serves to highlight what is most important about a Rawlsian 'reflective equilibrium'; we are using *common sense* moral assumptions, theorizing from them and then evaluating them against the principles that they may be said to instantiate.[23] Communitarian writers, most obviously Walzer and Sandel, similarly emphasize the 'authenticity' of an interpretation of a community's shared values as the way in which such 'reflection' is performed.[24]

The point here, of course, is that such a view links the epistemological and the political halves of the debate in that each depends upon the same general assumption, to wit that quarrels in moral and political theory can only be settled or resolved through the proper understanding and/or reshaping of our *existing* moral convictions and political institutions.[25] Moreover, as Bonnie Honig has pointed out in a powerful recent book, both liberals and at least some communitarians (let us say, with Bellamy, 'communitarian liberals like Walzer and Sandel') seek in important ways to 'silence' politics, in the sense of the site of conflicts in society.[26] For Honig, both Rawls and Sandel (the two thinkers she concentrates on) seek to 'displace' politics, 'Rawls for the sake of a justice that is well administered, Sandel for the sake of an identity that is sustained by stable communities'.[27] One effect of such displacement is, of course, the impossibility of radically rethinking the nature of that society or of moving outside the 'settled convictions' that exist in such a powerfully symbiotic relationship with political and social forms of a society.

The significance of this is that it suggests that the 'rebirth' of Anglo-American political theory has come to consist in a 'debate' in which the validity of any position is dependent almost entirely on seeing the existing social world in a certain way as generative of a set of social 'norms' or 'values' that are, firstly, all we have and secondly, all that can be assessed as true or false. This is as true of orthodox Marxists, I think, as it is of the liberals, utilitarians, Kantians and others who dominate contemporary Anglo-American political theory. The only difference being a characteristically Marxian reversal; rather than focus on the norms or values, such Marxist thought focuses on the 'social forms' themselves almost independently of such 'norms or values'.[28] In neither case is the possibility or desirability of radically other norms or values explored.

The question would then arise, however, how can we explore such ideas? Surely, to be at all realistic, political and ethical ideas have to have reach and reference within a given community, however large or small that community may be said to be. This is true, of course, but the point is not whether we can create such ideas *ex nihilo*, as it were, but what the appropriate reference should be for where we might turn to assess 'our' ideas or convictions. This will lead directly into a discussion of the character of our contemporary politics – in other words into the modernity debate.

Before I can make the implications of this claim fully apparent, however, I want to discuss a second area of contemporary political thought that we shall also need to engage: the question of the character, type and meaning of the history of ideas in general and of political thought in particular.

## The Contextualization of Political Thought

It has always seemed to me that it was in certain respects incorrect to talk about the 'death' of political philosophy. Throughout the period during which political philosophy was supposedly 'dead', an enormous amount of work was being done in a great variety of different areas of political thought.[29] On this view, the growth of the distinctive 'Anglo-American' political theory discussed above is expressive not of the resurgence of 'proper' (i.e. substantive) political theory but of the growth of a *different* way of looking at political theory and doing it. It is a change in the *direction* of much political theory certainly, but not the rebirth or revival of a previously moribund area.

However, what linked together many of the writers rejected by the newer political theory was a commitment to the history of philosophy, political thought and indeed ideas generally; not just for our understanding of the past but for the activity of political theory in the present. They saw discussions of past political thinkers as a contribution to debates about political issues in general. This view was, of course, rejected by the protagonists of the 'rebirth' of substantive political theory. As Brian Barry has put it in a fascinating and witty introduction to the re-issue of his *Political Argument*, 'when I began work on [his doctoral thesis, later *Political Argument*] I had no real idea of what I wanted to do, except that it should be theoretical in a constructive and analytical way rather than being about what somebody else had said'.[30] Later in the same passage Barry

draws an explicit contrast with two of the writers just mentioned when he says that both John Plamenatz and Isaiah Berlin
were primarily concerned with 'the history of political thought',
and their interests therefore did not correspond with his.

The more interesting question, however, concerns the history
of political thought itself. It too has moved away from this older
conception of its task. Why? In part, I think that this is due to
the growth of debates in literary studies more generally and the
interpenetration of social theory and literary theory which has
helped to produce a series of discussions about the appropriate
methodology for studying past thought and various different
attempts to construct (or deconstruct) a new canon of great
texts or to suggest that any such canon must needs be seen in the
context of its general intellectual milieu.

This latter view has become something of a new orthodoxy of
late and is especially (though by no means completely) associated in Britain and North America with a group of scholars
who, because of a generally shared link with the University of
Cambridge (virtually all of them at some time or other were
students or teachers there) can conveniently be referred to collectively as the 'Cambridge School'. These scholars are, or have
included (amongst others), Quentin Skinner, J. G. A. Pocock,
James Tully, Richard Tuck and the writer I shall come back to
in a moment, John Dunn.[31]

The general assumptions these writers share can be quickly
outlined. From an emphasis on particular texts, a canon of
'great books', they choose to focus on the contexts in which
such books were written and the 'languages' that both shaped
the contexts of their writing and were in turn shaped by the
contexts. Writing and thinking in this way gives us the chance,
as Quentin Skinner puts it, to formulate 'a history of political
theory with a genuinely historical character'.[32]

This has given rise to the widely shared view that the 'new
history of political thought', as it is also sometimes called
(though this is much wider than simply the Cambridge School),
has become the dominant approach in the last few years and
that while 'philosophers, political scientists, economists and
even lawyers' are getting on with their 'reborn', 'substantive'
political theory the new historians are busy rubbishing the

'great texts' and/or re-inventing the canon in such a way that the 'history' of political thought and its current practice are increasingly divergent. Thus, it is sometimes said, that we have two Thomas Hobbeses in the contemporary literature. First we have the Thomas Hobbes written about by the new historians, deeply embedded in the engagement controversy, the English Civil War and the theological and scientific disputes of the mid-seventeenth century; that is to say, the Hobbes of Richard Tuck, Johann Sommerville and, indeed, Skinner himself.[33] Secondly we have the Hobbes who is at the centre of the concerns of a lot of the new, 'reborn' analytical political theory, Thomas Hobbes the incipient game theorist, the analyst of power politics and the source of pragmatic (sometimes called 'economic') social-contract theory; in other words, the Hobbes of David Gauthier, of Gregory Kavka and of Jean Hampton.[34]

However, notwithstanding its truth at times, this appearance can, I want to suggest, be rather deceptive. As one of the leaders of the 'historical party' (though emphatically not one of the 'Cambridge School'), Iain Hampsher-Monk has put it, 'whilst an understanding of the identity of the conceptual 'language' being deployed is necessary to understand historical meaning, an exclusive pre-occupation with it can distract attention from the fact that it is being used to make a statement'.[35] and this is part of an attempt at understanding the dynamics of political agency which, as Hampsher-Monk goes on to say, 'is as important for present as for past political theory'.

What is more interesting still is that such views appear also in the views of the Cambridge School themselves. As I mentioned above, Skinner is unquestionably the most influential of these writers, at least methodologically, and as Tully rightly emphasizes, he has also had an increasing influence on the way that the history of political thought is written and taught more generally.[36] Thus, before moving on to Dunn, the most interesting of these writers for my purpose here, I want to look briefly at Skinner's general set of assumptions. Skinner is especially fascinating as he combines methodological assumptions taken from philosophers as diverse as Collingwood, Austin, Grice and Searle, the last three of whom certainly helped to create the atmosphere which led mainstream Anglo-American philosophy to abandon systematic discussions of ethico-political topics in the 1940s and 1950s. However, as will be seen, Skinner's views on the relation of the history of political thought to contemporary practice defy easy summary.

Tully, in perhaps the best recent summary of Skinner's position, has emphasized that Skinner's procedure can best be seen as comprising five distinct parts. First, asking what an author is doing in writing a text in relation to other available texts which make up the ideological context; second, asking what an author is doing in writing a text in relation to available and problematic political action which makes up the practical context; third, asking how ideologies are to be identified and their formation, criticism and change surveyed and explained; fourth, asking what relation exists between political ideology and political action which best explains the diffusion of certain ideologies; and fifthly, what forms of political thought and action are involved in disseminating and conventionalizing ideological change.[37]

Tully then goes on to articulate three theses about Skinner's work. The third of these concerns what Tully calls the 'primacy of practical conflict' in Skinner's work,[38] and the second concerns what Tully calls Skinner's theory of 'historical pragmatics' – that is, his 'theory of the universally valid conditions under which claims to know what is right and true could be advanced and rationally adjudicated'.[39] (Tully's view is that Skinner advocates an 'historical pragmatics' that differs from Habermas' 'universal pragmatics' by being anti-foundational and that the defence of this is found in Skinner's account of how critical discourse works.) I shall return to both of these assumptions later on, but for now I want to focus on the first thesis. This alleges that Skinner's 'genuinely historical' account of the 'foundations of modern political thought' is, in ways very similar to the work of Foucault, a 'history of the present' in that the foundations with which Skinner is mainly concerned in his (so far) major work, *The Foundations of Modern Political Thought*, are in fact how the period that Skinner discusses lays the 'foundations' for modern political thought *after that period*. Tully summarizes Skinner's position on this by showing that Skinner attempts to outline a dominant and a subordinate ideology, both of which he examines. The dominant ideology, which Tully calls 'juridical', is held to contain the following elements:

> the state is represented as an independent, territorial monopoly of political power. Political power is the right to kill in order to enforce universal rule of either objective right or subjective rights, such as rights, natural law, common good, tradition, majority will, modernisation or the constitution. Political power is exercised either directly by some sovereign body . . . or indirectly by some representative body . . . Also, political power is exercised through the law over a legally undifferentiated population and is limited by the standard of right.[40]

For Skinner, this ideology dominates conservative, liberal and Marxist social theory 'from Bodin and Buchanan to Rawls and Habermas', and is the product of four hundred years of political thought and action. It is his task to trace the interpenetrations and interrelationships that have helped to formulate it. In doing so, however, he begins to suggest ways in which the 'new history of political thought' can help us to articulate positions in contemporary politics *as well as* allowing us to develop a 'genuinely historical' history of political thought.

One way in which Skinner attempts to do this is by also detailing the subordinate ideology, which is that of civic republicanism, which becomes overlaid and overwritten by the juridical ideology but is still 'available' to us in certain ways. Skinner's explicit writings on this subject are still, however, relatively sketchy, and so in order to more fully examine how this ideology might be perceived and deployed in contemporary terms I want now to take up the case of Skinner's Cambridge colleague, John Dunn, who in many respects advances a similar thesis.

## John Dunn and 'The Tasks of Political Theory'

Given the obvious differences between 'Anglo-American' political theory and the contextualized history of political thought, it is hardly surprising that very few figures straddle more than one of these general areas. One person who manages this feat, however, is John Dunn. Whatever the truth about the

Cambridge School as a whole, nobody could say of Dunn that he has been a theorist concerned only with what the illustrious dead had to say about politics. His work has covered modern revolutions,[41] the politics of West African states,[42] socialism[43] and political economy,[44] as well as the history of political thought and political theory in the substantive sense.[45]

Much of Dunn's work has been published as collections of essays that contain articles on virtually all of these concerns,[46] and it is from these that we can begin an examination of how Dunn links the historical and practical parts of his project. Let me start with Dunn's conception of the enterprise of political theory itself. For Dunn, 'The purpose of political theory is to diagnose practical predicaments and to show us how best to confront them.'[47] To do this, Dunn argues, it needs to train us in three relatively distinct skills:

> Firstly, in ascertaining how the social, political and economic setting of our lives now is and in understanding why it is as it is; secondly, in working through for ourselves how we could coherently and justifiably wish that world to be or become; and thirdly in judging how far, and through what actions, and at what risk, we can realistically hope to move this world as it now stands towards the way we might excusably wish it to be.[48]

Dunn uses this formulation to build an analysis and critique of modern political theory, especially of the Anglo-American type discussed above, coming to the conclusion that it is deeply flawed. I shall, of course, return to this again, but let me just summarize his critique before examining its presuppositions. Given inevitable disputes over the nature of all of the three tasks of political theory, he suggests that most contemporary Anglo-American political philosophers emphasize 'the systematic conceptual analysis of the sole component of (their) subject matter that permits precise and controlled analysis: the theory of human value. Most contemporary political philosophy, accordingly, consists largely in the application of ethics to practical topics: the bringing of philosophy as an achieved academic practice to bear upon the sorry conceptual disorder of public affairs.'[49]

This is a clear reference to that body of political theory most strongly influenced by Rawls' *A Theory of Justice* and the

'Rawls industry' that now accompanies it. The reason that Dunn dissents from this project, despite an obvious respect for a good deal of it, is that for him such a project cannot properly understand the nature and depth of the problems that face us. As he says:

> At present there is every reason to believe the bearers of official, amateur and professional social theory to be equally feckless in their grasp of the prospective consequences of enacting their own presumptions and equally regrettable contributors, accordingly, by their agency to the impairment and imperilling of collective human life. The essence of my complaint about contemporary academic consciousness is its systematic unsuitability for defining this predicament, let alone for contributing to its alleviation.[50]

Why does Dunn think that most extant forms of political and social theory are 'systematically unsuitable' for defining our predicament? There are, of course, a number of reasons. One of the main problems with much contemporary social theory, Dunn thinks, is that it is founded, at least in part, on the assumption that true understanding of politics is analogous, at least in some respects, to true understanding in natural science. Dunn's whole corpus (and he shares this with the other advocates of the new history of political thought, of course) has indicated an especial scepticism about this view. However, in *Interpreting Political Responsibility* he also emphasizes the fact that, right or wrong, it offers a very poor prognosis for political theory achieving the tasks Dunn has set for it. A third reason is that the narrowness of the focus on human value is dwarfed by the scale of the problems of modern politics, a charge to which I shall return in a moment.

The consequence of this systematic unsuitability, Dunn thinks, is that our contemporary circumstances, ranging from the risk of nuclear annihilation (a reduced military risk now, perhaps, but Dunn is clearly also including the ecological risks of domestic nuclear programmes as well), to economic collapse and/or ecological devastation, all bespeak the need for a rearticulation of the well-known (but lately much ignored) virtue of prudence,[51] but that contemporary social and political theory is singularly ill fitted for this job. This view is expressed most powerfully in the final essay of *Rethinking Modern Political Theory* and virtually all of the essays in Dunn's most recent collection, *Interpreting Political Responsibility*, speak to it.

In *Rethinking Modern Political Theory*, he argues that 'What a political philosophy for the turbulent world of today and tomorrow needs at its centre is a theory of prudence – a theory adequate to the historical world in which we have to live.'[52] The later volume is clearly an attempt to explore the contours of this rearticulation of prudence rather more thoroughly. 'What modern politics most pressingly requires,' he says in the concluding essay of *Interpreting Political Responsibility*,

> is a democratization of prudence, a spreading out of the burden of judging and choosing soberly about political questions across the entire adult populations of particular societies. A modern political community – the only genuine form of political community now possible on the scale of the nation state – would be a community which faced and accepted the need to judge and choose together, a community whose members were reared and educated on the premise that this was the responsibility which lay ahead of them at the core of adult life.[53]

It is in this context that we should see the other essays in the volume. Those essays that revisit other aspects of Dunn's interests (revolution in chapter 6, African politics in chapter 9 and, perhaps most significantly, Locke in chapters 2 and 3), as well as those essays that merge several concerns (chapter 7 on country risk, for example, which links his interest in revolution with his interest in political economy), all assert the centrality of the virtue of prudence in order to make sense of contemporary political life.

However, it is his opening two chapters on Locke that perhaps indicate most clearly the trajectory of Dunn's thought since his original and highly influential reading of Locke in the late 1960s, and therefore locate why prudence has come to play so significant a part in his work and, overall, how as a result he tries to weld together the historical sensitivity of the new history of political thought with his concerns in substantive political theory. In 'What is Living and What is Dead in the Politics of John Locke', Dunn announces that his argument is an effective repudiation of 'a single (and particularly ill considered) sentence' in the preface to his earlier book on Locke. The offending sentence reads as follows: 'I simply cannot conceive of constructing an analysis of any issue in contemporary political theory around the affirmation or negation of anything which Locke says about political matters.'[54]

This view was, in other words, the corollary in the history of political thought, of the Anglo-American belief that 'susbtantive political theory' must of necessity be largely (though perhaps not exclusively) contemporary. Dunn prefaces his repudiation of this view by acknowledging that his intent in the book had been to emphasize the alien character of Locke's thought as a particular example of a wider thesis about how 'to understand the thinking of another human being in a very distant and in some respects culturally exceedingly alien environment'.[55] This wider thesis essentially asserts that such thinking needed to be seen as an integrated whole in a particular time and place, not simply as an assemblage of discrete individual propositions readily detachable from the others. As he remarks, such a view is, to a greater or lesser extent, akin to Quinean anti-realism in philosophy,[56] precisely that for which Dunn is methodologically best known, which he shares to a large extent with Skinner,[57] and which shaped the early work of the Cambridge School, at least to a large extent.

Dunn certainly does not repudiate this general view. What emerges in *Interpreting Political Responsibility*, however, is that he no longer thinks that all of Locke's thought is dead in the sense of being 'culturally distant from us'. In a brief survey of those areas of Locke's thought still widely regarded as being 'alive' in contemporary political theory, Dunn expresses scepticism about the Christian foundation of Locke's thought (which, of course, Dunn was most concerned to stress in the original book), natural rights, the theory of property and toleration and so on, on precisely the grounds of historical interpretation just alluded to. On one, however – the contractarian approach to the understanding of legitimate political authority – he thinks differently. Here, he thinks that Locke put his finger on what is still crucial for our sense of the political as much as it was for his.

His view of *what* precisely is so crucial in this understanding is, however, one of the things that most separates him from the fashionable contractarianism of Rawls and other prominent Anglo-American political theorists. What Dunn argues is that the three categories through which Locke interprets the role of men and women in history are detachable from many other assumptions that Locke makes and acutely pinpoint the dilemma of modern politics in a way that goes well beyond the 'contractarianism' of Rawls, or his followers.

These three categories are a conception of what it is to be a person and an agent, an insistence that any human society is the unintended consequence of a vast array of past human contrivances, and 'the degree to which the political texture of any decent human society depends – and must depend always – upon trust'.[58] This third category is by far the most significant for Dunn. It separates Locke, he thinks, both from those Natural Law theorists that preceded him and from the far more influential and variegated thinkers that followed him.

In the course of articulating this view, Dunn engages in an oblique but none the less powerful critique of much contemporary contractarian theory that echoes his earlier critique of the Rawlsian tradition in particular and Anglo-American political theory in general. Trustworthiness, on his reading, is far more the first virtue of social institutions than is justice. Trust must be seen as being located in the 'deep ambiguities of human nature', not just in the largely cognitive capacity for giving and receiving undertakings. 'For Locke,' Dunn says, 'the political task is always principally an exercise in practical skill. But what that skill consists of is the construction of moral order in the face of the permanent possibility of chaos . . . it is a view which captures – captures most evocatively – what politics is still like.'[59]

It is this way of seeing politics, this emphasis on trust and trustworthiness and on what he thinks it implies, that leads Dunn to stress the importance of prudence. Dunn's version of the Lockean view leads ineradicably to the view that politics as a practical skill, under contemporary conditions, requires an historically and theoretically sensitive notion of prudence. In a separate essay, Dunn calls this 'trust as policy (the properly sceptical choice of human political expedients)'.[60]

This form of prudence ('modern prudence', as he calls it[61]) is most emphatically not to be equated with the instrumental rationality that has stamped its mark on Anglo-American political theory, even though many of its leading practitioners are critics of it. For Dunn, it 'shows human beings why they need to see the settings of their lives in certain ways – and what sorts of practical implications follow from seeing these settings thus – and not as they at present happen to do'.[62] Most forms of instrumental rationality influential in Anglo-American political theory, in contrast, make an assumption about the way people actually behave (one version) or how they would behave if they were truly 'rational'[63] (a second version).

The notion of prudence, used in this sense, has an illustrious history, of course. It is a well-known hallmark of aspects of classical thought,[64] and in modern political thought has most often been invoked by the tradition of political realism, especially in international affairs.[65] However, Dunn inverts usual realist positions in that he stresses the need for more people, not (as realists have usually suggested) less, to be involved in the process of decision. This leads him to a position similar to that described by writers such as Ken Booth and Anthony Giddens as utopian realism.[66] These writers have also placed considerable emphasis on the notion of trust.[67] However, it is another aspect of the intellectual history of prudence that is perhaps most significant here, i.e. its association with the classical republican tradition, stemming from Roman writers, most especially Cicero, and flowering most especially during the Renaissance. It is precisely this tradition, of course, that Skinner suggests is the 'subordinate' ideology of modern political thought.

In order for us to have any chance of displaying the necessary 'prudence', however, we must know what our political circumstances are and how we should see them. It is this task, crucially, that the history of political thought can help us to perform. Dunn shows how significant he thinks this can be with his repudiation of his earlier view that Locke's thought is completely 'dead', and by using the perspective derived from this reading to analyse and discuss many of the substantive themes he is concerned with, such as revolution, political risk and the analysis of post-colonial states.

For Dunn, then, the 'historical turn', if we may so term it, is emphatically not a turning away from the tasks of political theory. It is, on the contrary, the indispensible beginning of those tasks. Contemporary political theory of the Anglo-American sort that is critical of, or perhaps simply uninterested in, historical work will simply never be able to perform the tasks of political theory as it will have no clear idea with what circumstances it has to deal, and therefore no way of setting out a clear programme of action to deal with them. That modern Anglo-American political theory has many strengths Dunn does not deny, but this central weakness undermines it in a crucial place.

Dunn's tasks of political theory, then, both dictate the centrality of history in general, and the history of ideas in particular, to his project. They also help to make it clear why he has been more ready than some in the 'historical school' to trespass on what might be regarded as alien territory (political economy, for example). Political theory is simply too important a task to be left to the (Anglo-American) political theorists. They cannot give us a way of attending properly to the tasks of political theory, and without being able to so attend, we will remain, as he once suggested, 'philosophically feeble and politically maladroit'.[68]

## A Critique

There can be no doubt, then, that Dunn's work constitutes one of the most wide-ranging contemporary accounts of the tasks and character of political theory. I certainly agree with a good deal of it, and I shall take some of it up again in chapter 4. However, for the moment I want to concentrate on what I think are the weaknesses in his argument.

The very breadth of his concerns and the care and sympathy with which he discusses them create the first reason to call into question Dunn's emphasis on prudence as the key component of modern politics that is lacking, and one whose rearticulation is central to any attempt to understand or act in modern politics.

As Dunn rightly comments, 'Modern political association ... exhibits a massive (though to be sure far from uniform) range of deficiencies. . . . human beings today live in an extravagantly complex world.'[69] Such a point, significantly, is also stressed by utopian realists such as Booth and Giddens,[70] and is most fully developed by Ulrich Beck's powerful *Riksogesellschaft.* However, are we really to assume that the uncertainties and vicissitudes of such a world can be reduced to an orderly whole by a rearticulated, reconceptualized understanding of prudence, even a prudence spread out from the elite to the citizenry as a whole?

One way of essaying an answer to this question is to consider whether Dunn is right to tie trust and prudence together in the way that he does. Let us grant that we live in a world of unparalleled complexity (such a view is one of the assumptions that go to build the notion of modernity, particularly its social form, that I shall be developing in chapter 2). Let us grant also that trust is a key component of our political lives, one that such complexity has helped to make increasingly problematic. Do the requirements of trust in a complex world mean that Dunn is right to insist on 'modern prudence' as the prerequisite to a satisfactory way of coping with this situation?

I think it is best to look at Dunn's claim as being open to both weak and strong interpretations. On the weak interpretation, Dunn is arguing that a generalized 'prudence' is part of a *process* whereby trust and hence political legitimacy and authority can be reclaimed for the modern world. On the strong interpretation, on the other hand, it seems that he is saying that it is a *prerequisite* for any attempted resolution of the dilemmas of modern politics, a necessary, and perhaps even at times sufficient, condition for such resolution.

Dunn's meaning seems to shift rather uneasily between these two views. In an essay discussing Roberto Unger's rather baroque theory of politics, for example, Dunn suggests that 'What to do in politics always depends on what can and will be caused to come about. Unger is quite right to insist that we can never know this. But what follows from such epistemic opacity is merely that we must learn to judge it better in practice: an endless task. For this purpose and over time, Unger's scepticism and his preoccupation with institutional form are likely to prove more instructive than the ardour of his faith.'[71] Here the implication is that Dunn's understanding of prudence (though it plays a relatively small role in this essay) is best interpreted in the weaker sense; where he agrees with Unger is that modern prudence will require a recognition of such 'epistemic opacity' and a determination to act prudently in the light of that knowledge.

At other times, however, the stronger sense seems clearly intended, as for example when Dunn concludes that 'over the generations to come (if there are indeed generations to come) the democratisation of prudence will be a *precondition* for anything at all resembling a good life to be in question for the vast majority of human beings' (emphasis added).[72]

The question, therefore, is whether contemporary politics implies either or both of these readings of modern prudence. I suggest that while it certainly implies the weaker sense, it does not logically imply the stronger, and that this has considerable implications for the rest of Dunn's substantive case. As Dunn himself remarks, 'The claim that trust is central to the understanding of political action ... needs to be stated with some care.'[73] Dunn sees this centrality in the idea of the mutual dependence of ruler and ruled, sovereign and subject, and in the fact that the complexity of modern life has made this relation enormously more complicated than it previously was. He has, therefore, very strong grounds for suggesting that prudence, as he treats of it, is a crucial component of any attempt to come to terms with modern political circumstances in a way that allows us any sense of trust at all. Good fences, it is said, make good neighbours; equally, prudent citizens (in Dunn's Lockean sense) would help to make more trustworthy governments and thus would the relation of trust between ruler and ruled be strengthened.

However, this is very different from saying that it is a *precondition* of such an attempt, or of seeing that such an attempt is even necessary. In order for this claim to follow from his argument Dunn would have to show that trust as a feature of political agency required prudence as *something that is the basis of all other aspects of meaningful political agency*. He does not do this, however; indeed, his emphasis on the complexity of modern life, the 'massive range of deficiencies' of modern political association, implies that no one aspect of life is likely to be (as Rawls might put it) lexically prior to all the others.

It is here that the significance of Dunn's original historical preoccupation becomes apparent. For, of course, it is Locke's reading of the importance of trust that generates Dunn's pre-ocupation with prudence. I will say at once that I have a good deal of sympathy with Dunn's interpretation of Locke, but in order for this reading to constitute the dilemma of trust as Dunn portrays it we must also agree with Dunn about the 'soundness of Locke's insight into what politics is really about'.[74]

Here I would differ from Dunn. While I agree that contemporary politics is in part constituted by the dilemmas generated by 'trust', and that, as a result, the Lockean-type arguments and concerns are important and manifestly relevant for contemporary politics (witness for example, the multifarious use of Locke by thinkers as diverse as Dunn, Gauthier and Nozick[75]), it is also the case that contemporary politics is characterized by much more diversity than is implied in this framework. Considerations that play a part in Dunn's own work (economic interdependence, decolonization and the globalization of aspects of politics, to name but three) are all changing the context in which politics takes place, and crucially, bringing into question, at least in certain places and under certain conditions, the character of the political association we call the state. This situation is one that is significantly different from that considered by Locke and from the Lockean dilemmas that Dunn uses as his starting point – in part because Locke is deeply involved in the development of Skinner's 'dominant ideology' of modernity and which – as I shall try and show in chapters 2 and 3 – is itself facing huge problems comprehending the nature of the political from within it.

What I think this implies is that while we might agree with Dunn that a reading of the importance and interrelationship of prudence and trust is one of the central axes of contemporary politics, it by no means follows that Locke's reading should be central, nor that it is the central one or the one on which all the others depend.

In saying this I do not mean to commit myself to any particular reading of this condition in advance. However, I would suggest that in addition to the questions raised by Dunn out of Locke, so to speak, this condition problematizes precisely that aspect of contemporary politics that Dunn argued in *Rethinking Modern Political Theory* was at the heart of the recognition of the distinctively modern character of politics. To wit, that 'the claim to know better . . . can be vindicated only within identities, that the only authority which it can possess is a human authority, an authority for human beings not an external domination over them. What it is to be modern . . . is simply to face up to this knowledge.'[76]

It seems to me that the character of modern politics is shaped not by the need to 'face up to this' but to ascertain *if* we have to face up to it in the way Dunn thinks we do. Trust and prudence are of course part of this debate. To assume the priority of prudence for the tasks of political theory, however, is to give as an answer what is, in fact, a central question for modern political theory.

Dunn's work, therefore, puts at the centre of the debate over the character of political theory how we are supposed to understand the relationship between the present and the past. Against those who claim such a concern is parochial or largely unimportant, Dunn argues that we can have no convincing account of modern politics and its predicaments without a knowledge of its past construction (intellectual and material). Against those who claim such an activity is largely (or only) an historical one, he points to the significance of historical readings (such as his of Locke) for contemporary political theory.

There, however, lies the rub. History is crucial for Dunn and yet his arguments do not really come to terms with the central problem of all such arguments. Does history here imply historicism?[77] Dunn recognizes, of course, that this is part of the implication of his moderate anti-realism and is at pains to stress on a number of occasions throughout his writings the paucity of our ability to 'know'; indeed, as we have seen, it is this that is characteristic of modernity for Dunn and part of the reason why prudence is so important.

However, the mere existence of such epistemic paucity does not mean that it is a necessary condition. Part of the appeal of the Anglo-American approach to political theory has been its claim to provide us with a relatively objective set of criteria (some of which are, of course, in dispute) from which to observe, explain and prescribe about our political circumstances. Dunn, I think, is right to question whether this much-vaunted explanatory and normative power is not bought at the expense of a philosophical and historical abstraction that blinds it to much that is central to our political predicament. However, he does not address the question of whether his chosen path leaves us any better equipped. While he undoubtedly diagnoses many of our political ills with great forensic skill, the suspicion remains that Dunn's prescriptive recommendation amounts to a rather baroque version of the old parable that says 'look before you leap', dressed up in an admittedly impressive and historically well-informed way.

The interesting thing to do here, however, is to look back at the analysis of Skinner's thought offered by Tully. For, if Tully is correct, as I remarked above, then Skinner's concern for the 'subordinate ideology' of civic republicanism that he traces to Machiavelli chimes in very much with Dunn's concern to elaborate a new theory of prudence which amounts also to a new theory of the responsible citizen. As I shall suggest in chapters 3 and 4, in fact, it is not really an account of 'prudence' that is required, rather it is a much fuller notion than we currently have of the character of political judgement and practical reason.

The question then arises, of course, now would it be possible to create such citizens in the modern world and what would the difficulties be, what other commitments must go with such a view and what implications would such a view have for our institutional/social and cultural forms, and last but certainly not least, would such a task create a better and more appropriate account of our contemporary situation than the various rearticulations of the 'dominant ideology' that dominate contemporary Anglo-American political theory?

In answering this question, however, I suggest that we need something that Dunn does not provide, to wit an account of our contemporary condition that displays the character (even, in a certain sense the *nature*) of its politics much more concretely than simply suggesting that it is highly complex and multi-faceted (which is true but trivial). It is this, I suggest, that can be provided by a consideration of the debate over modernity.

## The Need for a Theory of Modernity

To elaborate this point more fully, let me return to Richard Bellamy's analysis of the problems of liberalism that I touched on briefly above. Bellamy's argument is especially useful because, like Dunn in certain respects, he combines a sympathy for the Cambridge School (he was a student of Skinner's and his methodological stance as far as intellectual history is concerned is clearly related) with a very definite departure in terms of normative position.

Recall that Bellamy's position is that modern liberalism suffers from failing to realize that the 'social thesis' that alone made ethical liberalism plausible in the absence of any overarching metaphysical schema is now discredited, and that liberalism must move from being an ethical to a political theory, where institutions take the place of liberal values and where democracy becomes the sole real guarantee of a liberal society. Bellamy ends up still a liberal but a chastened and, he would say, a more realistic one. He admits, indeed, being strongly influenced by the 'democratic realism' of Danilo Zolo and the anti-foundational (and therefore non-ethical) liberalism of Richard Rorty (of whom more later on).[78]

I do not want to discuss the specific merits of Bellamy's argument about liberalism here.[79] Rather, what interests me is the way in which he mounts his argument. Contemporary liberalism, he suggests, is theoretically problematic largely because it flies in the face of a changing social reality. This is a point that Dunn emphasizes as well. We need his 'modern' conception of prudence at least in part because of the changing nature of modern society; its complexity, its size and the dangers and risks held to be inherent in it.

In both cases, these theorists deploy a very sophisticated understanding of the historical evolution they refer to; in both cases they each reject an alternative account that seems too 'metaphysical' to command acceptance today; and in both cases they seem to want to remain within the ambit of liberal thought but seek to supplement it in various ways. In both cases, however, the theoretical positions they outline depend for their validity upon a distinct *historical–sociological* claim about the nature of contemporary reality. In important ways, as we shall seen in chapter 4, I agree with much of their argument about the character of the changes currently shaping modern politics. However, they do not suggest why we should frame our response to these changes as they do. Bellamy tries to save liberalism by making it more consistent with 'reality' but does not say why liberalism deserves saving. Dunn argues we should be prudent, but does not say why we should be prudent. The point is not to suggest that they *could* not provide interesting defences of their respective strategies, rather it is to ask why they *do* not. The answer, I think, lies in the character of their descriptions of the changing character of the modern world that they hope their political theories address. To put it in terms I shall explain more fully in the next chapter, they run together, I think, claims about modernity as a socio-cultural form, with theoretical perspectives that depend upon a reading of modernity as a 'mood'. As a result, their argument constantly oscillates between one perspective and the other and loses focus and clarity.

I agree, therefore, with both Bellamy and Dunn that, important and powerful though they undoubtedly are on their own terms, the sorts of arguments that characterize 'analytical political theory' are fundamentally attenuated in quite crucial ways, and that the result is conceptual sophistication of a very high order, albeit one which, as Dunn rightly emphasizes, is a sophistication bought at the price of a damaging narrowness of focus. I think a weaker version of the same charge can be levelled at Dunn and Bellamy themselves.

With one or two honourable exceptions, the characteristic champions of Anglo-American political theory run around a very small cage as far as the issues that engage their attention are concerned. As Allan Bloom said of Rawls' *A Theory of Justice*, 'its horizon does not seem to extend to the abysses which we have experienced in our own lifetimes . . . rather [it] is a correction of utilitarianism . . . the problems he addresses are those of civil liberties in nations that are already free and the distribution of wealth in those that are already prosperous'.[80] This is not true to anything like the same extent in the cases of thinkers like Dunn or Bellamy; none the less, there is an uncomfortable echo.

Of course, to say this is not to say that such questions are not important; it is merely to suggest that they do not constitute the whole of political theory. However, a key determinant is the assumption, which Bellamy and Dunn largely share, that political theory must be rooted in 'our common convictions' at least in some sense. If political theory starts from 'moral argument' that rests ultimately on 'our considered convictions', several questions arise. Who, in this context, are 'we'? A state, a culture, a civilization, a religion, a sub-national community (of whatever sort), any or all of these or what? And if we are to make sense of the disparate nature of 'our' convictions (however we answer the first question) how can we avoid going beyond what they currently are, reaching for a standard by which they can be adjudicated, evaluated or (at least) ranked?

One answer to this question, as we shall see in chapter 2, is to suggest that there is no way we can do this, and so we must abandon the style of thought that suggests there is a problem if we do not, a style, that is to say, that is distinctively 'modern' in its views of knowledge, politics and the world. Other views, in contrast, seek to defend the 'modern' style by showing how it can be made relevent to our changing political circumstances and philosophical assumptions. The debate between these two views is that 'modernity debate' whose course I shall seek to outline and assess in the next two chapters. To close this chapter, however, I want to briefly explore what we are left with if, while accepting that modernity has created something different as far as our political circumstances are concerned, we do not take either the self-consciously 'modern' or 'postmodern' paths to address them. By doing this, I hope to flag issues the importance and significance of which I shall return to in Part II of this book.

Let me begin by making one observation. Virtually all the political theories that I have discussed above ask two central questions, though the priority and emphasis on each varies according to the theory or theorist who is addressing them. The relation between the two questions is also one of the central issues of modern political theory. These two questions are, 'what should I do?' and 'who am I?'.

The first question is, of course, a standard question of ethics. However, it sees the 'ethical' in a very particular way. It emphasizes the contextual setting of ethical action by focusing on the 'rules' (so to speak) of such action. As Kymlicka says, political theory of the Anglo-American type is moral argument depending on 'our considered convictions', and those convictions set the context of ethical and political action. On these assumptions we cannot 'break out' of that context and nor should we try. In this kind of political theory, moreover, there is an implied assumption about who the 'we' are, an implied answer in other words to the second question 'who am I?'. 'I' am a citizen of country $x$, with obligations $y$ and rights $z$; this is my context, the setting for my 'considered convictions'.

When Dunn argues that contemporary Anglo-American political theory 'concentrates on questions of value' it is to this, I think, that he is referring; and in this respect there is a very clear fact/value link – rather than the distinction that many positivist social scientists famously declared was appropriate. The 'facts' tell us what state we are citizens of, *and therefore, at least in a certain sense, what 'values' are appropriate to us.* It is important to see that this is true of both liberals and communitarians, of historians of political thought and 'substantive' political theorists. It is an area where the differences between so-called liberals and so-called communitarians are far less important than the basic similarities.

'Communitarian' writers (say Taylor or Sandel) emphasize the centrality of the 'community' (not necessarily the state, of course) in shaping the 'convictions' that are to be considered, and they argue further that 'liberal' writers either unfairly de-emphasize or completely ignore the framing of the context. Liberal writers (such as Kymlicka or Barry) respond that they emphasize the context because it is the context that mostly sets the parameters of our action, important though the framing of the context unquestionably is. Both groups, however, are asking the same two questions, what should I do? and who am I?

It is significant that the third question, one that is not really asked, is perhaps the oldest ethical question of all and the one that in a very powerful sense subsumes the two previous and much more common questions; who or what *should I be*? Of course, on the assumptions of Anglo-American political theory such a question does not really make sense. Our contexts are given and our rules are set and so we can only try to properly understand who we are and how we should act, not try and become something other than that. Moreover, the 'we' in modern political theory is everyone in a given community – and possibly even in a community of communities; all citizens, in other words (a point to which I shall return in the final chapter). I agree again with Kymlicka, though he is here himself agreeing with Ronald Dworkin, to the effect that virtually all modern political theory of the Anglo-American sort has a common core value – to wit equality, defined as 'the treating of people as equals'.[81] This view has recently been given a 'communitarian' twist by Charles Taylor, who has referred to it as 'the politics of recognition',[82] and who has emphasized that it is because this idea has become increasingly public in contemporary societies, especially Western ones, that so much of contemporary liberal political theory seems problematic. This 'common core' of Anglo-American political theory is traceable, Taylor thinks, to the great political theorists of the Enlightenment; in sum, it is the story of the evolution of modernity or of the evolution of that 'dominant ideology' of which Skinner spoke.

I shall be examining the truth of this contention in Part I of this book, but if we reject or at least seek to heavily modify the answers that the moderns and their postmodern critics give, we will find, I want to suggest, that we shall be forced back to that question 'is there anything I should seek to become?', to attempt to structure a political theory that can give us any chance of pursuing Dunn's three given tasks for political theory. Where that will lead us is what I shall then attempt to explore in Part II of this book. However, in doing this it is important to realize that the other two questions are not silenced, merely asked in a different context, and that even though I move some way from the modernity debate initially in my exploration of what these questions mean for political theory, it is to that debate that I shall, in the end, be forced to return.

## Notes

1 In what follows I shall use this term to indicate adherents of a set of approaches to political theory (of which more later), rather than to designate a particular national origin or location. Thus, Phillipe Van Parijs, who teaches in Belgium, does, in my terms, 'Anglo-American' political theory.

2 See, for example, Brian Barry, 'The Strange Death of Political Philosophy', in *Democracy and Power: Essays in Political Theory 1* (Oxford: The Clarendon Press, 1991); David Miller, 'The Resurgence of Political Theory', in *Political Studies*, 38, no. 3, Sept. 1990; David Held (ed.), *Political Theory Today* (Cambridge: Polity Press, 1991), introduction.

3 See Barry, 'The Strange Death of Political Philosophy', p. 18.

4 The revival of substantive political theory in what is usually called an 'Anglo-American' mode, is widely held to have been sent into overdrive by the publication of John Rawls' *A Theory of Justice* (Oxford: Oxford University Press, 1972) and the launching of the journal *Philosophy and Public Affairs* in 1971. As Barry remarks in the article cited above, the rebirth of analytical political theory also benefited from much work in political economy and economics, especially that in game theory and other forms of formal theory. Recent representative selections of analytical political theory in this vein would include Alan Hamlin and Philip Pettit, *The Good Polity: Normative Analysis of the State* (Oxford: Blackwell, 1989); John Broome's *Weighing Goods* (Oxford: Blackwell, 1992); Will Kymlicka, *Liberalism, Community and Culture* (Oxford: The Clarendon Press, 1991); and Brian Barry, *Theories of Justice* (vol. 1 of A Treatise of Social Justice) (Hemel Hempstead: Harvester, 1989).

5 A good brief discussion is in Chris Brown, *International Relations Theory: New Normative Approaches* (Hemel Hempstead: Harvester, 1992).

6 See, for example, the collection of much of the work of Smart in his book with Bernard Williams, *Utilitarianism: For and Against* (Cambridge: Cambridge University Press, 1973). Singer's work rather later culminated in his book *Practical Ethics* (Cambridge: Cambridge University Press, 1979; 2nd edn 1991).

7 See Michael Sandel, *Liberalism and the Limits of Justice* (Cambridge: Cambridge University Press, 1982).

8 Stephen Mullhall and Adam Swift, *Liberals and Communitarians* (Oxford: Blackwell, 1992), p. 40.

9 Alisdair MacIntyre, *After Virtue* (London: Duckworth, 1981; 2nd edn 1987).

10 The book most usually cited is Taylor's *Sources of the Self* (Cambridge: Cambridge University Press, 1989). However, it is worth saying that

Taylor is very difficult to fit into the 'communitarian' frame as he himself has pointed out and as perceptive critics such as Mullhall and Swift have also emphasized.

11  Walzer's 'communitarianism' is usually held to be displayed most obviously in *Spheres of Justice* (Oxford: Blackwell, 1983), though aspects of it are present in his *Just and Unjust Wars* (Harmondsworth: Penguin, 1977).

12  Jean Cohen and Andrew Arato, *Civil Society and Political Theory* (Cambridge: MIT Press, 1992), p. 8.

13  See his 'Cross Purposes: The Liberal–Communitarian Debate', in Nancy Rosenblum (ed.), *Liberalism and The Moral Life* (Cambridge: Harvard University Press, 1989).

14  For Dworkin see *Taking Rights Seriously* (Cambridge: Harvard University Press, 1977); for Ackerman see *Social Justice in The Liberal State* (New Haven: Yale University Press, 1980).

15  See Judith Shklar, 'The Liberalism of Fear', in Nancy Rosenblum (ed.), *Liberalism and the Moral Life* (Cambridge: Harvard University Press, 1989).

16  This section draws on my more detailed analysis of the liberal–communitarian debate in Nils Sorensen et al. (eds), *European Identities* (Odense: Odense University Press, 1994).

17  See Taylor, 'Cross-Purposes', p. 182.

18  Richard Bellamy, *Liberalism and Modern Society* (Oxford: Polity Press, 1992).

19  Ibid., 2.

20  Will Kymlicka, *Contemporary Political Philosophy: An Introduction* (Oxford: Oxford University Press, 1990), p. 7.

21  See, for example, Rawls, *A Theory of Justice*, pp. 48–51; discussed also in *Political Liberalism*, also as due reflection (New York: Columbia University Press, 1993).

22  Rawls, *A Theory of Justice*, p. 51.

23  Rawls also says in a footnote to this passage of *A Theory of Justice* that this view of moral deliberation goes back to Aristotle, at least in its essentials. There are powerful reasons for questioning this and I shall return to them in chapter 3, but it is worth noting this given the alleged Aristotelean emphasis of many communitarians and also of the change in the presentation (at least) of Rawls' theory between *A Theory of Justice* and *Political Liberalism*.

24  For a canonical interpretation see Michael Walzer, *Interpretation and Social Criticism* (Cambridge: Harvard University Press, 1986).

25  The one exception to this view in the 'liberal–communitarian debate' is MacIntyre. I shall come on to his version of the problem and the debate in a moment.

26  See Bonnie Honig, *Political Theory and the Displacement of Politics* (Ithaca: Cornell University Press, 1993).

27  Ibid., 10.

28 In referring to 'orthodox Marxism' here, I chiefly have in mind those who work self-confessedly as 'historical materialists', such as Perry Anderson. There is, of course, the whole question of the relationship of writers such as Gramsci to Marxism more generally which I do not discuss, and I am exempting for the moment the work of the Frankfurt School (which I will take up again in chapter 3) and also of so-called analytical Marxism (G. A. Cohen et al.) which seems to me to be so close to certain forms of 'reborn' Anglo-American political theory as to make no difference. My main point is simply to stress that the choice here seems to be between taking the basic convictions and assumptions of our 'norms' as the starting point, or on the other hand of ignoring them altogether. Each, as I shall seek to show, is a mistake.

29 Consider, just as a sample, the work in the United States of scholars like Leo Strauss, Eric Voeglin, Reinhold Niebuhr, Hans Morgenthau, Sheldon Wolin and Hannah Arendt. In France of Alexandre Kojève, Raymond Aron, Jean-Paul Sartre and a little later, Michel Foucault, Louis Althusser and Paul Ricoeur. In Germany, of Adorno and Horkheimer, Heidegger, Habermas and Gadamer. In Italy of Norberto Bobbio, Vattimo and, more recently Danilo Zolo; and in the UK of Michael Oakeshott, John Plamenatz and Isaiah Berlin. It is fair to say, of course, that much of this work was not explicitly done in 'political philosophy' and that much of it appeared (at least) to be done in the history of ideas, a point recognized by the likes of Barry and Miller. Their point is precisely that it was non-historical substantive political theory that was 'dead'. However, most of the above-mentioned writers (and, indeed, many others) were not exclusively concerned with the history of ideas or had a conception of political philosophy that saw the history of ideas as a crucial component of any substantive theory. This was certainly the view of, for example, Strauss, Gadamer and Oakeshott, though naturally in different ways. This might be incorrect; it does not, however, indicate that political philosophy was dead.

30 Brian Barry, *Political Argument* (Hemel Hempstead: Harvester, 1990; first publ. 1965), p. xxi.

31 For a general discussion of Skinner's position, methodologically the most influential and certainly the best known, see James Tully (ed.), *Meaning and Context: Quentin Skinner and his Critics* (Cambridge: Polity, 1989). Pocock's essay 'Languages and Their Implications: The Transformation of The Study of Political Thought', in his *Politics, Language and Time* (Chicago: University of Chicago Press, 1971) outlines his methodological views. Dunn's views I shall discuss more fully in a moment. For a good general survey of competing methods in the history of political thought see David Boucher, *Texts In Context: Revisionist Methods For Studying the History of Ideas* (Dordrecht: D. Reidel, 1983), and a useful additional collection and survey is Preston King (ed.), *The History of Ideas* (London: Croom Helm, 1983). In addition to the Cambridge School, there is some analogous (though often different) work being done in Europe, especially

in Germany. See, for example, the *Geschichtliche Grundbegriffe: Historisches lexikon zur politische-sozialen Sprache in Deutschland* (eds. Otto Bruner, Werner Conze and Reinhart Koselleck [five volumes to date: Stuttgart, 1972– ] ). For a general discussion of the similar yet differing versions of the 'historical turn' in the history of political thought see Melvin Richter, 'Reconstructing the History of Political Languages: Pocock, Skinner and the Geschlichtliche Grundbegriffe', in *History and Theory*, 29, no. 1, 1990, pp. 38–70.

32 Quentin Skinner, *The Foundations of Modern Political Thought* (Cambridge: Cambridge University Press, 1978), vol. 1, The Renaissance, p. xi.

33 See, for example, Richard Tuck's introduction to his new Cambridge Texts in the History of Political Thought edition of *Leviathan* (Cambridge: Cambridge University Press, 1991), his Oxford Past Master, *Hobbes* (Oxford: Oxford University Press, 1989) and Skinner's articles, 'The Ideological Context of Hobbes' Thought', in the *Historical Journal*, 9, 1966; 'Conquest and Consent: Thomas Hobbes and The Engagement Controversy', in G. E. Aylmer (ed.), *The Interregnum: The Quest for a Settlement, 1646–1660* (London: Macmillan, 1972), 'Thomas Hobbes on the Proper Signification of Liberty', *Transactions of the Royal Historical Society*, 5th series, 40, 1990.

34 See, for example, David Gauthier, *The Logic of Leviathan* (Oxford: The Clarendon Press, 1969); Gregory Kavka, *Hobbesean Moral and Political Theory* (Princeton: Princeton University Press, 1986); Jean Hampton, *Hobbes and The Social Contract Tradition* (Cambridge: Cambridge University Press, 1986).

35 Iain Hampsher-Monk, *A History of Modern Political Thought* (Oxford: Blackwell, 1992), p. xi.

36 See Tully's discussion in his 'Overview', pp. 3–6 of *Meaning and Context*.

37 Tully, *Meaning and Context*, pp. 7–8.

38 Ibid., 22.

39 Ibid., 19.

40 Ibid., 17–18.

41 John Dunn, *Modern Revolutions: An Introduction to the Analysis of a Political Phenomenon* (Cambridge: Cambridge University Press, 1972; 2nd edn 1989).

42 John Dunn (ed.), *West African States: Failure and Promise* (Cambridge: Cambridge University Press, 1978); John Dunn, Donal Cruise O'Brien and Richard Rathbone (eds) *Contemporary West African States* (Cambridge: Cambridge University Press, 1989).

43 John Dunn, *The Politics of Socialism* (Cambridge: Cambridge University Press, 1984).

44 John Dunn (ed.), *The Economic Limits to Modern Politics* (Cambridge: Cambridge University Press, 1990).

45 John Dunn, *The Political Thought of John Locke* (Cambridge: Cambridge University Press, 1969); *Political Obligation in its Historical Context*

(Cambridge: Cambridge University Press, 1980); *Western Political Theory in the Face of the Future* (Cambridge: Cambridge University Press, 1979); *Rethinking Modern Political Theory* (Cambridge: Cambridge University Press, 1985). Hereafter *RPT*.

46 The most recent being John Dunn, *Interpreting Political Responsibility* (Cambridge: Polity Press, 1990). Hereafter *IPR*.

47 *IPR*, 193.

48 *IPR*, 193.

49 *IPR*, 195.

50 *IPR*, 8.

51 See *IPR*, 197.

52 *RPT*, 189.

53 *IPR*, 214.

54 *IPR*, 9, quotation is from *The Political Thought of John Locke*, p. x.

55 *IPR*, 9.

56 This is not the place to go over the many and variegated turns of the realist vs. anti-realist argument in twentieth-century philosophy. Suffice to say that as opposed to the realist view which sees fixed, determinate existing objects for social investigations, anti-realism suggests that there are only particular interpretations or assumptions embedded in still further assumptions and so on. The assumptions of anti-realist arguments are clearly compatible with the emphasis on context of Dunn and others of the Cambridge School. There are, of course, a wide number of possible anti-realist views (as there are realist views) and one should not assume that Dunn would subscribe to them all.

57 See, for example, Skinner's views as developed in the essays gathered together by James Tully in *Meaning and Context: Quentin Skinner and His Critics* (Cambridge: Polity, 1988).

58 *IPR*, 23.

59 *IPR*, 25.

60 *IPR*, 43.

61 *IPR*, 200.

62 *IPR*, 200.

63 A good general introduction to the way in which these models are used can be found in Iain Maclean, *Public Choice: An Introduction* (Oxford: Blackwell, 1987). Of course, the techniques and assumptions are used in a wide variety of ways by different theorists; I do not mean to imply anything other than the fact that Dunn's usage of 'prudence' is very different from these theorists' use of the term 'rational', with which it might be confused.

64 See, for example, the discussion in Aristotle's *Politics*, Bk. III, 1277a, though of course 'prudence' in our sense does not quite adequately translate the Greek word *phronimos*, for which it is usually used.

65 I refer, of course, to those versions of realism associated with thinkers such as Hans Morgenthau, Reinold Niebuhr and Raymond Aron, rather than the more recent school of 'neo-realism' advocated by Kenneth Waltz. For

discussions see Michael Joseph Smith, *Realist Thought from Weber to Kissinger* (Baton Rouge: Louisiana State University Press, 1986); Joel Rosenthal, *Righteous Realists* (Baton Rouge: Louisiana State University Press, 1991); and, for neo-realism, R. O. Keohane (ed.), *Neo-Realism and Its Critics* (New York: Columbia University Press, 1984).

66 See Ken Booth, 'Security in Anarchy: Utopian Realism in Theory and Practice', in *International Affairs*, 67, no. 3, July 1991; Anthony Giddens, *The Consequences of Modernity* (Cambridge: Polity, 1990), especially chapter 5.

67 See for example Giddens' *Consequences of Modernity*, pp. 114–24, and Booth's emphasis on common security.

68 See *RPT*, p. 1.

69 *IPR*, 209.

70 See Booth, 'Security in Anarchy', esp. pp. 532 and 535; and Giddens, *Consequences of Modernity*, pp. 70–8.

71 *IPR*, 178.

72 *IPR*, 215.

73 *IPR*, 26.

74 *IPR*, 43.

75 See obviously the works of Dunn cited above, and David Gauthier, *Morals by Agreement* (Oxford: Oxford University Press, 1986) and Robert Nozick, *Anarchy, State and Utopia* (Oxford: Blackwell, 1974).

76 *RPT*, p. 153.

77 By which, of course, I do not mean the belief in the inevitable laws of history or anything of this kind, simply the relativistic point that values and beliefs that change through time is all there is; i.e. that there is no independent conception of truth or value outside history.

78 See Bellamy, *Liberalism and Modern Society*, p. 303 n. 1.

79 I have done so elsewhere, however. See my 'Migrating Communities: Minority Rights in World Politics'. Paper to the School for Slavonic and East European Studies Conference on Minority Rights, University of London, May 1994.

80 Allan Bloom, 'Justice: John Rawls vs. the Tradition of Political Philosophy', in Bloom, *Giants and Dwarfs: Essays 1960–1990* (New York: Simon and Schuster, 1990), p. 316. The review article was originally published in the *American Political Science Review*, 69 (2), June 1975, pp. 648–62.

81 See Kymlicka, *Contemporary Political Philosophy*, p. 5. He is citing an argument from Dworkin's *Taking Rights Seriously* (London: Duckworth, 1977).

82 See Charles Taylor (ed. Amy Gutmann), *Multiculturalism and 'The Politics of Recognition'* (Princeton: Princeton University Press, 1992).

# PART I:
# THE MODERNITY DEBATE

*What you have inherited from your forefathers you must first win for yourself if you are to possess it*

Goethe

# 1

# TWO SENSES OF MODERNITY

*Modernity is that which is ephemeral, fugitive, contingent upon the occasion.*

Baudelaire

*Philosophy rests on the texts it criticizes.*

Adorno

'Modernity' is a concept that does not have a fixed, easily delineated meaning or provenance. As it has been increasingly widely used of late, by an increasingly wide variety of writers, this is not, of course, very surprising. However, in this chapter I want to suggest that, for all this variety, there are two broad senses of the term modernity that can usefully be distinguished from one another. I shall term these two 'senses' of modernity, modernity as mood and modernity as socio-cultural form.

In particular, I shall be concerned to prepare the ground for the argument that I shall develop in the next chapter to the effect that what I shall describe as the 'modernity debate' in contemporary philosophy and political theory has primarily (and rightly) been a debate about modernity as mood, though there are writers who emphasize modernity as socio-cultural form as well. Moreover, I want to suggest that the discussion of the *two* senses of modernity has often been elided, conflated or simply ignored and that the result of this has been detrimental to our understanding of modernity as a phenomenon, but also – and more importantly for my purpose here – seriously detrimental to our ability to frame a response to the question of modernity that can give us direction in political theory and thus help resolve the impasse described at the end of the introductory chapter.

My first aim in this chapter, then, and the purpose of the first section below, is to sketch out these two senses of modernity and say something about each. Following this, in the middle section of this chapter, I want to begin by pursuing two different ways of reading modernity as mood, those of Alisdair MacIntyre and Stephen Toulmin, and then explore what I take to be the implications of their arguments both for the way in which the modernity debate has been framed and for the problems of political theory discussed in the introductory chapter above. This will help to situate the issues raised by modernity and will allow me to develop an account of the setting for the modernity debate and what is at stake in it.

In the final part of this chapter, then, I shall concentrate on developing an account of this sense of modernity which can help frame the critique of the modernity debate that follows and to which I shall return in my final chapter. While I shall argue that it is important – indeed, vital – to keep the two senses of modernity distinct, it is also central to any proper understanding of this phenomenon that we can meaningfully relate them. It is the failure to do this (or alternatively the tendency to conflate them) that has largely led, or so I want to suggest, to many of the problems inherent in the modernity debate that I shall try to point up in my next chapter. To frame my discussion here, I shall especially focus on Hans Blumenberg's discussion of the character of modernity and contrast it with some arguments of Leo Strauss. This will then provide the context and the framework for the discussion of the modernity debate itself, to which I shall turn in chapter 2, as well as for some of the alternative suggestions that I shall start to pursue in Part II of the book.

## Two Senses of Modernity?

Let me start, then, with two quotations:

> Even if modernity is not unique (it is too early to tell) it is at least
> distinctive. In its optimistic moments it defines itself by contrast

to earlier periods which are darker, more superstitious, less free, less rational, less productive, less civilized, less comfortable, less democratic, less tolerant, less respectful of the individual, less scientific and less developed technically than it is at its best . . . modernity is an epoch with no well defined beginning or end . . . it gives modern articulations to persistent questions of meaning, the relation of human life to nature, the relation of the present to the past and the future, the form of the well grounded order and the relation of life to death.[1]

Modernity refers to modes of social life or organization which emerged in Europe from about the seventeenth century onwards and which subsequently became more or less worldwide in their influence. This associates modernity with a time period and with an initial geographical location.[2]

These two statements clearly reflect different ways of looking at the shared concept with which they each begin. In the first, William Connolly's, 'modernity' is given almost a personal character. It has 'optimistic moments' and 'defines itself' in a certain way. It is also, while obviously temporally located, not *defined* by that temporal location. In the second, Anthony Giddens', modernity is much more obviously tied to a time and a place (at least in origin) and is also focused on 'modes of social life or organization'. Giddens is also aware, as he makes clear just before the passage quoted, that this view is an 'institutional analysis of modernity with cultural and epistemological overtones' and that this is different from many received views about modernity 'in which these emphases are reversed'.[3]

This distinction is what I shall refer to as modernity as mood (Connolly) and modernity as socio-cultural form (Giddens). The characteristics of each are relatively clear. Connolly's speaks to the sense of modernity as what Richard Bernstein has called, borrowing a phrase from Heidegger, a *Stimmung*, a mood which is 'amorphous, protean and shifting but which nevertheless asserts a powerful influence on the ways in which we think, act and experience'.[4] Giddens, on the other hand, wants to emphasize the institutional, social and economic nature of modernity, the sense of modernity as *the structure of* modern life rather than a sense of it as *a response within/to* the structure of modern life.

This distinction unquestionably has implications for the way in which we treat modernity. On the first view, modernity is fundamentally a philosophical (ethico-political) question, on the second it is a sociological (historical, anthropological) one. Like both Connolly and Giddens, I want to accept that both these are important senses of modernity. Unlike Giddens, however, I do not want to give priority to one view (modernity as socio-cultural form) over the other; each, or so it seems to me, is important, and to give causal priority to one would be to assume an answer to one of the major questions that modernity throws up; the appropriate relation between theory and practice. Instead, what I want to do is to assume the validity of each of these two senses of modernity and say something about each before going on to say rather more about the first sense, with which I shall be chiefly concerned in this book, the sense of modernity as a mood.

## Modernity as socio-cultural form

Because I shall be mainly concerned in this book with modernity as mood, I want to talk first here about the other sense, that of modernity as socio-cultural form. Typically, such a view of modernity takes the form of general analyses of our condition that emphasize the changing character of the material forces of society, and which emphasize the unique, or at least radically different, character of the modern age from previous ages. Thus, for example, Marxist analyses of modernity might stress the changes in the capitalist world economy,[5] other writers might stress the growth of information technology, the spread of computerization, fax machines and so forth,[6] or the evolving character of modernization and the structural changes to which it gives rise.[7]

Of course, such accounts need not be totally unconcerned with cultural, epistemological or philosophical questions. As Giddens explicitly states, they will certainly have 'cultural or epistemological overtones' and may have very sophisticated and nuanced accounts of the less tangible elements of modernity. However, their fundamental concern will be with structures, processes and 'conditions'. As David Harvey has put it, in one of the best explorations of (in his case) 'postmodernity', 'we can begin to understand postmodernity as an historical–geographical *condition*'.[8] This, incidentally, expresses a distinctive aspect of this sense of modernity – the sense in which '*postmodernity*' is an historical condition; the current phase *of* modernity, in other words, rather than a rejection of, or move 'beyond', the modern. I shall return to the question of postmodernity in chapter 4.

This sense of modernity begins to shade into the sense of modernity as mood, however, in some of the writing of the Frankfurt School. In the work of, for example, Walter Benjamin and Theodor Adorno we find both a sense of modernity as mood and the sense that it is an historically generated condition.[9] It is indeed the tension between these two aspects of modernity that often gives much of Adorno's work, especially, its particular power. In this writing the two moods are not 'confused', nor are they 'conflated'; at their best writers like Adorno and Benjamin hold the two senses in an uneasy and always unstable tension, where neither has priority; though the risk is always there that one aspect will come to dominate the other. Indeed, I think that one can argue that the project of 'Frankfurt School' critical theory has had, from its beginnings, something of a divided self as regards modernity, and that this has been the source of much of its power and intellectual fecundity, but also of its instability and tendency to fragment. I shall discuss this point in more detail in the next chapter.[10]

## Modernity as mood

However, let me now turn to 'modernity as mood'. As I remarked earlier, I borrow this phrase from Richard Bernstein, whose analysis of it in the opening chapter of his recent book *The New Constellation* cannot, I think, be bettered as a starting point. The phrase 'new constellation' itself, he tells us, is in fact taken from Benjamin and Adorno, and he cites Martin Jay's description of their usage of it as a 'juxtaposed rather than integrated cluster of changing elements that resist reduction to a common denominator, essential core or generative first principle'.[11] This, Bernstein says, is how he sees our contemporary situation. He also makes another suggestion, however, one that I shall be particularly concerned to develop in Part II of this book, but which I will simply describe for now.

Throughout the book, he uses the hyphenated expression 'ethical-political' to invoke and recall, he says, the classical (Greek) understanding of the symbiotic relation between ethics and politics. His description of this relationship is worth quoting in full, because while I agree with it in many respects, I shall later disagree very strongly with one aspect of it.

> Ethics is concerned with ethos, with those habits, customs and modes of response that shape and define our praxis. Politics is concerned with our public lives in the polis – with the communal bonds that at once unite and separate us as citizens. *The essential link between ethos and polis is nomos.* Though we can distinguish ethics from politics they are inseparable. For we cannot understand ethics without thinking through our political commitments and responsibilities. And there is no understanding of politics that does not bring us back to ethics. Ethics and Politics as disciplines concerned with praxis are aspects of a unified practical philosophy.[12] [emphasis added]

As I say, with this in broad terms I completely agree. As Bernstein also points out, an appeal to this conception (in many different ways, of course) has recently been a feature of ethical and political theory amongst the likes of Alisdair MacIntyre, Martha Nussbaum, Hans-Georg Gadamer, Bernard Williams and many others. Some of these writers will indeed be my point of departure in Part II of this book. However, it is this sense of challenge to contemporary modes of being and thinking (Bernstein cites also Hegel's notion of *Sittlichkeit* as a central site of this context) that has fed into what he calls the *Stimmung* of 'modernity/postmodernity'.

It is indeed this aspect of modernity as mood that I want to reflect on; the sense, that is, of challenge and response, of the attack on and defence of modernity, of 'the modern project'. Before this makes much sense, however, we must understand what 'the modern project' in this sense can be said to be; an understanding, in fact, of the parameters within which this mood can be said to exist.

## The Mood of Modernity: Two Reflections

In order to best capture the sense of modernity as mood, I want to take two presentations of modernity as an initial starting point. I choose these two partly because of their intrinsic interest and partly because they present significant disagreements about the character or nature of modernity which are highlighted, so to speak, by some very profound areas of agreement. These two views are those of Alisdair MacIntyre and Stephen Toulmin. MacIntyre is perhaps the best-known contemporary critic of modernity who is not a 'postmodern' (in the sense I shall discuss in the next chapter), and Toulmin, though a defender of modernity of sorts, is not a defender that most of the champions of the modern (also discussed in the next chapter) would recognize or applaud. In terms I shall use in the next chapter, MacIntyre is a 'disturber of the peace' in ways that postmoderns would find as disturbing as (even perhaps more disturbing than) moderns, while Toulmin is a 'defender of the faith' in modernity in a way that the more prominant defenders of modernity could take little comfort in. The differences and similarities in their accounts of modernity are, therefore, likely to be instructive. Moreover, both – at least in a certain sense – are aware of the difference between modernity as mood and modernity as socio-cultural form and try, though in markedly different ways, to address it. Let me look first, then, at the arguments of Alisdair MacIntyre.

### *MacIntyre and the collapse of 'the Enlightenment project'*

Alisdair MacIntyre has rightly been seen as one of the most interesting and acute critics of 'modernity' in contemporary philosophy. For him modernity is the creation of that period of thought referred to as the 'Enlightenment' and its immediate ancestors and descendants, roughly speaking between 1630 and 1880.

'It is only in the later seventeenth and the eighteenth century,' he writes in his magnum opus, *After Virtue*,[13] 'when [the] distinguishing of the moral from the theological, the legal and the aesthetic has become a received doctrine that the project of an independent rational justification for morality becomes not merely the concern of individual thinkers, but central to Northern European Culture'.[14]

This project is what MacIntyre refers to as 'the Enlightenment project' and it is the chief player in his view of the origin of modernity. However, it is not just the growth and increasing power of this view that is characteristic of modernity, but its breakdown and collapse. Famously, MacIntyre begins *After Virtue* with an excoriating portrayal of a society and a culture in terminal and irrevocable chaos because its categories of moral judgement are locked in interminable and unending conflict. This situation MacIntyre refers to as 'emotivism'. The emotivist view, MacIntyre argues, 'envisages moral debate in terms of a confrontation between incompatible and incommensurable moral premises and moral commitment as the expression of a criterionless choice between such premises, a type of choice for which no rational justification can be given'.[15]

This view of ethics is, for MacIntyre, that which finds its philosophically most acute expression in the thought of Nietzsche, and thus for MacIntyre 'modernity' is a project doomed to failure, doomed in other words to collapse in upon itself, though only Nietzsche and his explicit followers (among the moderns anyway) realize this. This is what leads MacIntyre to pose his famous stark choice halfway through *After Virtue*: Nietzsche or Aristotle. For if Nietzsche correctly recognizes that the game is up for modernity and modernity was erected upon the rejection of what was still fundamentally an Aristotelean world view, then the choice that confronts us is either a Nietzschean nihilism or a conviction that the rejection of Aristotle (which ineluctably leads to it) was mistaken in the first place. As MacIntyre expresses it:

> Either one must follow through the aspirations and the collapse of the different versions of the Enlightenment project until there remains only the Nietzschean diagnosis and the Nietzschean problematic or one must hold the Enlightenment project was not only a mistake but should never have been conceived in the first place. There is no third alternative.[16]

Modernity, then, for MacIntyre, consists in two main theses about the 'Enlightenment project': (1) its desire to construct an 'independent, rational justification for morality' and (2) the collapse of this attempt. It is important also, however, to ask *why* it had to collapse. MacIntyre argues that 'any project of this form was bound to fail, because of an ineradicable discrepancy between their shared conception of moral rules and precepts on the one hand and what was shared – despite much larger divergences – in their conception of human nature on the other'.[17] Both of these conceptions, claims MacIntyre, have a history and cannot be understood except through that history.

The nub of MacIntyre's argument here is that a new – and fundamentally anti-teleological – view of reason evolved into the mainstream of European thought with the Reformation and the movements that immediately prefigured and anticipated it, and that it was this conception of reason which, allowing for some differences in content and temper, dominated the Enlightenment and the project to which it gave rise. What is this view of reason? It is reason as purely instrumental.

'Reason is calculative,' MacIntyre has this view assert,

> it can assess truths of fact and mathematical relations but nothing more. In the realm of practice, therefore it can speak only of means. About ends it must be silent . . . Even Kant retains [this concept's] negative characteristics; reason for him, as much as for Hume [in most respects for MacIntyre, *the* Enlightenment philosopher], discerns no essential natures, and no teleological features in the objective universe, available for study only by physics. Thus their disagreements on human nature co-exist with striking and important agreements and what is true of them is true also of Diderot, of Smith and of Kierkegaard.[18]

This view, however, conflicts with the contextual setting of the moral schema which was the historical ancestor of the framework of moral values within which the philosophers operated, that which Aristotle analysed in the *Nicomachean Ethics* and which, argues MacIntyre, required three main elements: 'untutored human nature, man as he could be if he realised his telos and the moral precepts which enable him to pass from one state to the other'.[19]

The new – Enlightenment-adopted – conception of reason, however, did away with the middle element and consequently was left with a view of untutored human nature as it is and a set of moral injunctions deprived of the context which gave them sense. 'The eighteenth-century moral philosophers,' argues MacIntyre, 'engaged to find a rational basis for their moral beliefs in a particular understanding of human nature, while inheriting a set of moral injunctions on the one hand and a conception of human nature on the other which had been expressly designed to be discrepant with one another.'[20] Given this, MacIntyre suggests, it is hardly surprising that the result was disaster.

Note, then, that on this understanding, it is the conception of reason that comes to dominate the Enlightenment that therefore plays the third key role in the creation of modernity for MacIntyre, along with the Enlightenment project itself and its collapse.

We appear to have then a fairly clear view of the *character* of modernity (moral and political confusion caused by interminably clashing ethical categories) and its *origin* (the 'Enlightenment project', its collapse and the role of reason in it). MacIntyre's preferred solution – a return to Aristotelean teleology – is something I shall return to later on, but for now let me move on to a very different, though equally interesting, presentation of the mood of modernity.

## Toulmin and the 'hidden agenda' of modernity

Stephen Toulmin, in his book *Cosmopolis*,[21] like MacIntyre and Giddens, tries to locate the emergence of modernity in a temporal shift made at a specific point in time – or rather two – (the sixteenth and seventeenth centuries) and with a specific physical location (Europe). In his opening chapter, indeed, he charts the rise of what he terms the 'standard account' or 'received view' of modernity, which bears more than a passing resemblance to MacIntyre's view just outlined.[22] Acknowledging that it is a multi-faceted account and that there are many aspects to it (and perspectives on it), there are a number of things on which the 'standard account' is agreed, he suggests:

Despite all the ambiguities surrounding the idea of modernity, the confusions and disagreements hide an underlying consensus . . . the arguments rest upon shared assumptions about *rationality*. All parties to the debate agree that the self styled 'new philosophers' of the seventeenth century were responsible for new ways of thinking about nature and society. They committed the modern world to thinking about nature in a new and 'scientific' way and to use more 'rational' methods to deal with the problems of human life and society. Their work was therefore a turning point in European history and deserves to be marked off as the true starting point for modernity.[23] [emphasis added]

This 'turning point' gave rise to a 'theory-centred' style of philosophy that followed Descartes and has continued to be the most important style in which philosophical reasoning is expressed to this day, though it has met with many challanges.[24] Toulmin argues that as the notions deriving from these assumptions have become more problematic, so the status of 'modernity' has suffered accordingly, especially in philosophy. However, his own argument is to suggest that the 'standard account' is in any case wrong to see modernity in the way that it does, and in order to argue for this view he attempts to link what I have called modernity as mood and modernity as sociocultural form.

This linkage begins with Toulmin criticizing the general historical and sociological assumptions underlying the received view. Essentially there are three of these. First, that by 1600 AD new levels of material prosperity and comfort had been reached and trade was growing. Second, that the hold of the Church on intellectual and cultural life was slackening. Third, a related point to the second, that the spread of literacy created a new secular source of ideas and potential change.

Contrary to these claims, Toulmin suggests that while in the sixteenth century Europe did enjoy relative prosperity and economic expansion, by the early years of the seventeenth century this had come to a grinding halt, leading to what a number of historians have termed the 'crisis of the seventeenth century'.[25] Moreover, rather than the Church and religion generally becoming less important in the early seventeenth century, it became more important and more demanding. Finally, while it is true that literacy was spreading and creating a literary and scientific culture separate from that of the Church, this was not a novelty. Printed books had been around for over a century by 1600, and the literary, though perhaps not the scientific or philosophical culture of modernity long pre-dated the seventeenth century.

These points lead to one obvious conclusion for Toulmin:

> we may therefore ask if the modern world and modern culture did not have two distinct origins, rather than one single origin, the first (literary or humanistic phase) being a century before the second. If we follow this suggestion and carry the origins of modernity back to the late Renaissance authors of Northern Europe in the sixteenth century we shall find the second, scientific and philosophical phase, from 1630 on, leading many Europeans to turn their backs on the most powerful themes of the first, the literary or humanistic phase.[26]

Toulmin fills in this idea by pointing out the very considerable difference between the philosophical agenda of the post-1630 world and that of the previous century. He sees the central difference in the thoroughgoing abstraction of the latter.

> Before 1600, theoretical inquiries were balanced against discussions of concrete practical issues, such as the specific conditions on which it is morally acceptable for a sovereign to launch a war, or for a subject to kill a tyrant. From 1600 on, by contrast, most philosophers are committed to questions of abstract, universal theory, to the exclusion of such concrete issues. There is a shift from a style of philosophy that keeps equally in view issues of local timebound practice and universal, timeless theory, to one that accepts matters of universal timeless theory as being entitled to an exclusive place on the agenda of 'philosophy'.[27]

The gradual abandonment of the humanistic view is what, for Toulmin, sets up the 'rationalistic', 'scientific', 'instrumental' aspect of modernity that MacIntyre and Connolly take to be its crucial feature, if not the whole of it (though he does not discuss them by name very much, Connolly not at all). He particularly suggests that four displacements took place that were of especial significance; a move from the oral to the written, the particular to the universal, the local to the general and the timely to the timeless. He goes on to deepen his socio-economic argument by suggesting that

> the early seventeenth century . . . saw a narrowing of scope for freedom of discussion and imagination that operated on a social plane with the onset of a new insistence on 'respectability' in thought and behaviour, and also on a personal plane. There, it took the form of an alienation quite familiar to the late twentieth century which expressed itself as solipsism in intellectual matters and as narcissism in emotional life.[28]

Toulmin continues this story into the seventeenth and eighteenth centuries. He discusses Leibniz's dream of an ideal language 'that could be learned and understood by people of any country, culture or religion', emerging out of Leibniz's reflection on the sorry state of Europe after the Thirty Years' War, and links it to Leibniz's more general ideas about a *characteristica universalis*, which would be not simply a general language (like Esperanto) but a language that would capture the processes of rational thought and perception through the use of formal (mathematical) symbolism.[29] 'It would,' Toulmin says, 'embody and codify all the valid modes of argument, so that people with different intellectual backgrounds could reason together without fear of confusion or error.'[30] Toulmin concludes here by pointing out that 'the dreams of a rational method, a unified science and an exact language, unite into a single project. All of them are designed to "purify" the operations of human reason, by decontextualising them, i.e. by divorcing them from the details of particular historical and cultural situations.'[31]

This led ineluctably, Toulmin argues, to the construction, through the power of Newtonian physics, of what he calls 'the new cosmopolis'. This was, as he outlines it, a social and political as well as a scientific creation. Toulmin expresses this important insight as follows:

> a cosmopolis . . . gives a comprehensive account of the world, so as to bind things together in political–theological, as much as scientific or explanatory terms. Those who reconstructed

European society and culture after the Thirty Years' War took as
guiding principles stability in and among the different sovereign
nation states, and hierarchy within the social structures of each
individual state[32] . . . it was important to believe that the principles of stability and hierarchy were found in all of the divine
plan . . . the more confident one was about subordination and
authority in nature, the less anxious one accordingly needed to
be about social inequalities.[33]

However, from the end of the eighteenth century onwards,
Toulmin argues, this edifice became more and more unstable
and the twin pillars of its success, doctrinal and experiential,
metaphysical and scientific, followed increasingly divergent
trajectories.

The formal doctrines that underpinned human thought and
practice from 1700 on followed a trajectory with the shape of an
Omega, i.e. after three hundred years we are back close to our
starting point. Natural scientists no longer separate the observer
from the world observed . . . sovereign states find their independence circumscribed; and Descartes' foundational ambitions
are discredited, taking philosophy back to the scepticism of
Montaigne . . . Meanwhile in experiential terms . . . the progress
of natural philosophy has been cumulative and continuous and
Descartes' cryptanalytical hopes have proved more than
justified . . . both philosophy and science are back in the intellectual postures of the last generation before Descartes . . . we are
freed from the exclusively theoretical agenda of rationalism and
can take up again the practical issues sidelined by Descartes'
*coup d'état* some three hundred years ago.[34]

Toulmin then develops his own analysis of the modernity
debate and his own prognosis and recommendations, which I
shall defer discussion of until the next chapter. However, a few
general comments on both MacIntyre and Toulmin's readings
seem in order at this point.

## Divergent readings of modernity?

It is quite clear that there is a substantial amount of agreement
between MacIntyre and Toulmin on the main characteristics of

modernity and on what is wrong with it. Both argue that it is *time bound* in a very specific sense; both argue that it depends upon certain conceptions of *rationality* that no longer command general acceptance; both argue that modernity prefers the universal to the particular, the general to the local; and both see the abandonment of these characteristic 'modern' assumptions as central to our ability to properly think, act and function as human beings.

For all that they share, however, Toulmin's presentation of modernity is sharply different in at least one key respect from MacIntyre's. Toulmin does not suggest that we either can or should 'retreat' from the modern; for Toulmin, understanding modernity aright means understanding its dual root and returning, to use Peter Euben's luminous phrase, to 'the path not taken', the path that is mapped out by Montaigne, Erasmus and the other 'humanists' who Toulmin believes were the first 'moderns'. Interestingly enough, in his epilogue to *Cosmopolis*, Toulmin suggests that 'we are the point of transition from the second to the third phase of modernity – or, if you prefer, from modernity to postmodernity'.[35] This 'postmodernity', however, would be a *return*; a return to the moderns that existed before Descartes; the civic, literary, humanistic moderns such as Montaigne and Erasmus.

Even with this difference, however, there is much that they agree upon. Like MacIntyre, Toulmin suggests that this 'transitional period' points us in the direction of a challenge to those intellectual and political modes of being most associated with modernity, most especially, in the narrowly political realm, the nation state. Again, however, there is a crucial difference. Toulmin argues that, 'Rather than deploring this change by blanket condemnation of, say, multi-national corporations or the international monetary fund, it is more useful to ask how the ideal of "representative government" can be extended to these institutions, so as to bring their activities under scrutiny from the people whose lives they most affect.'[36] His view, like that of the Montaigne he celebrates, is tolerant and optimistic.

MacIntyre's view, certainly in *After Virtue* and, I would argue, in his later writings as well, is far more pessimistic. We are told that today the barbarians 'are not waiting beyond the frontiers, they have already been governing us for quite some-time',[37] and the elegiac conclusion – that we await another St Benedict – is another comment in the same vein.

One could put this down in part, of course, to the temperamental differences between Toulmin and MacIntyre and no doubt there is some truth in this. However, I suggest that there is a much deeper problem here. It consists, I think, in the feeling that dominates MacIntyre's work that modernity is somehow *illegitimate as a whole*, that it can never succeed in what it promises and, in failing to do so, carries away all standards and possibilities of legitimate judgement. As Stephen Holmes has recently alleged,[38] such a view is by no means unique to MacIntyre, it has a long history – and arguably a whole tradition of thought – associated with it. I shall return to this view in chapter 3 of the present study, but for now it is important to note that the central difference between MacIntyre and Toulmin is precisely this: MacIntyre thinks modernity fundamentally illegitimate; Toulmin believes it to be legitimate *if understood correctly* and that so understood it is, indeed, our best and only hope of 'facing the future again', to use his own phrase from the epilogue to *Cosmopolis*.

These views have significant implications for the problem of political theory sketched in the introductory chapter. On either Toulmin or MacIntyre's account of modernity the 'Anglo-American' agenda of political theory is in deep trouble. If MacIntyre is correct, then virtually *all* contemporary (Anglo-American) political theory is misconceived and will be unable to either properly analyse our contemporary political condition or properly advise us on how to act within it. If Toulmin is right, then at least in principle, liberalism (for example) is salvageable, but it will be the liberalism of a Judith Shklar, a Richard Flathman or a Richard Rorty, a 'liberalism of fear', a 'willful liberalism' or a 'liberal ironism' derived perhaps from Montaigne,[39] not a juridical liberalism derived, as in the case of Rawls, at least allegedly, from Kant.[40]

On both views, however, the history of political thought (and indeed, of ideas generally) is central to the tasks of political theory and philosophy as such. This clearly links their claims with the writings of the Cambridge School discussed in the introductory chapter. However, their arguments go much further than the Cambridge School would seem to accept, in that for both MacIntyre and Toulmin it is not just that the character of our political thought (and indeed much else besides) can only be properly understood historically – though this is also true – rather it is to claim that such understanding is the *only* kind of understanding relevant to our political and moral thinking.

Again there are some differences. MacIntyre requires there to be a sense of transhistorical survival, through the medium of tradition – otherwise Aristotle could have no relevance for us. Toulmin is less concerned with this but agrees that the local, the particular and the specific are far more important than the universal, the timeless or the general.

What matters in either case, however, is the centrality for each of the above presentations of the characterization of modernity as time-bound, primarily focused on a particular understanding of human reason and the subsequent sense of modernity's legitimacy or otherwise. Thus it is to this question that I must now turn if I am to complete my presentation of modernity as mood.

## Reconceiving the Modern Frame?: Blumenberg and Strauss

To frame this discussion I first want to consider two further presentations of modernity that differ quite substantially from those given above. The first, Hans Blumenberg's massive and magisterial *Die Legitimät der Neuzeit*,[41] is unquestionably one of the most important books to be written on the general theme of modernity. As William Connolly has noted, Blumenberg's central claim is that 'the problem of the legitimacy of this age is latent in the modern age's claim to carry out a radical break with tradition and in the incongruity between this claim and the reality of history which can never be entirely new'.[42] The second is Leo Strauss's well-known argument that (in a sense even more radical than MacIntyre's) modernity is 'illegitimate'; founded upon a fundamental error that has developed and evolved over the last few centuries in a series of 'waves'.[43]

The first point to make, however, is that Blumenberg and Strauss are not quite addressing the same question. As Robert Wallace points out, Blumenberg is responding to a wide range of (largely) German thought that culminates in 1949 with the publication of Karl Löwith's powerful *Meaning in History*.[44] In this work Löwith argues that 'modern' philosophies of history (from Voltaire through to Hegel, Marx and Proudhon) are best interpreted as 'secularisations' of the eschatological pattern set up by the Jewish and Christian religions, of their faith in the fulfilment of the world's history through 'final' events (coming of the Messiah, Last Judgement etc.), a faith whose essence he describes as 'hope', 'living by experience' or simply 'futurism'.[45] Löwith presents this as a fundamental contrast to the classical worldview which was founded, he suggests, on 'a reverence for the past and the ever present . . . exemplified by organic life and the revolution of the heavens'. The problem with the modern age for Löwith is that having now abandoned the religious underpinnings of an eschatological worldview it has the sharp focus of neither Judaeo-Christian or Greek thinking. The idea of 'progress' which results is therefore fundamentally flawed; hence illegitimate.

Before moving on to Blumenberg's reponse to this argument it is worth pointing out that, on this reading, 'modernity', in a certain sense at least, might be said to begin with the triumph of Christianity. The point of this, of course, is that it raises a question about seeing modernity as something that in any meaningful sense can be 'dated'. If 'modernity' can in any sense be seen as beginning in the fifth or sixth centuries AD then it is manifestly odd to call it 'modern'. This is another reason, I suggest, for seeing 'modernity' as, in important senses, a mood, a response to certain issues in (at the moment) contemporary life and thought. It should also be noted, as Wallace notes, that Löwith's ideas have distinct echoes of the work of Leo Strauss, though there are also I think quite crucial differences. As I shall argue in chapter 3, both similarities and differences have to do with their response to the figure who was in many ways central to both, Martin Heidegger.[46]

Blumenberg, however, is critical of this whole line of thought. *Die Legitimät der Neuzeit* is, amongst other things, an enormously detailed development of a critique of Löwith's secularization thesis first delivered at the Seventh German Philosophy congress in 1962 and later greatly expanded. Blumenberg's critique of Löwith is conducted on a number of levels and we do not need to discuss them all, but in brief he argues that, firstly, Christian (and indeed, Judaic) eschatological schemes assume an 'outside, transcendental intervention' to bring about the 'final end', whereas modern ideas of progress are really 'inside' accounts of 'immanent' development. He also argues that Christian approaches to the final judgement are (to say the least) as much characterized by fear (of Hell) as by hope (of Heaven).[47]

Secondly, for Blumenberg, progress arises out of the two early-modern experiences of 'overcoming': the overcoming of the 'authority' of Aristotelean science; and the gradual overcoming of the belief that classical literature and art were models of perfection only to be aspired to, and its replacement by the belief that ages created their own 'perpetually valid' models that were potentially every bit as 'perfect' as classical ones. These two developments are primarily seventeenth-century ones and are built upon in the subsequent centuries.

The most original argument in the book for my purposes here, however, is that which Blumenberg unfolds in part 2, entitled 'Theological Absolutism and Human Self Assertion'. As Wallace recognizes, this argument is a highly original interpretation of the role of Christianity in bringing about modern 'human self assertion' of which 'progress is to be understood as a mode of implementation'.[48] Blumenberg himself puts it more strikingly:

> The modern age is the second overcoming of Gnosticism. A presupposition of this thesis is that the first overcoming of Gnosticism, at the beginning of the middle ages, was unsuccessful. A further implication is that the medieval period, as a meaningful structure spanning centuries, had its beginning in the conflict with late antique and early Christian Gnosticism and that the unity of its systematic intention can be understood as deriving from the task of subduing its Gnostic opponent.[49]

Gnosticism, in this context, should be understood to mean the most radical disjunction between the world and the spirit. As Blumenberg notes, this then challenges both classical thought and early Christian thought at its roots. With respect to the Ancient World, he writes, Gnosticism 'disputed the status of the cosmos as the embodiment of all reality that is binding in itself; with respect to Christianity it disputed the combination of creation and redemption as the work of a single God'.[50] Its purpose was to explain the nature of badness and evil in the world.[51]

Blumenberg's argument is that the first 'overcoming' of Gnosticism was 'accomplished' by Augustine's synthesis of Neoplatonism and Christianity but that within that overcoming Gnosticism remained intact (though transformed) in Augustine's equally important doctrines of original sin and predestination, which by separating out a 'predestined' elect and a corrupt many, solved the problem of the lasting corruption of the world by blaming those who would never participate in the heavenly city. In doing this, he sowed the seeds for the 'return' of a translated 'gnosticism' to plague the Middle Ages. As Blumenberg goes on to argue, 'In many ways the scholasticism of the Middle Ages travels Augustine's path over again. Its attempt to hold the God of creation and the God of salvation together in one system rests, in the full range of its variants, on the ground plan of *De libero arbitrio*.'[52]

The second overcoming of Gnosticism at the end of the Middle Ages, – which for Blumenberg inaugurates, so to speak, the modern age – marks a different turn. For now, what he calls 'the escape into transcendence' is not an option. Instead it is marked by a 'disappearance of order' (*Ordnungsschwund*). This causes 'doubt regarding the existence of a structure of reality that can be related to man [and] is the presupposition of a general conception of human activity that no longer perceives in given states of affairs the binding character of the ancient and medieval cosmos . . . [instead it] is bound up with a new concept of human freedom'.[53]

This 'new concept' turns on the increasing emphasis on self-preservation and what, for Blumenberg, goes with it. It is not, of course, that 'self-preservation' was in any sense the *invention* of the modern age, rather that 'the second overcoming of Gnosticism' made it appear in a remarkably different light. As Blumenberg puts it, 'the "disappearance of order" that was brought about by the disintegration of the Middle Ages pulled self-preservation out of its biologically determined normality, where it went unnoticed, and turned it into the theme of human self comprehension.'[54] As he goes on to argue, this had an enormous influence on the shape and character of modernity; as a result 'it is also the case that the modern stage of human technicity can no longer be grasped entirely in terms of the anthropological structure of wants. The growth of the potency of technique is not only the continuation – not even the acceleration – of a process that runs continuously though the whole history of humanity. On the contrary, the qualitative increase in technical achievements and expedients can only be grasped in relation to a new quality of conciousness'.[55] This new 'quality' became central to the modern age, Blumenberg believes. It regards self-preservation in this sense as a 'fundamental category of everything in existence and has found this borne out all the way from the principle of inertia in physics to the biological structure of drives and the laws of state building'.[56]

As we shall see in the next chapter, there is a good deal in the defence of modernity that builds on this insight of Blumenberg's (though not always consciously). Note, however, for the moment how we might incorporate both Toulmin and MacIntyre into Blumenberg's thesis. On Blumenberg's analysis, the differences that we noted between both MacIntyre and Toulmin can be resolved in the sense that each is concentrating on one major aspect of the 'second overcoming of Gnosticism', the debate between science and humanism in the case of Toulmin, and the project of attempting an 'independent justification of morality' in the case of MacIntyre.[57] In both cases, however, they were unable to see the most appropriate way of conceiving of modernity as they were looking for something distinctively new, a break or a discontinuity, rather than something distinctively *different* but somehow organically related to its past. Blumenberg suggests, famously, that the modern age 're-occupies' the terrain of the Middle Ages and that it is this 're-occupation' in which the 'second overcoming of Gnosticism' consists. 'Re-occupation', here, should be understood as Blumenberg's attempt to explain how the modern age deals with questions inherited from its past but now understood differently, phrased differently or, perhaps most significantly, *felt* differently. Wallace suggests, and I agree, that for Blumenberg the modern age tries, not so much to answer a question as *to satisfy a need*, the need to understand, comprehend and give order to the world, and that it is the process of attempting to satisfy this need in the aftermath of the failure to properly overcome Gnosticism that produces the distinctive character of modernity. As such it is not necessarily the case that modernity is a *timebound* concept (i.e. that it occurs at a specific point in time and develops from there), though, of course, it is temporally located *in* a given time. What Blumenberg refers to as the 'epochal threshold' is not, therefore, necessarily something that requires a linear view of time; it marks the boundary between two world views, two different epochs in this sense.

This gives rise to another feature of Blumenberg's argument. For him 'self-assertion' and its corollaries become the defining feature of modernity, and as such much else that we think of as distinctively modern is in fact seen as 'the durability of the *not yet modern* in the modern age, the fundamental delay of Enlightenment' (emphasis added).[58] Wallace suggests this implies that in the course of his argument Blumenberg has come around to presenting not just an interpretation of modernity but a defence of it, but whether this is so or not it marks another crucial aspect of Blumenberg's argument, to wit the extent to which the modern age is, rather than being over or collapsing, *still becoming*, as it were.

Before I can sum up this theme, however, I want to look at one last aspect of it that can be best brought out, I think, by focusing on a different argument entirely; specifically, Leo Strauss's argument in his well-known essay 'The Three Waves of Modernity'.

## Leo Strauss: Modernity as 'The Crisis of the West'

Strauss is famous, of course, for having argued what might at first sight seem the exact opposite of Blumenberg's case. For

Strauss, 'the modern age' is characterized not by the deferral of modernity but by its gradual, though unquestionable appearance and subsequent dissolution into fragments; a dissolution that threatens even the good things that modernity has brought with it. However, such a trajectory is not to be wondered at, Strauss thinks, if only we remember in what modernity chiefly consists.

In 'The Three Waves of Modernity' he outlines a prospectus for an understanding of modernity and its trajectory and it is no accident that the first work he cites is as famous a text in the critique of modernity as any, Spengler's *Der Untergang des Abendlandes*.[59] The corner-stone of Spengler's argument, for Strauss, is that the 'West' that is said to be declining is 'a culture which emerged around the year 1000 in Northern Europe. It includes above all, modern western culture.'[60] In other words it does *not* include the origin of 'western culture' to be found in Ancient Greece. As he puts it, 'Modernity was understood from the beginning in contradistinction to antiquity; modernity could therefore include the medieval world.'[61] The full significance of this I shall come back to in a moment.

The nub of this modern crisis reveals itself, however, in the fact that 'modern western man no longer knows what he wants – that he no longer believes that he can know what is good or bad, what is right or wrong'.[62] This implies, Strauss says, that on the modern presumption political philosophy – 'what is the just or the good or the best order of society' – is impossible. The crisis of modernity is, then, the crisis of modern political philosophy. Strauss puts it thus: 'By modernity we understand a radical modification of pre-modern political philosophy – a modification which comes to sight first as a rejection of pre-modern political philosophy.'[63]

This rejection is first propounded by Machiavelli, organized and deepened by Hobbes and broadened and generalized by two changes which, Strauss says, 'occurred after [Machiavelli's] time but were in harmony with his spirit'; to wit the emergence of specifically modern natural science and the reconnection of politics and natural right, sundered in Machiavelli but reconnected in a very specific way by Hobbes. The sense of all of these changes, Strauss thinks, can be put in two ways. First, they reduced the 'moral and political problem' (how to arrive at the best, most just, community) to a technical problem. By this Strauss means to imply that the 'moderns' rejected the sense of hierarchy in 'pre-modern' thought and its accompanying sense of the centrality of chance in political life, which led the ancients to prescribe prudence and moderation and urge attention to nature. For the moderns, the 'political problem' may be difficult but it is in no way impossible, and it merely means 'getting the institutions right'.

The second sense is the view that the concept of nature is in need of being overlaid by 'civilisation as a mere artifact'. As Strauss puts it, 'conquest of nature implies that nature is the enemy, a chaos to be reduced to order; everything good is due to man's labour rather than to nature's gift . . . the political society is in no way natural; the state is simply an artifact, due to covenants'.[64] Like Blumenberg, Strauss emphasizes that a key part of this argument is the increasing centrality of the idea of individual 'self-preservation' (especially in Hobbes) and, therefore, of course of 'self-assertion'.[65]

The above represents what Strauss calls the 'first wave' of modernity. The second wave begins crucially with Rousseau.[66] He problematizes each of the above two senses of modernity and in doing so produces a serious fissure in the evolving structure. He confronts us with 'the antinomy of nature on the one hand and of civil society, reason, morality, history, on the other, in such a way that the fundamental phenomenon is the beatific sentiment of existence – of union and communion with nature – which belongs altogether on the side of nature as distinguished from reason and society'.[67]

However, Rousseau's thought also had powerful implications for his great German successors Kant and Hegel. Radicalizing the notion of the state of nature inherited from Hobbes, Locke and their contemporaries, Rousseau suggests that it is through the historical process that we become fully human. In the work of Kant and Hegel, Strauss suggests, this becomes the view that moral laws as laws of freedom are no longer understood as natural laws; indeed, they are understood as fundamentally 'anti-natural', established without reference to nature, and so the only basis becomes a (de-natured) reason: reason alone ('pure' reason) in Kant; reason historicized in Hegel.

If this is the trajectory of the second wave, however, then the third wave is more problematic still. Here the siren voice is that of Nietzsche: the third wave may be described as being constituted by a new understanding of the sentiment of existence: 'that sentiment is the experience of terror and anguish rather than of harmony and peace, and it is the sentiment of historic existence as necessarily tragic; the human problem is indeed insoluble as a social problem as Rousseau said, but there is no escape from the human to nature; there is no possibility of genuine happiness or the highest of which man is capable has nothing to do with happiness'.[68]

The argument here is dependent on seeing the century between Rousseau and Nietzsche as the century of the philosophy of history *par excellence*, the central thinker of which was, of course, Hegel. For Hegel, according to Strauss, there is (at least in a sense) a 'secularization' process going on in that there is a 'peak and end' of history, and it is this which allows Hegel to 'reconcile the idea of philosophical truth with the fact that every philosopher is a son of his time: the true and final philosophy belongs to the absolute moment in history, to the peak of history'.[69] However, if the idea of an 'end' or 'peak' to history is rejected (as, by and large it was, Strauss thinks, after Hegel), then the whole edifice of belief in progress rests on the edge of an abyss.

> Nietzsche was the first to face this situation. . . . all ideals are the outcome of human creative acts, of free human projects that form that horizon within which specific cultures were possible; they do not order themselves into a system; and there is no possibility of a genuine synthesis of them. Yet all known ideals claimed to have objective support; in nature of God or in reason. The historical [second-wave] insight destroys that claim and hence all known ideals. But precisely the realisation of the true origin of all ideals – in human creations or projects – makes possible a radically new [third-wave] kind of project, the transvaluation of all values.[70]

This project is the third wave of modernity for Strauss and, as his remarks at the end of the essay make clear, he sees in it the origins of fascism.[71] Liberal democracy and communism, on the other hand, he sees rooted in the soil of the first and second waves. However, the point is that the whole project of modernity is in doubt and that this doubt cannot simply be ignored or turned away from, it must be faced. In the very last sentence of the essay Strauss suggests that liberal democracy – unlike the other regime forms he traces to modernity – can receive some support from 'a way of thinking that cannot be called modern at all: the pre-modern thought of our western tradition'. This point is one I shall return to in chapter 3, but for now let me look at how Strauss's portrayal fits into the picture of 'modernity as mood' that I have been trying to sketch in this chapter.

## Integrating Strauss and Blumenberg: Self-assertion, Self-preservation and the Turn Away from Nature

The centrepiece of Blumenberg's argument, it will be recalled, was to see modernity as coterminous with a different way of answering questions that had been posed in different ways almost from the beginning of Western thought. While Blumenberg obviously does think that the 'epochal threshold' was crossed at a particular time (that is to say, roughly speaking in the fifteenth and sixteenth centuries), it was not *causally related* to its time.

Despite their differences, a similar argument is discernible, I think, in Strauss. Strauss talks of modernity as being seen in contradistinction to 'antiquity' and, therefore, as possibly including the medieval period. However, in his account of the 'crisis of modernity', he identifies it with the rejection of classical political philosophy and claims that the first thinker who *explicitly* did this is Machiavelli. Note that the key word here would seem to be 'explicitly'. In other words, there might have been others who 'less explicitly' did this in the medieval period, and thus, as such, there is no necessary contradiction here.

Modernity for both Strauss and Blumenberg, then, is – in contradistinction to MacIntyre and Toulmin – *not* timebound, though it is, of course, temporally located. It is rather best seen as a way of thinking about certain problems and issues; or, perhaps more accurately for them both, as a related and expanding set of ways of thinking. Most interesting of all perhaps, is the surprising commonality between Blumenberg and Strauss over what the central assumptions of modernity is. For Blumenberg it is the emphasis on self-assertion that is the key to the 'modern age' and much else in the 'modern age' is not properly modern, so to speak. For Strauss, the key aspect of modernity is its turning away from classical notions of nature, the change of focus from the 'natural' (however that is understood) to the 'human'. The crucial link between these two views is, however, as we have seen, the centrality of 'self-preservation' for both; not, of course, as a simple fact (it is after all part of 'our nature' for Strauss and a feature common across the epochal threshold for Blumenberg), but as the most important 'fact' of human social life and as a crucial turning point in the evolution of modernity.

It is significant that the key thinker in this respect is the same for both Strauss and Blumenberg: Hobbes. For Strauss, Hobbes is the writer who reunites the sundered halves of political science, politics and natural right, but does so in Machiavelli's spirit and thereby allows the Machiavellian revolution to develop its full power. He describes this as follows:

> whereas prior to [Hobbes] natural law was understood in the light of a hierarchy of man's ends in which self-preservation occupied the lowest place, Hobbes understood natural law in terms of self-preservation alone ... natural law came to be understood primarily in terms of the right of self-preservation as distinguished from any obligation or duty – a development which culminates in the substitution of the rights of man for natural law, nature replaced by man, law by rights ... eventually we arrive at the view that universal affluence and peace is the necessary and sufficient condition of perfect justice.[72]

Blumenberg sees it slightly differently, of course, but the centrepiece of the argument is remarkably similar:

> The classical proposition that nature has given everything to everyone (*natura dedit omnia omnibus*) becomes the point of

departure of the construction of political order . . . in terms of
the context in which it originated this proposition had an unambiguously teleological intention . . . It was meant to say that
nature had arranged her goods adequately in relation to man's
needs and that only their just distribution is still required in
order to achieve nature's ends . . . Hobbes made of this axiom
something radically different and foreign to its origin. As the
principle of the pre-political state of nature, the proposition not
only defines for each individual his right to insist on the satisfaction of his needs . . . but it also designates the unlimitedness
and unlimitability of his claim to everything at all that he finds
within his reach . . . natural law gives rise to its antithesis,
lawlessness.[73]

In both cases, therefore, this turn away from a conception
focused on 'nature' to one focused on 'man'[74] is what is most
significant for the evolution of a distinctive view that can be
called modern.

To say this, however, is obviously to raise another question.
Whereas Strauss believes that the turn away from classical
thought was a mistake, Blumenberg believes that self-assertion
is the correct strategy for resolving the problems that gave rise
to the modern age. The question then surfaces, however, of
exactly what form of self-assertion is most appropriate. For, in
important ways, as Strauss's argument in 'The Three Waves of
Modernity' shows (whether or not we agree with his position),
'modernity' has hardly spoken with one voice on the topic.
Rousseau and Nietzsche, for example, are critics of Hobbes and
Machiavelli as much as they speak in their voice.

However, around this particular point the contemporary
'modernity debate' speaks with one accent (if not, of course,
with one voice). As I shall try to outline in the next chapter the
'defenders of the faith' and the 'disturbers of the peace' alike
have all relied on some version of the self-assertion thesis. They
have all seen modernity as a turn away from the classical sense
of nature and towards the human. Moreover, they have all
agreed – more or less – with this turn. In this respect, therefore,
it seems to me that Blumenberg's argument is quite correct,
though few, if any, understand it in quite the way that
Blumenberg himself does.

Thus we have found two very distinct issues – though they are, of course, connected – on which the modernity debate in this sense (modernity as mood) revolves: the character of the *temporality* of modernity and the question of *nature*. Or, to put these issues in an interrogative form: Can we talk about 'nature' and what are its implications for politics? (to which different answers are given by Blumenberg and Strauss); and how significant are the time frames and periodizations (that we recognize anyway as simplifications and perhaps arbitrary orderings) for political thought and practice? (To which Strauss and Blumenberg on the one side and MacIntyre and Toulmin on the other give different answers.)

In the next chapter, however, I want to suggest that the protagonists in the modernity debate have allowed these two central issues to become blurred by a range of other issues that, at least in the sense discussed here, have little or nothing to do with 'modernity' *per se* at all.

One major reason why the major issues are blurred, I think, is that modernity as mood is either run together with the notion of modernity as socio-cultural form, and issues which emerge in the latter context become inappropriately confused with issues that are supposed to be the provenance of the former; or one sense of modernity alone is discussed and the issues which are appropriately the province of the other become confused or, worse, ignored completely. Before I move on, then, to sketch in the parameters of the contemporary modernity debate I want to say something about the relation between the two senses of modernity I have referred to, and finally suggest how the implications of this relationship affect the three 'tasks of political theory' I discussed in my opening chapter.

## Relating the Two Senses of Modernity

Modernity as socio-cultural form is without doubt also a central aspect of the 'modernity debate'. Unquestionably, the late twentieth century is witnessing some very profound cultural and socio-economic changes which have enormous implications for politics and therefore for political theory. As Scott Lash and

John Urry have recently argued, characteristic mechanisms of production are becoming increasingly linked with communication and information structures and this fact, coupled with increasing mobility and time–space compression is changing many of the most significant ways in which politics is conducted as well as the arenas in which it is conducted.[75]

Unquestionably also, because of the likely effects they are going to have on political and social structures, these changes will be of enormous importance for political and social theory. However, it is important, I think, to emphasize that they will not have any *necessary* or *determinate* effect. How we choose to respond to these developments is a matter for us; *that* we must repond to them is what I would argue cannot be gainsaid, if political theory is to have any chance of performing those three 'tasks' that I suggested in the last chapter, following John Dunn, that are its *raison d'être*.

The relation between modernity as mood and modernity as socio-cultural form is then an ambiguous and symbiotic one. Changes in the latter do not necessitate any particular view or perspective in the former – save, I think, for one, to which I shall have to return (as I suggest above this is simply the view that we all do live within these changes and cannot pretend otherwise whether we like it or not).[76]

However, the way in which this relationship has been conceived (or, more often I think, misconceived) has meant that certain issues are given a particular importance that they do not always deserve *as part of the discussion about modernity*. One danger is to run the two issues too closely together. This has happened, I think, to one issue that is particularly pertinent for my argument in the next chapter, i.e. what is usually called 'relativism'. This is, of course, an important and highly charged philosophical and methodological issue in the human sciences. However, it is also a very *old* issue and does not, I suggest, have anything specifically to do with 'modernity', though it is certainly relevant to issues that arise out of a consideration of modernity. It is the running together of modernity as mood and modernity as socio-cultural form that has lent this issue the spurious significance it has come to have for the modernity debate, or so I shall seek to argue in the next chapter.

An opposite danger comes from holding the two senses of modernity, when they are recognized as distinguishable, too far apart, or from privileging one over the other, or even effectively denying one and asserting the other. Much materialist historical sociology of late seems to me to run this risk.[77] Much of this work is extremely sensitive to the issue that I have termed modernity as socio-cultural form.[78] The problem, of course, is that an avowedly materialist history cannot do justice to the way in which modernity as mood can shape human preferences and expectations and, as such, that history cannot be a good understanding of modernity *tout court*; it can only ever be partial.

Of course, an equal mistake can be made the other way around. An over-concentration on modernity as mood can produce equally dislocating or corrupting effects, as I shall seek to show in the next chapter. While this book is primarily concerned with discussing modernity as mood, it does not seek to suggest that one should do anything other than attempt to relate together the two senses of modernity – indeed, the agenda for such an attempt is what chapter 4 of the present study will seek to outline.

## Conclusion

Before I move on to the modernity debate itself, I want just to summarize my argument so far and link it with the account of Anglo-American political theory I gave in the introductory chapter. I agreed, in broad terms, with John Dunn's suggestion that political theory consists in a threefold task – offering an interpretation of where we are and how we got here, giving us a suitable goal to aim at and providing some idea of how we might get there from here. However, for the various reasons I outlined, I was unconvinced that either the 'reborn' Anglo-American political theory or the 'new history of political thought' could very adequately perform these tasks, whatever their (very real) individual merits. Taking cognizance of the notion of modernity might, on the other hand, provide us with just such an opportunity. As I have interpreted it here, modernity might indeed provide us with a way of interpreting the 'three tasks' in that it asks us two fundamental questions which any attempt to fulfil the three tasks would have to answer. First, does modernity (taken as *both* mood and sociocultural form, remember) have a fixed or delimited spatio/temporal character? And, second, is there anything to the idea that we, as humans, have a 'nature' that has some sort of effect on how we act in ethics and politics and should, in any case, influence our actions and our politics?

These two questions raise a third, and in this context it bears remembering that it is one that lies at the heart of the difference between MacIntyre and Toulmin; to wit the character of rationality. This too is a central part of being able to tease out the significance of modernity for political theory, and it is also, of course, central to any way of relating our conception of our situation to how we act and what we act to create or realize. Again, I shall return to this in chapter 3.

Of course, no particular answer is necessarily forthcoming from those three questions. However, before I can return to them, I need to substantiate my claim, made several times in different contexts in this chapter, that the current participants in the modernity debate have moved the debate on to areas not particularly helpful for considering these questions. I have to further suggest why and in what way these questions might be superior to the ones they in fact have been concerned with.

## Notes

1 William E. Connolly, *Political Theory and Modernity* (Oxford: Blackwell, 1988), pp. 1–2.
2 Anthony Giddens, *The Consequences of Modernity* (Cambridge: Polity Press, 1991), p. 1.
3 Ibid., 1.
4 Richard Bernstein, *The New Constellation: The Ethical-Political Horizons of Modernity/Postmodernity* (Cambridge: Polity Press, 1991). Bernstein actually describes his 'mood' as modernity/postmodernity. I shall defend my adaptation of this at the end of this chapter.
5 See, for examples of differing versions of such Marxist accounts, Fredric Jameson, *Postmodernism, or, The Cultural Logic of Late Capitalism* (London: Verso, 1991); David Harvey, *The Condition of Postmodernity* (Oxford: Blackwell, 1989). It is worth observing that both Jameson and Harvey describe 'postmodernism' as an aesthetic, cultural response to the

condition of late capitalism; one, incidentally, that they reject in the name of Marxism.

6 See, for various examples of these styles of argument, Roland Robertson, *Globalisation* (London: Sage Publications, 1992), Scott Lash and John Urry, *The End of Organised Capitalism* (Madison: University of Wisconsin Press, 1987); Scott Lash and John Urry, *Economies of Signs and Space* (London: Sage, 1994); James Rosenau, *Turbulence in World Politics; A Theory of Change and Continuity* (Hemel Hempstead: Harvester, 1991).

7 This is most obviously associated with Ulrich Beck's now well-known thesis about the evolution of a 'Risk Society', which he subtitles 'towards a new modernity'. See Ulrich Beck, *Risikogesellschaft: Auf dem Weg in eine andere Moderne* (Frankfurt: Suhrkamp Verlag, 1986). It is worth emphasizing that Beck's analysis has much in common with Giddens' and, in fact, their work over the last few years has increasingly run on parallel lines.

8 Harvey, *The Condition of Postmodernity*, p. 359.

9 I return to this briefly in the next chapter. To see the sense in which this remark is true of these writers see Walter Benjamin's 'Theses on the Philosophy of History', and perhaps his best-known essay, 'The Work of Art in the Age of Mechanical Reproduction', both included in *Illuminations* (London: Fontana, Collins, 1970). For Adorno, probably the best work to consult is *Negative Dialektik* (Frankfurt: Suhrkamp Verlag, 1966).

10 For general (and secondary) discussions of the Frankfurt School, to which I shall return in the next chapter, see David Held, *Introduction to Critical Theory: Horkheimer to Habermas* (Cambridge: Polity Press, 1980); Martin Jay, *The Dialectical Imagination: A History of The Frankfurt School and the Institute of Social Research 1923–50* (Boston: Little-Brown, 1973); Raymond Geuss, *The Idea of a Critical Theory* (Cambridge: Cambridge University Press, 1978); Fred Dallmayr, *Polis and Praxis: Exercises in Contemporary Political Theory* (Cambridge, Mass.: MIT Press, 1984), esp. chs 2, 5 and 6; Axel Honneth, *A Critique of Power* (Cambridge, Mass.: MIT Press, 1989); and, perhaps most comprehensive of all, Rolf Wiggerhaus, *The Frankfurt School, Its History, Theories and Political Significance* (Cambridge: Polity Press, 1993).

11 See Bernstein, *The New Constellation*, p. 8. He is citing Martin Jay, *Adorno* (Cambridge, Mass.: Harvard University Press, 1984), pp. 14–15.

12 Bernstein, *The New Constellation*, p. 9.

13 Alisdair MacIntyre, *After Virtue: A Study in Moral Theory* (London: Duckworth, 1981; 2nd edn 1987). Unless indicated otherwise all references here will be to the first edition.

14 Ibid., 36.

15 Ibid.

16 MacIntyre, *After Virtue*, p. 111. It seems fair to suggest that there has been a slight change, if not of view then at least of emphasis, in MacIntyre's argument between *After Virtue* and *Three Rival Versions of Moral*

*Inquiry*, where he suggests that there are three broad positions available to us. His own (neo-Thomistic) position, what he calls a 'genealogical' (meaning Nietzschean) position, and an 'encyclopedist' (meaning Enlightenment/Liberal) position. If this is so, then, there is a third way (though strictly speaking, of course, one cannot have a third alternative).

17  Ibid., 50.

18  Ibid., 52.

19  Ibid.

20  Ibid., p. 53.

21  Stephen Toulmin, *Cosmopolis: The Hidden Agenda of Modernity* (Chicago: University of Chicago Press, 1990).

22  Though it is worth pointing out that MacIntyre is usually enlisted as an ally in Toulmin's argument. This is certainly true of the three occasions in *Cosmopolis* when he is specifically referred to (pp. 12, 189 and 199).

23  Toulmin, *Cosmopolis*, pp. 9–10.

24  Obviously it is the style that received its most potent twentieth-century endorsement from the development of analytical philosophy, and as I suggested in the introduction, it has continued to have ramifications throughout the human sciences. Anglo-American political theory, by no means accidentally, sees itself as 'substantive' precisely in so far as it deals with 'problems' and 'theories' in this sense. Criticisms of this view have, however, also proliferated during the century, taking a wide variety of forms: idealist, hermeneutic, and post-structural being perhaps the most common.

25  Toulmin, *Cosmopolis*, p. 17. Toulmin cites a variety of work in support of his case, perhaps the most important being Roland Mousnier's well-known *Les XVI$^e$ et XVII$^e$ Siècles* (Paris: Gallimard, 1953); Eric Hobsbawm's equally well-known essay 'The Crisis of the Seventeenth Century', in *Past and Present*, 5 and 6; and Theodore Raab's excellent and penetrating *The Struggle for Stability in Early Modern Europe* (New York: Oxford University Press, 1975). A work that also illustrates his point, while introducing qualifications and refinements, is the masterly survey of the period offered in Joshua Goldstein, *Long Cycles: Prosperity and War in the Modern Age* (New Haven: Yale University Press, 1988), esp. pp. 296–313.

26  Toulmin, *Cosmopolis*, p. 23.

27  Ibid., 24.

28  Ibid.

29  It is worth pointing out here that Toulmin's analysis of the link between Leibniz's political and metaphysical and scientific writings would benefit from a study of the writings of Patrick Riley on Leibniz, which he does not cite. See, especially, Riley's introductory essay to his *Leibniz's Political Writings* (Cambridge: Cambridge University Press, 1989).

30  Toulmin, *Cosmopolis*, p. 101.

31  Ibid., 104.

32  I shall return to this particular point in the final chapter. I shall also be

discussing it in rather more depth in a forthcoming book: see N. J. Rengger, *Duties Beyond Orders: Towards a Political Theory of World Order* (London: Routledge, 1995, forthcoming), see esp. ch. 2.

33 Toulmin, *Cosmopolis*, p. 128.

34 Ibid., 167–8.

35 Ibid., 203.

36 Ibid., 208.

37 MacIntyre, *After Virtue*, p. 245.

38 Stephen Holmes, *The Anatomy of Anti-Liberalism* (Cambridge, Mass.: Harvard University Press, 1993).

39 See, for Shklar's presentation of her liberalism, Judith Shklar, *Ordinary Vices* (Cambridge, Mass.: Harvard University Press, 1986), and her essay 'The Liberalism of Fear', in Nancy Rosenblum (ed.), *Liberalism and The Moral Life* (Cambridge, Mass.: Harvard University Press, 1989). For Rorty see *Contingency, Irony and Solidarity* (Cambridge: Cambridge University Press, 1989). For Flathman, see his *Willfull Liberalism* (Ithaca: Cornell University Press, 1992).

40 I say 'allegedly' to indicate that I am very unhappy about seeing Rawls' theory as a Kantian one. That Rawls perceives himself to be strongly influenced by Kant I do not of course deny, but that the theory which results is Kantian in anything other than a very formal (and very weak) sense I would most certainly deny. I do not have time to go into this here, however.

41 Hans Blumenberg, *Die Legitimat der Neuzeit* (*erweiterte und uberarbeitete neuausgabe*) (Frankfurt: Suhrkamp Verlag, 1966). Based upon the second paperback German edition published in three volumes in 1973, 1974 and 1976, it has been translated into English as *The Legitimacy of the Modern Age*, trans. Robert M. Wallace (Cambridge, Mass.: MIT Press, 1985). I shall use this translation throughout, though I shall occasionally alter or rephrase certain passages in the interests of clarity. Where I do this I shall indicate in the notes.

42 Connolly, *Political Theory and Modernity*, p. 183.

43 Leo Strauss, 'The Three Waves of Modernity', in Hilail Gildin (ed.), *Political Philosophy: Six Essays by Leo Strauss* (New York: Bobbs-Merrill, 1975).

44 Karl Löwith, *Meaning in History* (Chicago: University of Chicago Press, 1949). German edition, *Wetgeschichte und Heilsgeschechen die theologischen Voraussetszungen der Geschichtsphilosophie* (Stuttgart: Kohlhammer, 1953).

45 Wallace, introduction to *The Legitimacy of the Modern Age*, p. xv.

46 Wallace refers to the affinities between Löwith and Strauss (and he adds Hannah Arendt) on p. xxxi of his introduction to *The Legitimacy of the Modern Age*. Though Wallace does not mention this, Arendt and Löwith were closely connected to Heidegger. Arendt was his student and also an intimate, if often distant (both physically and intellectually) friend. Löwith was one of his principal philosophical assistants at Marburg in the 1920s

(the other significant philosophical one being, of course, Gadamer). Strauss's admiration of, and hostility to, Heidegger is well known and attested to, for example, in *The Return of Classical Political Rationalism* (Chicago: University of Chicago Press, 1989; ed. Thomas Pangle). An excellent discussion of Arendt's relationship to Heidegger (both personal and philosophical) is contained in Elizabeth Young-Breuhl's, *For Love of The World: The Life of Hannah Arendt* (New Haven: Yale University Press, 1983). A wonderfully atmospheric portrait of Löwith is given by Hans-Georg Gadamer in his *Philosophical Apprenticeships* (Cambridge, Mass.: MIT Press, 1986), which also contains a memorable chapter on their joint 'teaching years' as assistants to Heidegger at Marburg in the 1920s. I shall return to the linkage between Heidegger, Gadamer and Löwith in chapter 3; however, I shall not be discussing Heidegger's philosophy as such in this volume. Important as he unquestionably is for discussions of modernity and postmodernity, to discuss Heidegger in the depth his thought deserves must await another occasion. In any case, for the relatively narrow task I have set myself here, reflecting on the importance of modernity for political theory, a full discussion is not necessary. I hope to address Heidegger's thought on some of the issues discussed here in a future book on political judgement and moral communities.

47 See Blumenberg, *Die Legitimät der Neuzeit*, part 1, ch. 3. An interesting contrast is presented by John Milbank in *Theology and Social Theory: Beyond Secular Reason* (Oxford: Blackwell, 1992). I shall return to Milbank's argument in chapter 3.

48 Blumenberg, *Legitimacy of the Modern Age*, p. xviii.

49 Ibid., 126. Blumenberg is not unique, of course, in emphasizing the relationship between Gnosticism and modernity. As he recognizes, it is a prominent theme in the work of Eric Voeglin (see especially his essay in the *Philosophische Rundschau* 1 (1953/4), though it is a theme his later writings pick up as well). I shall return to Voeglin's use of the idea in chapter 3.

50 Blumenberg, *Legitimacy of the Modern Age*, p. 129.

51 Wallace uses 'badness' to translate Blumenberg's use of 'des Ubels', usually translated, as he admits in a note (Blumenberg, *Legitimacy of the Modern Age*, p. 136) as 'the problem of evil'. His reason for this translation is to differentiate the centrepiece of Gnostic concern, which is the existence of evil in the world – 'what is simply not good' as he puts it – from the usual use of evil, meaning individual human-willed wrongdoing. As he also says, the usual Latin term, *malum*, does not prejudge this issue. I agree with the sense of Wallace's translation here; however, as I shall try and explain in chapter 3, I think there is a sense in which we should use the notion of evil in – so to speak – a structural sense. I will therefore use 'Evil' (with a capital 'E') to refer to what Wallace translates as 'badness' and evil (with a small 'e') to refer to acts of will and their results.

52 Blumenberg, *Legitimacy of the Modern Age*, p. 135.

53 Ibid., 137.

54 Ibid., 139.
55 Ibid.
56 Ibid., 143.
57 Both of these areas are touched on independently by Blumenberg in his splendidly original presentation of two figures from either side of what he calls 'the epochal threshold'; Nicholas of Cusa (the cusan) and Giordano Bruno (the nolan). See *Legitimacy of the Modern Age*, especially Part IV.
58 This passage is from the first German edition of *Die Legitimät der Neuzeit*, cited by Wallace, *Legitimacy of the Modern Age*, p. xxiv.
59 Originally published, of course, in two volumes in 1919 and 1921. A standard English translation is by C. F. Atkinson, *The Decline of The West* (New York: 1932).
60 See Strauss, 'Three Waves', p. 81.
61 Ibid., 93. The similarity to Löwith's position here is obvious and, I think, not incidental in that Heidegger was clearly an important influence on both. For the most radical (though I think too extreme) presentation of Strauss as a Heideggerian/Nietzschean see Shadia Drury's *The Political Ideas of Leo Strauss* (London: Macmillan, 1988). The charge is made more temperately, though still inaccurately I think, in Luc Ferry's *Political Philosophy 1, Rights – The New Quarrel Between the Ancients and The Moderns*, trans. Franklin Philp (Chicago: Chicago University Press, 1990); and most subtly and interestingly in Stanley Rosen's *Hermeneutics as Politics* (Oxford: Oxford University Press, 1987). I shall return to Rosen's argument in more detail in chapter 3.
62 Strauss, 'Three Waves', p. 81.
63 Ibid., 83. I shall not, for the moment, take issue with Strauss's characterization of 'pre-modern political thought', which for him essentially means Ancient Greek thought. However, I shall try and make clear in chapter 3 that for all the power of Strauss's interpretation of Greek thought, there are some very serious problems with it.
64 Ibid., 88.
65 Ibid., 88–9.
66 Now is not the time to join the debate over the interpretations of Rousseau offered by Strauss and by some of his followers and disciples, most especially and influentially Allan Bloom. I hope to say something about this on another occasion, however, and have made a start in chapter 3 of the Ph.D. thesis that was the distant ancestor of this book. For a prospectus of what we might call the 'Straussian' view of Rousseau see, especially, Leo Strauss, *Natural Right and History* (Chicago: University of Chicago Press, 1968), and Allan Bloom, introduction to his (excellent) translation of *Emile* (Harmondsworth: Penguin, 1978). More general treatments of Rousseau that provide alternative interpretations that I find extremely valuable can be found in: Judith Shklar, *Men and Citizens: A Study in Rousseau's Social Theory* (Cambridge: Cambridge University Press, 1968); Maurizio Viroli, *Jean Jacques Rousseau and the 'Well Ordered Society'* (Cambridge: Cambridge University Press, 1988); John Charvet,

*The Social Problem in the Philosophy of Rousseau* (Cambridge: Cambridge University Press, 1974); Patrick Riley, *Will and Political Legitimacy: A Critical Exposition of Social Contract Theory in Hobbes, Locke, Rousseau, Kant and Hegel* (Cambridge: Harvard University Press, 1982); Stanley Hoffmann and D. Fiedler (eds), *Rousseau on International Relations* (Oxford: Clarendon Press, 1992). My own very sketchy treatment of Rousseau comes in chapter 3 of *Reason, Scepticism and Politics* (Doctoral dissertation, University of Durham, 1987).

67 Strauss, 'Three Waves', p. 94.

68 Ibid., 94–5.

69 Ibid., 95.

70 Ibid., 96.

71 Ibid., 98.

72 Ibid., 88–9.

73 Blumenberg, *Legitimacy of the Modern Age*, pp. 218–19.

74 And, as many feminist writers have pointed out, of course, it most certainly is 'man' and not 'man and woman'. See, for example, Carole Pateman, *The Sexual Contract* (Stanford: Stanford University Press, 1988).

75 See Scott Lash and John Urry, *Economies of Signs and Space* (London: Sage, 1994). This aspect of modernity as socio-cultural form is one that plays a considerable role in the first part of my forthcoming book *Duties Beyond Orders*.

76 What it does seem to me that it means for us is that talk of 'rejecting' modernity is not plausible. We are all moderns, for good or ill, in the sense we all inhabit the modern world, though, as I shall seek to show, we are by no means all required to subscribe to what modernity's self-conscious defenders suggest as the best or only way of seeing ourselves now we live in modernity's shadow. I shall return to this in chapter 4.

77 This point, and my elaboration of it in the next couple of paragraphs, is discussed in a good deal more detail in my 'Clio's Cave: Historical Materialism and the Claims of Substantive Social Theory in World Politics', *The Review of International Studies*, forthcoming. See also part one of *Duties Beyond Orders*.

78 See, for example, Justin Rosenberg, *The Empire of Civil Society* (London: Verso, 1994); and Michael Mann, *The Sources of Social Power*, vols 1 and 2 (Cambridge: Cambridge University Press, 1986 and 1994). Rosenberg's is an excellent, thoroughgoing Marxist materialist account of the evolution of discrete social forms within modernity. Mann's exhaustive (and exhausting) *magnum opus* of comparative historical sociology emphasizes the economic and political sources of social power in modernity, in contrast to the ideological and military sources dominant in earlier periods. For a full discussion see Rengger, 'Clio's Cave'.

# 2

# DEFENDERS OF THE FAITH, DISTURBERS OF THE PEACE

*Difficult though it may be to detect it, a certain polemical thread runs through any philosophical writing. He who philosophises is not at one with the previous and contemporary worlds' ways of thinking of things.*

Goethe

With the above discussion as a background let me now turn to what I have been calling the 'modernity debate' in contemporary social and political theory. Obviously, given all that I have said, the terrain the debate can and has covered is vast and I could not possibly attempt to discuss it all. Instead, I shall try and give a broad overview of certain aspects of the debate, as it is relevant to the concerns that emerged in the last chapter. As I said above, therefore, this chapter will focus very largely on 'modernity as mood', though I shall say something about the relation between the two senses of modernity in my conclusion.

Of course, as Geoffery Bennington has rightly pointed out, there are very real problems with attempting an 'overview' of a 'debate' where most of the contributions are themselves already 'overviews' (of a sort), and where one of the hallmarks of at least one way of viewing the 'postmodern' is that it celebrates disagreement and that it is therefore not trying to 'resolve' the 'debate' precisely because such a view would be irreconcilably 'modern'.[1] Equally, I agree also with Bennington that a good deal of what passes for 'debate' in this area is astonishingly prone to misinterpretations, partiality and simple mistakes.

However, I do not think that in the current context this is too much of a problem, partly because I do not offer my reading of the exchanges that I shall refer to as the 'modernity debate' as the only one (though naturally I think it is a helpful one), but also because I want to suggest that it is because certain aspects of the 'debate' are *common* to 'moderns' and 'postmoderns',[2] but that this is rarely noticed. As such, I can bracket at least for the moment questions such as whether or not, for example, I think 'consensus' or 'dissensus' are the most appropriate stances.

In brief, the argument I shall pursue here is that while many of the themes within the modernity debate are rightly central to understanding and evaluating our conceptions of politics, the manner in which they have been discussed has often served to obscure, rather than illuminate, this point. By manner here I do not mean simply style or literary skill (though it is unquestionably true that some of the contributions to the modernity debate are about as far away from that as it is possible to get). Simply put, my argument will be that the structure of the so-called 'debate' itself has generated more heat than light. Most especially, I think that the debate has become fixated on questions to do with the alleged 'relativism' or 'nihilism' of the postmodern or the 'rationalistic' or 'totalizing' ('logocentric') ambition of the modern, to the considerable disadvantage of our ability to develop an account of politics that speaks to those themes discussed in the introductory chapter and in chapter 1; that is to say, the sense in which we can appropriately consider politics and ethics together and properly perform the 'tasks of political theory'.

As I indicated above, my usage of 'moderns and postmoderns' is meant to imply a certain set of responses to the question of modernity. In what follows the 'moderns' will be understood as those whose understanding or interpretation of 'modernity' is such as to suggest a defence; they defend the 'faith' that distinctively 'modern' conceptions of life and politics are an advance on pre-modern ones, and reject the claim that the characteristic stances of modernity must be radically re-thought or even rejected (though, of course, in some sense they may need completion, continuance or even radical rearticulation).

The postmoderns, on the other hand, attempt to disturb, disrupt or dislocate what they take to be an unwarranted set of assumptions about (amongst other things, and not always together) truth, value, science, progress or ethics. For them the 'modern' must be problematized, challenged and disrupted, and it is *in this process* that the 'postmodern' comes into existence and *because of* this process that we must rearticulate and reimagine many of our most cherished political assumptions and beliefs.

Of course, both moderns and postmoderns are many and varied; the issues that they are debating have been part of European cultural sensibility at least from Weber's time (and arguably, indeed, from Hegel's), and as the last chapter suggested, the themes of the 'modernity debate' in a more general sense have been with us much longer still. However, in this chapter I shall be concerned with those writers who have picked up on these issues since the end of World War II and especially with those who have self-consciously seen themselves as 'defending' or 'attacking' some other position. As with the rise of 'Anglo-American political theory' and the 'new history of political thought', so with the modernity debate; it is in the last thirty or so years that the issues and the debate have taken on the shape they now have.

I shall start my *tour d'horizon* of this debate by focusing on what we might call the 'challengers', the disturbers of modernity's 'peace'. It is, indeed, largely the postmoderns who have set the agenda of the debate as a debate, and so it seems fair to begin with them.

## The Disturbers of the Peace: Postmodern Moods and Political Theory

As is well known, of course, 'postmodernism' is a very loose term for a very wide collection of ideas and movements in aesthetics, architecture, literary theory, philosophy, social and political theory, and increasingly other areas as well.[3] While there are many reasons for being suspicious of such all-inclusive understandings of the postmodern (as I explained in note 2), I think it is probably helpful that I offer a very brief general interpretation of this style of thinking before I come on to examine the implications of postmodern assumptions for political theory.

Perhaps the best general statement of what we might call the postmodern tendency in contemporary thought is that of Huyssens. Let me quote it in full:

> What appears on one level as the latest fad, advertising pitch and hollow spectacle is part of a slowly emerging cultural transformation in Western societies, a change in sensibility for which the term 'postmodern' is actually, at least for now, wholly adequate. The nature and depth of that transformation are debatable, but transformation it is . . . in an important sector of our culture there is a noticeable shift in sensibility, practices and discourse formations which distinguishes a postmodern set of assumptions, experiences and propositions from that of a preceding period.[4]

It is worthwhile noting three things about this description to which I shall return. First, that 'postmodernism' is held to be constitutive of *Western* societies (by implication, therefore, it is not necessarily the case in non-Western ones); secondly, it is primarily seen here as a shift in *assumptions*; and thirdly, that it constitutes a transformation whose nature and depth are debatable but the fact of which is not.

Before moving on from this let me just note that, at least from the perspective on modernity outlined in chapter 1, there are some problems with this presentation. For example, Huyssens seems to conflate what I have referred to as modernity as mood (his second point) and modernity as socio-cultural form (his first point) and is thus running the risk of making the error I discussed at the end of chapter 1, i.e. supposing that accepting some interpretation of the one has determinate implications for the other.

Let me turn now, however, to how we might characterize these 'sets of assumptions' that constitute postmodern thinking. As Michael Ryan has said, the postmodern emphasizes 'reflexivity, irony, artifice, randomness, anarchy, fragmentation, pastiche and allegory. Cynically regarding the progressivist dreams of modernism, which hoped to shape the cultural world in the image of technology, industry and science, postmodernism is resolutely ironic with regard to the enabling myths of art, culture, society and philosophy . . . the emphasis shifts from content to form or style.'[5]

Within this general framework, a bewildering number of contemporary thinkers, writers or artists can, of course, be subsumed. It is usually said to include post-structuralism in French and American thought (for example Barthes, Foucault, Derrida, de Man, and perhaps Stanley Fish),[6] literary criticism running from Frederico de Onis in the 1930s to figures such as Hassan, Sontag, Derrida (again) and Eco today,[7] musicians and composers like Cage, Holloway, Glass, Stockhausen and Briers, architects like Jencks, Venturi or Bolin, geographers and social critics like David Harvey, and philosophers as different in other respects as Lyotard and Rorty.[8] This is to say nothing of works of film (still and moving), drama and fiction, like the novels of Rushdie, Eco (again) and Hutcheon.

Such is the disparity between this huge and multi-faceted group that many have, understandably, become increasingly unhappy with trying to tie them together. Richard Rorty, for example, has 'given up on the attempt to find something common to Michael Graves' buildings, Pynchon and Rushdie's novels, Ashberry's poems, various sorts of popular music and the writings of Heidegger and Derrida'.[9]

As I indicated above, I have a good deal of sympathy with this view. However, despite this enormous variety and heterogeneity, it is interesting, I think, to look at what might be said to be common to this large and very disparate group of thinkers, writers and artists – if anything. To begin with, I suggest that there is a common belief, though it is expressed in various ways and to different degrees, that in contemporary culture we are observing a general crisis of 'representation'. By this term is meant simply that there is 'a series of crises . . . in which older 'modernist' modes of defining, appropriating, and recomposing the objects of artistic, philosophical, literary and social scientific languages are no longer credible and in which one common aspect is the dissolution of the very boundary between the language and its object'.[10]

From this general belief, it is held, flows the set of assumptions listed above. If you merge language and object then the characteristic assumptions about 'truth', 'value', 'knowledge' and so on made by art, science, philosophy and social and political theory since (at least) the late eighteenth century become very problematic.

Here of course we reach the crux of the 'postmodern' for many of the writers who self-identify with it. It is precisely a rejection of 'the legacy of the Enlightenment' that was so instrumental in creating the sets of assumptions that go along with the view of representation that sees a key distinction between the world and the language we use to describe the world.

In this sense, the finest philosophical expressions to date of the postmodern mood have been Lyotard's *La Condition postmoderne*[11] and Rorty's *Philosophy and the Mirror of Nature*.[12] Rorty, in a luminous image, has captured the essential postmodern claim about knowledge, language and the world: the modernist assumption was that we had a 'glassy essence' that could be rationally perceived and interpreted through particular techniques. Postmodern thinking smashes that glass.

## Playing the Fool to the Academic Priest?: Three Postmodern Moods in Political Theory

Such a broad set of assumptions will obviously have a very wide referent, then, when it comes to political and social theory. As is fairly obvious, however, and as, for example, Boyne and Rattansi and Michael Ryan have each recently elaborated, postmodern thinking is, of its very nature, 'political'. Any approach that questions the substance of the way we understand 'the social' inevitably questions the social (and, of course, the political) itself; as Wittgenstein presciently reminded us in the *Tractatus*, to alter ways in which we look at the world is to alter the world.[13] To realize this, however, does not mean that there is any particular agenda that postmoderns have in common when it comes to politics (though I shall suggest that their different agendas will still have at least some marked similarities).

However, the above set of assumptions possess, I think, one common feature: all reject or at least problematize essential aspects of those assumptions that have generally been seen as the distinguishing hallmarks of Enlightenment thought and practice. Indeed, there are some postmoderns who would go much further than this and reject more general features of the 'Western', 'metaphysical' styles of reasoning and many others (Toulmin, for example, and perhaps even, in a certain sense, Lyotard[14]) who would want to suggest that the 'postmodern' is in fact a 'return' – to literary or humanistic forms of reason and relation.

None the less, and despite this variety, I want to suggest that out of this general set of assumptions and reactions one can identify two forms of postmodern response to the question of 'modernity' in political thought (though one of these needs to be seen in two different senses),[15] at least if modernity (in this sense) is understood primarily as depending on the confluence of the three questions I suggested it did in the last chapter; to wit, temporality, nature and reason.

These two approaches are, of course, as I present them here, ideal types. Often writers will display elements of both in their work even if one is paramount. With apologies to certain giants of Hellenistic philosophy then, and in anticipation of a reading I shall defend in more detail in chapter 3, I will term these two broad approaches the Sceptical and the Epicurean and look at each in turn.[16]

## The postmodern sceptics

By identifying a powerful sense of the 'postmodern' reading of modernity with scepticism, I do not mean to imply that such postmoderns are necessarily guilty of the 'nihilistic', 'anything goes' attitude often attributed to them and which, in much (loose) critical writing on postmodern thought, is one of the most frequently cited reasons for viewing them with suspicion or outright distaste.

An aspect of this has been brought into very powerful relief, I think, by the discussion and debates that have surrounded the lives and personalities of two individuals widely thought to be leading influences on 'postmodern' thought, Paul de Man and Martin Heidegger. The discovery that de Man, one of the leading literary critics associated with deconstruction (often – and wholly erroneously it seems to me – equated with 'postmodernism') had an uncomfortably unheroic, even collaborationist, past (i.e. he wrote for a pro-Nazi journal in his native Belgium during the war and later covered it up), appears to have thrown both friends and enemies into a collective fit.[17] Heidegger's case is even graver. He not only collaborated with the Nazis but actively supported them, most notoriously during his period as Rector of Freiburg University between 1933 and 1934, but he clearly remained attached at least to his version of what national socialism meant long afterwards, and in any case he never directly repudiated it.[18]

These cases are interesting in themselves and clearly relevant to any general assessment of the thinkers in question. What they most certainly do not show, I think, is any necessary or direct connection between either of the authors concerned and the 'postmodern' responses to the question of modernity that concern me here. Nor do they demonstrate that 'postmodern' thinking about political theory must necessarily be 'relativist' or 'nihilist' (whether or not such terms can plausibly be deployed in the context of Heidegger and de Man). To aver otherwise is simply to try and play a very old and rather dull game of guilt by association which avoids the unquestionably much more difficult task of actually reading what these and other writers have to say, and assessing how accurate or important it is as a response to certain important questions about ethics and politics.

As I interpret them, the postmodern 'sceptics' are simply those postmoderns who harbour most doubts about the assumptions characteristic of modern social and political thought, including aspects of modern political thought held to be 'progressive', such as liberal ideas about openness, tolerance, equality and so on. As a result, the sceptics go on to problematize and rethink these assumptions.

An archetypal postmodern sceptic in this sense is Michel Foucault. While it is certainly true that Foucault's position hardly remains the same across a career with more than its fair share of ideological and normative shifts, it is also true that a consistent part of Foucault's work consists in the problematizing of the characteristic stances of modernity, both at the level of what I have called 'mood' and at the level of socio-cultural form (it is probably fair to say that Foucault would have been equally suspicious about this distinction), particularly at the level of those aspects of modernity that have become difficult to properly analyse or sometimes even to see.

Famously, the position that Foucault adopts is essentially to suggest that 'Truth is a thing of this world: it is produced only by virtue of multiple forms of constraint. And it induces regular effects of power. Each society has its own regime of truth, its general politics of truth: that is the type of discourse which it accepts and makes function as true.'[19] As a number of Foucault's critics have argued, Foucault appears to be saying that there can never be an exit from this particular cage and that, as a result, as Charles Taylor has said, we are left to adopt the stance of a soul in Plato's myth of Er.[20] Even fellow postmoderns, for example Rorty,[21] seem happy to accept this portrayal of Foucault, and many writers who offer similar interpretations of aspects of our social life seem to echo this. For Taylor it is, of course, a critique (and one to which I shall return later in this chapter), but for many it is an affirmation. Here, for example, is Richard Ashley: 'Poststructuralism cannot claim to offer an alternative position or perspective because there is no alternative ground upon which it might be established.'[22] This position can be characterized as sceptical in that it emphasizes this aspect of postmodern social theory, the claim that the collapse of representation has left us only with the realization that our categories are merely infinitely different and more or less preferable, never better or worse.

However, it is very easy to oversimplify Foucault's views. In one of his last interviews, Foucault emphasized that 'my attitude . . . is . . . on the order of problematization – which is to say, the development of a domain of acts, practices and thoughts that seem to me to pose problems for politics. For example, I dont think that in regard to madness and mental illness there is any politics that can contain the just or definitive solution. But I think that in madness, in derangement, in behaviour problems, there are reasons for questioning politics; and politics must answer these questions, but it never answers them completely.'[23] This argument is, I suggest, an extension of an earlier remark Foucault made in another interview to the effect that he is concerned with 'politics as an ethics' and that 'ethics is a practice . . . a manner of being'.[24]

Of course, these remarks are hardly models of clarity. There is much that needs to be interpreted and teased out in Foucault's positions. On the other hand, they do not sound like a man who has no ethical sense, who believes that 'anything goes'; on the contrary, they seem to me to be deeply ethical (though of course they might still be dangerous, or simply wrong). Scepticism, here, is what Foucault calls the 'problematization' of politics, and it is this sense of perpetual critique which I suggest is characteristic of the postmodern sceptics. I shall come back to it again in a moment.

However, there are, I think, at least two versions of this scepticism. The first version, which I will call the 'hard-sceptical version', has among its best (and best-known) exponents, Lyotard, at least in some moods, and more recently Baudrillard.[25] It tends to be marked by a running together of the two senses of modernity I outlined in chapter 1 and by a suggestion that, in that context, traditional forms of (amongst other things) art and politics will radically change their character and form, or even perhaps 'disappear'.[26]

To do justice to the complexity of the arguments of either of these authors would require at least a book each, and so here I shall simply take a couple of examples out of context to indicate the sort of thing I have in mind. It is necessary to emphasize that this does enormous violence to the subtlety and nuance present in both writers, to say nothing of the fact that they obviously evolve and change over time. However, it does indicate a certain way of responding to modern conditions which allows us to say something, I think, about the assumptions that make up their own idea of modernity, and this is my primary concern here.

In *Driftworks*,[27] for example, Lyotard inveighs against reason as the main instrument of repression and stresses the free play of both language and action that leads to what Michael Ryan has called the 'plurality of singularities' that Lyotard himself calls 'Driftworks'. A similar concern is shown in Lyotard's emphasis on developments in modern science, such as catastrophe theory, chaos theory and so on, all of which display, he thinks, the bankruptcy of traditional, Enlightenment-derived forms of epistemology.[28]

The other most influential presentation of this form of postmodern social thought has, I think, been Baudrillard's recent work.[29] The central concern of all Baudrillard's work, of course, is the proliferation of communication through the media and the transformation that this has wrought in our social lives. In his work in the 1980's, however, Baudrillard has taken an increasingly pessimistic tone about what this transformation means for us. The key work for an understanding of this aspect of Baudrillard's work is *Les Stratégies fatales*.[30] Here Baudrillard refines the notion of 'hyperreality' that he discussed originally in *Simulations*. Originally this term was simply designed to describe the world of self-referential signs that Baudrillard believed to be the world of the media. In *Les Stratégies fatales*, however, Baudrillard sees the world of the hyperreal as the new fact of the social world. As Mark Poster has put it: 'The concurrent spread of the hyperreal through the media and the collapse of liberal and Marxist politics as master narratives, deprives the rational subject of its privileged access to truth.'[31]

Baudrillard's view is, then, a pessimistic one; though another term often used (for example by Ryan), i.e. nihilistic,[32] seems to me at least to be simply polemical and as such rather unhelpful. It is also very much the view that Pauline Rosenau has called 'sceptical', though her presentation of Baudrillard seems rather one-sided to me. In a recent essay, for example, Baudrillard himself has mitigated his pessimism by suggesting that 'one can still attempt to analyse [society] – with growing difficulty – from a critical point of view', while adding that 'society itself, because of its internal structure, does not produce a critical point of view. It only produces a sort of positivity, an immanent operationality which is self justified and self fulfilling.'[33]

This 'scepticism' is, then, certainly not 'fatalism' or 'nihilism', however pessimistic it might be. Some writers in this sceptical vein push in a rather more overtly celebratory direction. This emphasis I shall call soft-sceptical. These writers would include, I think, writers as different in other respects as Homi Bhabha,[34] Michael Shapiro, James Der Derian, Rob Walker, Bonnie Honig, Chantal Mouffe and, perhaps most importantly for political theory in general, William Connolly.[35]

Connolly is especially interesting here as he has also suggested ways in which this form of postmodern political theory differs from at least some versions of the 'hard-sceptical' type. In the course of a friendly exchange with Ashley, for example, Connolly takes issue with Ashley's characterization of the project. Rather than simply advocating 'positions' or 'perspectives' (which Connolly thinks is a modern strategy), postmodern thought 'thinks within the code of paradox because only attentiveness to paradox can loosen the hold monotonic standards of identity have over life'.[36] For Connolly, the job of the postmodern writer is to play the fool to the academic priest.

An essential aspect of this role, for Connolly, is to problematize the relations that exist in modern societies. For example, in his recent book *Identity/Difference*[37] Connolly places enormous weight on the problem of evil, focusing on the problem of responsibility. 'Before suffering can be called evil,' he writes, 'some agent must be responsible for it. This may be a fateful shift. It simultaneously exerts pressure to exclude some injuries from the category of evil and to intensify the search for agents who can be said to be responsible for those forms of suffering we most abhor.'[38] Connolly traces this shift to Augustine and much of the book is concerned to trace its implications in the ethico-political realm.[39] In particular, he thinks, it gives rise to 'two problems of evil'. The first consists in the result of Augustine's attempt to save his God from any responsibility for evil in the world though both the delimitation of 'sites at which responsibility can be located' and the 'intensification of the demand to identify agencies of responsibility'.[40] The second problem, continuing from this, 'is the evil that flows from the attempt to establish security of identity for any individual or group by defining the other that exposes sore spots in one's identity as evil or irrational . . . The Augustinian definition of Manicheanism as heresy and of Greek Polytheism as paganism provides two exemplifications of the politics of identity and difference. That politics contains the second problem of evil moving silently inside the first one. The question now becomes: is it possible to counter the second problem of evil without eliminating the functions served by identity?'[41]

In many ways this is the defining question of the book, and one of the central ways in which the sceptical postmodern temperament is manifested. It is worth, therefore looking briefly at Connolly's conclusion. Late modernity, Connolly argues, is a 'systemic time without a corresponding political place'.[42] In saying this, he suggests, he means to bring into question the 'sufficiency of sovereignty', the site of the supposedly universal political space, and he moves on to argue in detail for the extension of democracy to non-territorial issues.[43] This inevitably leads to the problematization of many of the aspects of contemporary political theory and practice most strongly held by moderns, as I shall come on to discuss a little later on. It is also worth emphasizing that Connolly's discussion of evil is very much one that links up with the comments of Blumenberg that I touched on in chapter 1. However, I shall save further comments on this until a little later on in the chapter.

Another good illustration of this approach in contemporary political theory (one, indeed, influenced by Connolly's position) and which also has relevance to my later argument can be found in Bonnie Honig's recent book, *Political Theory and the Displacement of Politics*.[44] As I briefly outlined in chapter 1, Honig begins by suggesting that most political theorists are hostile to what she calls the 'disruptions' of politics. They assume, she says, 'that the task of political theory is to resolve institutional questions, to get politics right, over and done with, to free modern subjects and their sets of arrangements of political conflict and instability'.[45] She offers in the book an account of how this became the project of political theory, whether it can succeed and, even supposing it could, whether we should want it to. She locates the primary site of the attempt to displace politics in the thought of Kant and considers this, along with modern derivatives such as Rawls (unsurprisingly) and Sandel (rather more surprisingly). Her primary figures for the contestation of this assumption are Nietzsche and Hannah Arendt. As she puts it, 'Whereas Kant looks to politics to support his rational grounding of morals for modernity, Nietzsche debunks the idols (which include reason and the modern state) to which Enlightenment thinkers like Kant turn in their effort to fend off what they perceive to be nihilism. Nietzsche counters that to confront and affirm the fact that the human world is not inherently valuable or meaningful – to announce the death of God – is to take a step away from nihilism, not towards it.'[46] Her own reading, as she says throughout the book, is Nietzschean, as is Connolly's.

This presentation of the sceptical postmodern view is what Rosenau picks out as one of the strands of what she calls 'affirmative postmodernism'. However, on my reading both hard and soft attitudes discussed above are framed by the acceptance of postmodern scepticism (towards most of the assumptions and characteristic aspects of the 'Enlightenment'). It is simply that as far as politics is concerned, there are a large number of different ways of reading the implications of such scepticism, and what determines what will be appropriate at any given time will be equally varied, but would certainly include the interplay between actors and context. There is a danger, however, to which I shall return, that in doing so the distinction between modernity as mood and modernity as socio-cultural form is elided.

However, neither form of scepticism, I suggest, is necessarily open to the charge that it is a 'nihilistic' advocate of 'anything goes'; on the contrary, both are seeking what they take to be the real conditions of affirmation in a world where those that are usually asserted are (in a non-Foucauldian sense) deeply problematic. As Judith Squires has suggested, introducing a recent collection of essays which contains contributions from a wide variety of 'postmoderns', 'A post Enlightenment defence of principled positions, without the essentialist or transcendental illusions of Enlightenment Thought, is both possible and necessary.'[47] Following Jane Flax, she also suggests that we should see 'postmodernism' as having a 'strong' and a 'weak' variety.[48]

'The Strong form holds that the subject is merely another position in language. It rejects any historical narrative that focuses on the macro rather than the micro and condemns all western metaphysics for an imputed grounding of Truth in the Real. The Weak form, on the other hand, posits an embedded, rather than a purely fictive subject. It also involves the rejection of not all macro-narratives but of essentialist and mono-causal grandnarratives.'[49] Squires, and at least most of the contributors to the book, adopt the weak version, and as such attempt to contribute to the sort of project that Connolly and Honig, in their different ways, are also essaying. Before I discuss this any further, however, I must look at a second 'postmodern' response to modernity and then move on to the defenders of the faith themselves.

## *A postmodern epicureanism?*

There is, I want to argue, another 'loop' to the 'postmodern turn'. I shall call this version of the postmodern 'Epicurean'. The leitmotif of classical Epicurean thought was, of course, its insistence that we avoid the fears that Epicurus believed dominated our everyday lives; fear of death, fear of the gods, fear of uncertainty. Our solution to these fears is to have hope not in transcendental solutions but in community with a rightly ordered soul and city.[50] This form of postmodern political theory is best seen, I think, in some recent versions of American pragmatism, especially that of Richard Rorty, though versions of it are also to be found in writers like Cornell West and in literary theorists and critics such as Stanley Fish.[51]

Rorty's own ideas about politics, building on the philosophical assumptions outlined in *Philosophy and The Mirror of Nature* and *The Consequences of Pragmatism*,[52] have been elaborated in a series of essays during the 1980s, in his recent book *Contingency, Irony and Solidarity* (a title which very neatly sums up his basic argument) and in his recent Amnesty lecture on human rights.[53] Rorty's philosophical position at one level is similar to Lyotard's: an abandonment of 'meta-narratives'. However, he has also emphasized that we need such stories as aids to the social solidarity he thinks is central to our status as social beings.[54] Rorty poses for us a vision of a 'postmodernist form of social life in which society as a whole asserts itself without bothering to ground itself'.[55] Now what Rorty himself believes is that we can best find the location (not, be it noted, grounding or foundation) for our social selves in a sense of solidarity with, and of our contribution to, a particular community.[56] For Rorty, therefore, there is nothing wrong with believing in the hopes of the Enlightenment since our societies are largely built on these hopes; we simply cannot have, and do not need, a transcendental grounding for them. He celebrates what many others (postmoderns included) have criticized (ethnocentrism and bourgeois liberalism, for example); asserts the lexical priority of democracy to philosophy, and in his most obviously Epicurean mood, succinctly expresses what separates the sceptical and Epicurean postmodern moods by suggesting that the difference between himself and Lyotard (and indeed, Foucault) is summed up in the claim that, for him, the abandonment of the notion of meta-narratives, of the belief in a 'grand commensurating discourse' simply means that what he calls 'one of the less important sideshows of western civilisation – metaphysics is closing down. It does nothing to cast doubt on the possibility (as opposed to the difficulty) of peaceful social progress.'[57] For Rorty, Deweyan pragmatists have never had what Bernard Yack has nicely called 'The Longing For Total Revolution',[58] and in this sense they are separated, he thinks, from writers like Lyotard and Foucault, despite accepting the general postmodern assumptions that they would also share. Rorty, indeed, christens what I have called the postmodern sceptics, the 'school of resentment', borrowing a phrase from Harold Bloom, and his critique of them is often sharp. His explanation of this is revealing, I think: 'If my criticism of this school seems harsh,' he says, 'it is because one is always harshest on what one most dreads resembling.'[59]

Of course, one should not take Rorty's own estimation of his own differences from the sceptics without qualification. There is a good deal in Rorty's appropriation of writers such as Lyotard and Foucault (and even more, I think, in his reading of Derrida) that displays a rather curiously partial view of their work, and some of it that seems to me at least simply mistaken.[60] However, that there are very considerable differences between his reading of the 'postmodern' and those of Lyotard and Derrida (for example) is clear, and the centrepiece of it lies in his relation to the Enlightenment as compared with theirs. In the language of Charles Taylor (and that I shall discuss in a moment) Rorty does not accept that recognizing that the experiential agenda of the Enlightenment has broken down implies that the public aspects of the Enlightenment legacy must also collapse. Indeed, like some other postmoderns (usually of the soft-sceptical kind, such as Chantal Mouffe[61]), he suggests that the failure of the epistemological and ethical aspects of the Enlightenment makes its political legacy all the more important, because if difference is important and if it is all we have then (liberal, democratic) ways of mediating and living with those differences are doubly important. Thus, both senses of the postmodern end up with at least a 'relatively' positive assessment of the possibilities of radical and democratic political action. The question, however, is obvious: are such assessments justified? Let me turn now to the defenders in the faith of modernity who try to show why they are not.

## The Defenders of the Faith: Affirming the Modern Mood

Marshall Berman, in *All That is Solid Melts Into Air*,[62] has given us a clear view of the modern perspective that the postmoderns seek to problematize:

> To be Modern is to find ourselves in an environment that promises adventure, power, joy, growth, transformation of ourselves and the world – and at the same time threatens to destroy everything we know, everything we are ... modernity can be said to unite all mankind. But it is ... a unity of disunity.[63]

The 'modern' project of modernity is to recognize this (a point argued by John Dunn, as I mentioned in chapter 1). However, the defenders of 'faith in the modern' seek to find ways of understanding and coping with this realization that do not mean that the optimistic hopes and assumptions – especially in the political and social realms – are nullified.

As will be obvious, this has some similarities with the position of Rorty outlined above. The dissimilarity, however, – and it is central – is that the 'moderns' do not feel that 'the legacy of Enlightenment' can be protected if all the foundational hopes that undergird it are removed. Thus, *some* grounding for our political and ethical norms and institutions is essential.

Of course, the variety of modern defences of the 'project of the Enlightenment' are huge. Many contemporary social scientists, for example, simply identify themselves as 'children of the Enlightenment' without offering any defence of such a position or seeming to realize that one might be necessary.[64] Others offer a bewildering variety of defences either explicitly or implicitly. In what follows here, however, I want to look at two explicit defences of the 'Enlightenment project' that seek to assert against the 'postmodern' a 'modern' reading of our contemporary situation, and suggest how it can be justified, interpreted and evaluated. The two writers in question are Jürgen Habermas and Charles Taylor.

## *Habermas and the reassertion of rationality*

Perhaps the best-known critic of the postmoderns in modern social and political theory is Jürgen Habermas.[65]

He has been blunt, to the point of rudeness, about the failings of the whole gamut of approaches that, in various ways, lead into 'postmodern' readings of contemporary politics. 'The radical critique of reason,' he writes in one of his most uncompromising attacks of the 'postmodern turn', 'exacts a high price for taking leave of modernity. In the first place, these discourses can and want to give no account of their own position. Negative Dialectics,[[66]] genealogy and deconstruction alike avoid those categories in accord with which modern knowledge has been differentiated – by no means accidentally – and on the basis of which we today understand texts.'[67] He goes on to argue that there is a second respect in which these approaches are deeply flawed: 'They are guided by normative intuitions that go beyond what they can accommodate in terms of the indirectly affirmed "other of reason".'[68]

What are the grounds on which Habermas launches this fierce attack on the postmoderns? To all intents and purposes,

Habermas's defence of modernity is bound up with his defence of the legacy of the Enlightenment that has been in a sense the leitmotif of his life work.[69] I cannot, of course, here do anything other than scratch the surface of what is, after all, one of the most impressive (and enormous) bodies of work in twentieth-century social and political theory. However, some brief summary must be attempted.

Briefly, then, Habermas argues that 'modernity' is the uncompleted project of the Enlightenment; that the Enlightenment, far from fully creating modernity, failed to adequately comprehend its problems, although they were right to diagnose those problems as they did. What is required, therefore, is to complete the Enlightenment-inspired project of modernity, not abandon it altogether.[70] His general argument is nicely expressed in a passage from *Der philosophische Diskurs der Moderne*, to the effect that

> The parties that have contended about the correct self-understanding of modernity since the days of the Young Hegelians all agree on one point: that a far-reaching process of self-illusion was connected with the learning processes conceptualized in the eighteenth century as 'enlightenment' . . . In the discourse of modernity, the accusers raise an objection that has not substantially changed from Hegel and Marx down to Nietzsche and Heidegger, from Bataille and Lacan to Foucault and Derrida. The accusation is aimed against a reason grounded in the principle of subjectivity . . . All parties are united on this point: *These glassy facades have to shatter.*[71]

This analysis Habermas describes as one of the history of the opposition to modernity and traces its focal point to Nietzsche, whom he calls 'the real challenge for modernity',[72] and through him to Heidegger, Bataille, Foucault and Derrida. In other words, as is quite obvious, he is quite explicitly criticizing what I have called in this chapter the 'sceptical postmoderns'.

His critique of this tendency is complex and not always consistent. It is first of all important to see what it is not. To begin with, Habermas certainly does not pretend that modernity is an undifferentiated whole or that, as he is sometimes accused of, he still believes in the notion of a universal subject. As Martin Jay has rightly pointed out,[73] Habermas can be read as defending a certain notion of *differentiation* against the

'postmodern' appeal to 'differance'.[74] His theory of communicative action, for example, 'calls for the nurturing of a
plurality of intersubjectively grounded speech communities'.[75]
Drawing on work as varied as Weber, Parsons and Luhmann,
Habermas develops an account of the evolutions (and they are
multi-faceted, hence evolutions in the plural) of modernity,
where what Habermas calls 'system integration' and 'social
integration' begin to diverge markedly in the late eighteenth
century. System integration is derived from an instrumental
relationship between humanity and its natural environment,
while social integration (also referred to as the *lebensweld*, or
lifeworld) refers to norms and values which have a communicative rather than an instrumental derivation. This process,
Habermas accepts, gives rise to enormous strains, but it is the
domination of system integration in modernity over social integration, what in his rather arcane philosophical terminology he
calls the 'domination of the lifeworld by the system', that needs
to be the focus of a critical theory.

In this, of course, Habermas is echoing concerns similar to
those expressed by his Frankfurt School mentors Adorno and
(especially) Horkheimer, although (as was indicated above) he
is also disagreeing quite strongly with the turn their work took
in the 1940s and which Adorno's retained thereafter.[76] Moreover, it is this situation, Habermas argues, that has produced
the crisis of modernity that the postmoderns mis-diagnose as a
crisis of subjectivity.

Habermas's chosen solution is to try and strengthen social
integration through harnessing the emancipatory potential inherent in each of the three separate spheres of reason marked
out by the Enlightenment – that is to say, technical (or instrumental) reason, moral reason and aesthetic reason – and which
much of his own earlier work was designed to discuss.[77]
Postmodern readings of this situation, Habermas suggests, are
intrinsically conservative, because by running together these
various strains of thought they find themselves in a self-con-
structed cul-de-sac from which there is no escape, and where
there can be no sense that value A is better/preferable to B,
except, perhaps, on purely aesthetic grounds. Whereas in
positivistic social science (the dominant mode of reasoning at

present, Habermas thinks) instrumental reason is given unwarranted priority, in postmodern thought it is the aesthetic that is
given an unnecessarily high priority, and it is, moreover interpreted not rationally but irrationally. It can therefore never find
a solution to the problems of modernity and is inevitably nihilistic.

The view is clearly mainly directed at the postmodern sceptics. However, he also criticizes Rorty, though his criticism of
Rorty is rather muted. In some respects, as I have already
pointed out, their conclusions are not all that far apart.
Habermas expresses sympathy for and solidarity with the pragmatic tradition in terms of its 'attempt to make concrete concerns with the daily problems of one's community'.[78] His
critique, however, is that Rorty's philosophical position is just
as seriously flawed as other postmoderns' for the simple reason
that 'Rorty takes Western logocentrism as an indication of the
exhaustion of our philosophical discourse and a reason to bid
adieu to philosophy as such'. However, 'this way of reading the
tradition cannot be maintained if philosophy can be transformed so as to enable it to cope with the entire spectrum of
aspects of rationality'.[79] It is precisely this, of course, that
Habermas believes that the shift to communicative rationality
and discourse ethics can accomplish.[80]

For Habermas, therefore, the defence of modernity takes the
form of a defence of the Enlightenment, specifically a defence of
the conception of rationality he thinks is anchored in the
Enlightenment and of what he thinks it implies.[81] His attack on
the postmoderns (all varieties) revolves around the idea that
their understandings of this is in the first place deficient, and in
the second place leaves the door open to a corrosive relativism
that would neuter social critique from the outset.

In a moment I want to come on to the problems with this
argument, but before I do I want to look at one further defence
of modernity, of a rather different kind.

## Charles Taylor and the trajectory of the modern self

This is the defence offered by Charles Taylor in his book
*Sources of the Self*.[82] Of course, Taylor's book is a large and

complex one and I could not possibly attempt to summarize it all. However, my aim is much more modest. I simply want to extract from it the kernel of its defence of the modern identity and its critique, sometimes explicit but often implied, of what I have here called the postmodern attempt to 'disturb the peace'. A second reason for looking at Taylor is that he, like me, wants to suggest that the 'modernity debate' (though he does not call it that) has actually obscured much of what it was supposed to illuminate, and that until this is recognized we shall not be able to get anything like a good view of that 'modernity' which we are all trying to understand. As he himself says in the preface, the modern 'identity is much richer in moral sources than its condemners allow, but this richness is rendered invisible by the impoverished philosophical language of its most zealous defenders. Modernity urgently needs to be saved from its most unconditional supporters . . . understanding modernity aright is an exercise in retrieval.'[83]

It is in his final chapter, however, where he tries to draw the threads of his long and involved argument together, that Taylor most obviously moves onto the terrain I am concerned with here. Taylor thinks that the self-understanding of the modern identity he has been developing brings three 'standing areas of tension or threatened breakdown in modern moral culture'[84] into bolder relief. These three are what he calls the issue about sources (specifically, about the uncertainty and division that exists about constitutive goods); the issue about instrumentalism (can it be a disengaged instrumentalism, what alternatives are there to it?[85]) and, thirdly and finally, the issue about morality. This last issue arises, Taylor thinks, out of the conflicts of both the first and second issues, and he expresses it like this: 'beyond the question about the sources of our moral standards, and the one which opposes disengaged instrumentalism to a richer fulfilment, there is the question whether these moral standards are not incompatible with that fulfilment; whether morality doesn't exact a high price from us in terms of wholeness. This is a question which has come to the fore with certain contemporary postmodern writers influenced by Nietzsche, like Jaques Derrida and Michel Foucault.'[86]

As this suggests, Taylor believes that the three issues are deeply intertwined with one another, and his discussion of them begins with the second, the issue of instrumentalism which, as he says, 'has been at the centre of the most influential theories of modernity over the last two centuries'.[87] The point, of course, is that again it is the Enlightenment that is said to be the target. Romanticism, which is the primary carrier of the critique of instrumental reason for Taylor,[88] contained reactions to the 'felt inadequacies of standard Enlightenment . . . naturalism'. Especially, Taylor suggests, the romantic critique of Enlightenment took two forms; the first, Kantian in inspiration, concentrated on the creation of significance for us in our *self-chosen* nature; the second view, called expressivist by Taylor, and just as clearly Rousseauean in inspiration, focuses on nature as a source. 'The instrumental stance involves our objectifying nature,' Taylor suggests in his account of this expressivist view, 'we see it as a neutral order of things . . . both without us and in ourselves. This stance of separation is what blocks us [for the expressivists] . . . and so among the great aspirations which come down to us from the Romantic era are those towards reunification: bringing us back into contact with nature, healing the divisions within and between reason and sensibility, overcoming the divisions between people and creating community.'[89]

This, of course, has particular resonance when we remember Taylor's own reputation as (at least in some senses) a communitarian, which I briefly touched on in the introductory chapter. However, Taylor also wants to suggest that these two areas of critique lead to two specific attacks on instrumentalism; that instrumentalism 'empties life of meaning and that it threatens public freedom; that is, the institutions and practices of self-government. In other words the negative consequences of instrumentalism are allegedly two fold, experiential and public.'[90]

Taylor's own view is that the problem with the modern inheritors of both instrumental and expressivist modes is that they are too narrow in their sympathies. Each offers too simplistic a reading of the complexities of the modern identity. Yes, instrumentalism is untenable, both on experiential and on public and consequential grounds, but even the more pessimistic versions of expressivism (amongst which, be it noted, Taylor includes the early Frankfurt School and especially Adorno, and with which Taylor admits a high degree of sympathy[91]) have too narrow a range of sympathies. They are still entirely anthropo-centric, treating all goods not anchored in human powers or fulfilments as illusions from a bygone age. In this, Taylor suggests, they show very clearly their roots in the radical Enlightenment.

It is worth pointing out here that this reading of Taylor's contains an interesting critique of Habermas. In criticizing Adorno's argument in *Dialectik der Aufklärung*, Habermas argues that the 'impossible conflict between instrumental reason and expressive fulfilment' comes from a faulty conception of the human agent dependent upon seeing agents in terms of a re-lation of subject to object. Habermas's argument in *Theorie des kommunikativen Handelns*, of course, is that in fact the agent is constituted by language and thus by exchange and inter-change between agents. As Taylor paraphrases Habermas here, 'significant others . . . are not simply external to me; they help constitute my own selfhood . . . [and] once we see that agents are constituted by exchange, we understand that reason also advances in another dimension, that of the rational search for consensus through argument'.[92]

Taylor agrees with Habermas that this gives us reason for supposing that Adorno (and many others) were far too pessi-mistic about the possibility that instrumental control over nature necessarily means a parallel growth of instrumental con-trol over people, and thus, in terms of public consequences, modernity may be nothing like as predisposed to domination as has often been thought. However, Taylor also wants to say that while he agrees with Habermas about the claim that the self is constituted through exchange in language,[93] he most certainly does not agree that this means that the experiential aspects of instrumentalism are not real enough.

The distinction between experiential and public attacks on instrumentalism, I should add parenthetically, has some simi-larities to aspects of the distinction between modernity as mood and modernity as socio-cultural form. I mention this to flag a theme I shall explore later in this chapter. The most interesting point here, however, is that Taylor believes that Habermas elides the distinction between the two, and in detailing his reason for supposing this Taylor clarifies his own differences both with Habermas on the one hand, and with the 'postmoderns' like Foucault and Derrida (who are responsible for 'the issue of morality', remember).

What gets lost from Habermas's picture, Taylor argues, is not the demands of expressive fulfilment, which he does discuss in the context of the 'aesthetic' sphere of rationality. 'Rather, what cannot be fitted into his grid . . . is the search for moral sources outside the subject through languages which resonate within him or her, the grasping of an order which is inseparably indexed to a personal vision.'[94]

In this, Habermas is in agreement with a very wide body of contemporary thought, Taylor thinks. This spreads across moderns, postmoderns and even some (so to speak) pre-moderns, specifically the 'followers of Leo Strauss', who are singled out as being opposed to the whole 'modern turn' in both its 'disengaged instrumental and Romantic expressive forms'. I think that, as a characterization of the thought of Strauss himself (whatever is true about his 'followers') this is both inaccurate and unfair, and I will return to it in a moment. However, it shows very clearly the lines of the argument Taylor is trying to make.

Most importantly, this allows me, finally, to come to Taylor's treatment of the postmoderns. What emerges from his discussion of instrumentalism, Taylor thinks, is that we need to recognize a plurality of goods (and often of conflicts) which other views tend to mask by delegitimizing one or more of the goods in contest. Both some (disengaged and instrumentalist) moderns and critics of modernity (both pre- and postmoderns) do this, Taylor says. However, this conflict has been 'further articulated', he says, 'by writers who have drawn on Nietzsche'.[95] As an example, he points out that 'one of the important themes one can find in the work of the late Michel Foucault is the understanding of the way in which high ethical and spiritual ideals are often interwoven with exclusions and relations of domination'; and, he adds, 'William Connolly has formulated this aspect of Foucault's thought very aptly'.[96] Again, however, Taylor thinks these views are too narrowly focused: 'Characteristically these take the self-destructive *consequences* of a spiritual *aspiration* as a refutation of this aspiration. They make . . . the cardinal mistake of believing that a good must be invalid if it leads to suffering or destruction' (emphasis added).[97]

Thus, Taylor's position emerges as one that rejects both the unthinking allegiance of modernity (which he characterizes as instrumentalism), the spuriously easy retreat to accounts of the good that are seemingly homogenous but treat modernity far too simply (Strauss and his followers), and both modern and postmodern attempts to ignore those aspects of modernity that point to something outside ourselves, however much it is mediated for ourselves through language and community. In this respect, it seems to me, Taylor too 'defends' modernity, because his whole argument depends upon the story he tells in the bulk of the book about the character and evolution of the 'modern identity'.

In point of fact, Taylor offers a defence of modernity predicated upon certain assumptions about our nature, just as Habermas offers a defence of modernity predicated upon certain assumptions about rationality – and the supposed views on rationality held by those who problematize it. In these writers, therefore, we meet again those issues which, in the first chapter, we suggested lay at the heart of questions about modernity; and they use them to try to problematize the positions adopted by various 'postmoderns'. It is time, therefore, to attempt an overall assessment of the arguments that we have examined here.


## A One-Sided Debate?

Let me start by returning to the questions about modernity that were raised at the end of chapter 1. There were three: the temporal character of modernity, the issue of nature and/or convention and the issue of rationality. We can now see, I think, that the modernity debate as I have discussed it here, has given clear answers to two out of the three but, I want to suggest, only a very partial, muddy and unhelpful one to the third.

On the question of temporality, both moderns and (at least most) postmoderns agree, in general terms, that modernity is, to all intents and purposes, bound up with the legacy of the Enlightenment,[98] though they give contrasting accounts of what that legacy is and take different sides on the question of 'the ethico-political'; the moderns asserting the centrality of both for an understanding of either (though sometimes, as in Habermas, favouring the political) and the postmoderns broadly favouring the 'ethical', though understood in a 'Foucauldian' sense and with some postmoderns asserting the necessary political consequences of this view.

On the question of rationality, too, there is no doubt as to its centrality and the battle lines are correspondingly relatively well drawn. The moderns defend 'modern', Enlightenment-derived conceptions of reason, though they do not defend them all and are perfectly clear that the most dominant conception of rationality in modernity (i.e. instrumental rationality) is deeply flawed and requires serious revision. There are very deep differences between moderns on how this might best be done; but that rationality in its 'Enlightenment-derived' sense is absolutely central to the tasks of political theory, they do not doubt.

The postmoderns, on the other hand, problematize these conceptions of rationality as such. Of course, many would claim (as Geoffery Bennington has recently done) that the point is that, for postmoderns, things can still be discussed 'rationally', simply not rationalistically.[99] However, other postmoderns would be suspicious even about this usage, and would want to be still more critical of all 'rational' arguments on the ground (for example) that it privileges one form of understanding over another (perhaps the aesthetic). This links up with the preference many postmoderns show for 'poetic', radically autonomous readings of ethos as – in Foucault's words, to which I shall return in a moment – a 'manner of being'.

However, it is on the third question raised in chapter 1 that there is a significant silence. On the question of 'nature/convention' virtually all the moderns and postmoderns discussed here *share* a view. To elaborate my argument here I want to return to one of the arguments I mentioned briefly at the very outset, to wit Richard Bernstein's usage of the phrase 'ethico-political' in his book on modernity. When I discussed his argument, it will be recalled that I quoted his reasons for his use of the term 'ethico-political' in some detail, with approval, but also pointing out that I intended to disagree with one aspect of this presentation. The relevant passage was as follows: 'ethics is concerned with ethos, with those habits, customs and modes of response that shape and define our praxis. Politics is concerned with our public lives in the polis – with the communal bonds that at once unite and separate us as citizens. *The essential link between ethos and polis is nomos*' (emphasis added).[100]

I would like to emphasize that I think Bernstein is right to see ethics and politics as linked in this way and, as I shall pursue in the next chapter, I think that this has profound implications for the way in which we think about both. However, I think that it is deeply significant that *both* moderns and postmoderns, as I have discussed them here, adopt a certain stance in relation to this conjunction of ethics and politics which is rightly picked up by Bernstein; that is to say *both* moderns and postmoderns do see the essential link between ethics and politics as *nomos*, the conventional, artificial structures and processes that we create[101] for our communal living.

Of course, while they agree about this in general, it is also true that they disagree about the *manner* of these conventional, artificial structures and processes, and before I come to what I take to be the most important implications of this agreement, I just want to outline what I take these disagreements to be.

The postmoderns tend to make a distinction between the 'political' and the 'ethical' based on their view of the character of this artificiality, or rather, they see the 'political' as *some version* of the ethical. As Foucault once remarked, in an interview shortly before his death and specifically in opposition to Habermas's political focus, 'I would more or less agree with the idea that in fact what interests me is much more morals than politics, or, in any case, politics as an ethics. . . . ethics is a practice, ethos is a manner of being.'[102]

A similar thrust is, I think, visible in Rorty's work. While, as we have seen, Rorty has no problems with the liberal politics that are the legacy of the Enlightenment in the public realm (indeed, he celebrates them), he also sees private 'ethical' features of our lives as not only not connected to such public things but possibly in competition with them, with neither side having priority over the other. As he remarks in *Contingency, Irony and Solidarity*, a central claim of the book 'is that our responsibilities to others constitute only the *public* side of our lives, a side which competes with our private affections and our private attempts at self-creation and which has no *automatic* priority over them'.[103]

Of course there are differences. The postmodern sceptic (and in this respect it matters little if they are 'hard' or 'soft') will often suggest that in this sense they are 'against ethics',[104] though they might more properly say that they are problematizing and inverting what has usually (according to them) been thought to be 'ethical'. Some (soft-sceptical postmoderns especially) will also often insist that readings of (for example) our ethical and cultural identities generate certain forms of politics,[105] and that, in this respect, their concentration on 'ethos' is indeed linked to the polis through *nomos*.[106]

If we look at the moderns, the focus is very different, though equally emphatic. Here there is what we might call a 'strong' link between the ethical and the political and often it is the political (at least in some sense) which is prior, and which organizes the sense of 'nomos' involved.

As Thomas McCarthy has said, in Habermas's case, one might see his view of the relation between ethics and politics as so close as to see 'his moral theory as a theory of "political morality" – of social justice rather than of moral virtue, character, feelings and judgement, or of ethical life, community and the good – and his political theory as being, at least at the core, a "moral politics" – as privileging strictly universal laws over the conflict and compromise of interests'.[107]

Habermas himself has been equally clear. For him one of the most central tasks for us today is 'the building up of restraining barriers for the exchanges between lifeworld and system'.[108] These 'restraining barriers', for Habermas, are, of course, what his realm of politics – the public sphere – should be all about. If they are, they are what he calls 'autonomous' public spheres which he defines as 'neither bred nor kept by a political system for purposes of creating legitimation'.[109] Such public spheres are how Habermas fills in the catgory of *nomos*, in the Bernsteinean equation and the relationship of these spheres to 'largely rationalised lifeworlds' is a mutually dependent one. They can only draw their strength from such lifeworlds, but at the same time, without them, the lifeworlds are prey to the logic of system which has produced the corrupted public culture of contemporary modernity.

Taylor's way of relating the categories of ethics and politics is different again. However, he too suggests that at least one aspect of the distinctions between the moderns and the postmoderns lies in the postmodern emphasis on the 'ethical' *over* the political. The postmoderns on his account, let us not forget, raise 'the issue about *morality*', and one (though not the only one) of his criticisms of this move is that it falsely assumes that some of the appalling public consequences of certain moral views invalidate those moral views. In fact, for Taylor, the public consequences of 'instrumentalism' need not be as terrible as the critics (whether they are postmodern or not) think; in that he agrees with Habermas. However, he also wants to make a distinction between the experiential and the public (directly political) aspects of modernity and suggests further that here, modernity has resources available to it not recognized by *either* moderns like Habermas *or* postmoderns like Derrida and Foucault. These resources, however, may not be free from pain for those who choose to adopt them. 'Do we have to choose between various kinds of spiritual lobotomy and self-inflicted wounds?', Taylor asks. 'Perhaps. Certainly most of the outlooks which promise us that we will be spared these choices are based on selective blindness.'[110] None the less, his view is clearly that the sources that have created the modern self have the 'resources' (if understood aright) to point us in the right direction. In a more recent study, he has given a political cast to these thoughts when he calls the politics that the evolution of the modern self has called up the 'politics of recognition', a subspecies of what he calls 'the politics of equal dignity', based on the idea that all humans are equally worthy of respect.[111] Such a politics depends, he argues, on the recognition that the 'crucial feature of human life is its fundamentally dialogic character',[112] and this in turn depends on the existence and construction of communities that can recognize and permit such dialogue. Here too, therefore, while the interrelationships between ethics and politics are very close, the postmodern assertion of the ethical (or perhaps the anti-ethical) over the political is seen as a primary weakness of their account.

In all these cases, however, the bedrock assumption is that *nomos* can be seen independently of *physis*, of nature or the natural. Yet in this respect, it seems to me Bernstein is incorrect. For the Greeks, what had to link ethics and politics was not simply *nomos*, it was the *question* of *nomos* and *physis*; that is to say, whether there were laws, conventions etc. that should reflect some natural state of things, in us, in our 'manner of being' or in the world in general (or indeed, outside the world at all). This aspect of the third question, present explicitly in Strauss and at least by implication in Blumenberg, is absent in the modernity debate almost entirely.

I say *almost* entirely, for there are, in truth, fragments of it scattered through the debate; nearly forgotten remnants of a once central question. In Foucault, for example, especially in his discussions of sexuality, the question of nature surfaces from time to time and it is raised in similar ways by some (though few) other postmoderns.[113] In Taylor's presentation of the sources of the modern self, the idea of nature also plays a central role, though chiefly in connection with 'naturalism' both in the Enlightenment and in the romantic opposition to it, though it also features briefly and elusively again in the concluding discussion, where Taylor is arguing for the centrality of a sense of spirituality as a core component of those elements of the resources of modernity that have been ignored by moderns and postmoderns alike.

I agree with Taylor here. Ignored it has been, and to the detriment not just of the participants in the modernity debate. For in many ways it is *the* central question if we are to perform the tasks of political theory I outlined in the introductory chapter, and as I shall come on to discuss again in chapter 4. Moreover, it is, I submit, a central question for adequately answering the question of rationality and also of relating modernity as mood to modernity as socio-cultural form, which in turn enables a much better perception of the adequacy of views of modernity as temporally bound.

Before turning to this question in the next chapter, however, I want to offer three further reasons for supposing that the participants in the 'modernity debate' have misunderstood the significance of at least some of the central issues involved.

## Three Problems

### First problem

The first question has to do with the role that the Enlightenment plays in the modernity debate. As is obvious from the above discussion, for both the moderns and the postmoderns the Enlightenment and its legacy is a central part of what is at stake. Yet, the character of the Enlightenment and its legacy is subtly different in many cases. MacIntyre, for example, has a very broad definition of the 'Enlightenment' effectively including much of the seventeenth and early nineteenth centuries as well as the eighteenth. For Habermas, in contrast, Enlightenment is a much more specific term and has not yet, of course, been fully realized. For Lyotard, to give a third example, the Enlightenment is the source for most of modernity's master narratives, the incredulity towards (and perhaps rejection of) which is the real signifier of *la condition postmoderne*.

There are two related problems, I think, which emerge from a consideration of the centrality of the Enlightenment in the modernity debate. The first is a definitional one; the second, growing out of this is, so to speak an historical one.[114]

The first problem has to do with the characterization of 'the Enlightenment' as such. As has frequently been pointed out, to speak of *the* Enlightenment is already to assume a particular answer to the question 'is there something that links the disparate and often quite contradictory writings of those figures most concerned with the Enlightenment in eighteenth century Europe?' Can we make a unity out of such diverse material or is this unity a chimera, a creature created, as Roy Porter suggests, by 'mingled academic imperialism and tidy mindedness'?[115]

It is well known, of course, that many leading scholars of the Enlightenment have indeed suggested that there was a conscious unity.[116] However, it is important, I think, to see precisely in what this unity might be said to consist. According to Gay, 'The Philosophy of Enlightenment insisted on man's essential autonomy, man is responsible to himself, to his own rational interests, to his self-development and, by an inescapable tension, to the welfare of his fellow man.'[117]

However, this indicates, I suggest, a unity of *aim*, and to an extent of *approach*, but certainly not of general philosophical outlook or ontological commitment. A distinction worth bearing in mind here is CharlesTaylor's suggestion (in the context of the liberal/communitarian debate) that we distinguish between ontology and advocacy.[118] Ontological questions, for Taylor, 'concern what you recognize as the factors you will invoke to account for social life . . . advocacy issues concern the moral stand or policy one adopts'.[119]

In this context, the self-conscious Enlightenment, while certainly differing greatly on issues of (for example) which form of government was most appropriate, held its unity in terms largely of its advocacy. As one of the age of Enlightenment's most distinguished followers put it, 'I should think myself a weak reasoner and bad citizen . . . were I not, though a royalist in London, a republican in Paris.'[120]

However, there were great differences at the ontological level, especially if the Enlightenment is taken out of its (relatively) narrow mainstream (French) setting and extended either spatially (to include Prussians like Kant and Lessing, Scotsmen like Hume, Smith and Ferguson and Englishmen like Gibbon) or temporally (to include writers in the seventeenth or nineteenth centuries). Moreover, there was, I suggest, a fundamental ontological division within even the mainstream Enlightenment, between, for example, the likes of Montesquieu and Rousseau.[121] Interestingly, given my earlier argument, much of this ontological dispute lay over the character and use of the 'natural'. The specifics do not really concern me, at least for the moment,[122] but the important point is to recognize that given the existence of these sorts of differences and disagreements within the Enlightenment it is rather difficult to see how one could be 'for' or 'against' the 'Enlightenment project' as such. One might find some aspects of it that one was in sympathy with and others that one was not. This, indeed, is what a good deal of the discussion of the Enlightenment in the modernity debate actually amounts to, I think.[123] To suggest that one particular assumption or even related set of assumptions was, somehow, 'dominant' or 'really significant' would have to depend on an argument about the legacy of the Enlightenment and 'what happened after'.

This brings me to my second point. The story that is often told, by moderns and postmoderns (though naturally in rather different ways) about the role of 'the Enlightenment' in the creation of 'our identity' or 'our society' is, I think, far too simple. In this respect (though not necessarily in what he derives from it) I agree with Taylor. It often amounts to claiming that a certain thinker, Kant, perhaps, or Hegel or Nietzsche, expressed the 'real logic of the Enlightenment position' in a way that no one else did.

It may, of course, be perfectly true that a thinker saw an aspect of a set of arguments that no one else has done, and that for that reason we should pay very close attention to what he or she says. It is even true, I think, that the three thinkers just mentioned are especially interesting in helping us to trace the philosophical problems of modernity. However, first of all, this is not to say that they (and they alone) represent the 'true legacy' of 'the Enlightenment' or can pinpoint its flaws, since, for the reasons given above, such a claim will make little sense.

Secondly, the significance of this sort of claim, even if it could be shown to have some plausibility, would depend upon it having a much wider reach than simply the world of philosophy. This point thus brings me on to my second general question: the relationship between the modernity debate as I have discussed it here and the question of the relationship between modernity as mood and modernity as socio-cultural form.

## Second problem

Another feature of the modernity debate as I have sketched it here is the relatively infrequent sense that modernity as mood and modernity as socio-cultural form are either separable in principle or can be separated in practice. Habermas's theory, for example, is dependent upon seeing 'modernity' as a complex relationship of what I have termed mood and socio-cultural form, but there is a strong sense that in fact the latter orders and organizes the former, and much of his critique of the postmoderns derives its force from his insistence that they have no real account of modernity as socio-cultural form.

In the case of a postmodern like Baudrillard, who clearly does, the case is rather different. Here it is unclear as to what his account of modernity leads to in terms of 'advocacy', but in any case there does not seem – at least to me – to be a clear sense of modernity as discussing the three questions I raised at the end of chapter 1.

If one accepts the point I made above in connection with the Enlightenment, then one can, I think, derive something very interesting from this. Effectively, the modernity debate as I have here construed it *ought* largely to be a debate at the level of ontological commitment. However, because of the elision of the two senses of modernity in a good deal of writing on these questions, both the ontological *and* advocacy levels have become confused and, as a result, the modernity debate itself has failed to properly address the very question it set itself to resolve: the character and implications of modernity.

This suggests another point. In fact, the consideration of modernity as socio-cultural form will be intimately related to modernity as mood in that our 'ontological commitments' will generate 'advocacy' *in the light of a reading of what the conditions for advocacy are.* At this level, in other words, I should like to amend Taylor's distinction and suggest that rather than a dual distinction between 'ontology and advocacy' we use a threefold distinction between ontology, advocacy and what we might perhaps call conditionality, seen as the conditions about which our ontological reflections revolve and in the light of which our advocacy is structured.

In other words, it is at the level of 'conditionality' in this sense that our discussions of modernity as socio-cultural form should largely take place, though our ontological reflections will also be oriented towards this in the sense that this will inform the understanding of the 'social' that is the focus of our ontology here. Equally, our 'advocacy' will arise out of the interplay of the ontological and condition-oriented levels and will have an impact on those levels, in that 'advocacy' may affect 'conditions' which will in turn change the sense of our ontological reflections.

This way of looking at things will become clearer in the next chapter. For now let me simply add that the implication of it is that the different levels need *both* to be kept separable *and* be understood together. Only if both these things are done consistently can we expect to reach an understanding of modernity that can help us perform the tasks of political theory. An illustration of this, though it also raises another important question, is provided by the third question I want to discuss.

## Third problem

To discuss the third question, I want to return to an issue raised most obviously by Hans Blumenberg and William Connolly; to wit, the question of evil. The significance of this is twofold here. In the first place, as was indicated during the discussion of Blumenberg in chapter 1, evil has two faces, so to speak, which I referred to as 'Evil' and evil. The latter sense of evil, the sense of willed evil, of human action and inaction, is largely unproblematic, in the sense that we can understand what is meant by it, even if we are inhospitable to terms such as evil because of their theological overtones. However, the former sense, 'Evil' – that is to say, the condition of evil in the world, which the Gnostics were concerned with – is rather more problematic.

Connolly's argument, it will be recalled, is that the former version of evil moves silently inside the first one, though he does not use the terminology I use here. I think in a certain sense at least Connolly is correct. If this is so, however, it makes it even more imperative that we have available a sense of 'Evil' that is comprehensible, for without it we will not be able to properly come to terms with the seemingly unproblematic use of the term, and as such our capacity for judgement will necessarily be weakened.

It is on this point, I think, that (some of) the postmoderns have been more acute than (most of) the moderns.[124] Yet, a fundamental question here is surely to ask if there is anything (which we might call 'Evil') which permits, encourages or creates the conditions for evil. This surely must be both a question of 'nature' (as I shall come on to discuss it later) but also of social form, as Arendt's analysis in *Eichmann in Jerusalem* shows with unanswerable power, I think.[125] Given the critique discussed above, it seems unlikely that the postmoderns could give us a very clear answer to this question. The problem with many moderns is that they do not even ask it.

However, 'Evil' (and evil) are surely central to any discussion of what we advocate for our contemporary societies. If there are aspects of modernity (as socio-cultural form) which, so to speak, encourage procedures, patterns of behaviour or activities which we might call evil, then, surely, we should avoid them. Yet only if we have an understanding of how 'Evil' and evil are related can we sensibly do that, and this requires an understanding of modernity that can allow us to reflect adequately on this relationship.

## Conclusion: Beyond Enlightenment and Critique?

Finally, let me try and draw the threads of this rather disparate chapter together. I do not think it can be denied that the modernity debate ought to be a central element of any political theory seeking to come to terms with the reality of our contemporary situation, whatever answer is given to the general question 'how should we understand modernity and what are its implications?' However, in order to do this, we must understand that there are two broad senses of modernity (mood and socio-cultural form), and they must be related to one another in ways that neither privilege one over the other nor elide the distinction between the two.

In most contemporary discussions of modernity, however, one or other of these moves are made, to the detriment of our ability to offer an understanding of modernity that can either do a very complex phenomenon justice or help reorient political theory in ways that would overcome the problems of forms of political theory that largely ignore modernity as such. Moreover, the modernity debate is beset with purely stipulative notions of 'the Enlightenment' that do a good deal to structure and organize the debate and yet about which there can be very little real agreement.

If we look at a wide range of discussion of modernity, however, then a number of issues stand out; most importantly, I suggested, three: whether or not modernity can or should be given a discrete temporal and spatial location; the role and character of rationality; and the possibility and importance of 'nature', however understood. While the modernity debate proffers many and various readings of the first two, differing both between moderns and postmoderns and within each broad group, on the third they are remarkably agreed: the central aspects of our politics and ourselves are and must be artificial and constructed; 'nature', however understood, has at best a secondary and derivative role.

However, as some moderns (for example Taylor) and some postmoderns (for example Connolly and Honig) have recognized, working through the implications of modernity as they understand it brings us up against questions such as the character and political implications of evil that raise the question of nature at least as much as those of temporality and reason. Thus, within the modernity debate, there are the beginnings of a new set of questions that start to problematize the hitherto under-examined question of whether 'nature' (leaving it undefined, for the moment) has anything to offer that we have so far ignored, and that can help to orient us in ways that allow us to interpret both modernity as mood and modernity as socio-cultural form, so as to allow us to perform the 'tasks of political theory', even if in an altered or reconstructed form.

Such a task, however, cannot even be begun, it seems to me, if we remain locked in debates about things called 'the Enlightenment project', and whether we are 'for it' or 'against it'. I agree with Gay, Cassirer and many others that the Enlightenment has an identifiable set of core values which allow us to speak of it as, so to speak, a 'mood' in itself. In this sense it is certainly one of the most powerful and important aspects of 'modernity as mood' and the concentration upon it by the epigones of the modernity debate is both understandable and, I think, correct.

However, the sense of those 'core values' is not such as to allow us to be simply 'for' or 'against' them. Many of them (indeed I would argue most of them) are properly seen as occupying the realm of advocacy, not of ontology; though there are clearly some shared ontological assumptions as well. Thus, it would be perfectly possible to disagree violently at the onto-logical level while remaining committed at the advocacy level to aspects of the 'Enlightenment project' and, indeed, vice versa. Indeed, this is what I think is true of a wide range of contem-porary thinkers who are often seen as critical of the 'Enlighten-ment' while sharing obviously 'Enlightenment-derived' political assumptions.

However, we must bear in mind also the 'conditional' level I mentioned above, which in many discussions of modernity is ignored, since the distinction between modernity as mood and modernity as socio-cultural form is not made at all. Effectively, as I shall explain in more detail in the next section, this level is the level where modernity as socio-cultural form most obviously manifests itself.

If we see this, then we can understand better the central role that the relationship between the two forms of modernity plays in our understanding. Modernity as socio-cultural form clearly does have a temporal location. How and in what manner we understand 'modernity as mood' will in part depend on how we see the relations between the ontological, advocacy and con-ditional elements of modern social life, and thus the relation between modernity as mood and modernity as socio-cultural form.

However, in trying to articulate this we inevitably have to look at the question of the most appropriate way of conceiving of these relations. This task is what I shall pursue in the next chapter. I want to look at the implications of taking 'nature' seriously and where that leaves our conceptions of modernity. It gives us, I shall argue, a very particular ethico-political impera-tive which suggests we should see rationality in a much larger sense than we are accustomed to do. In the final chapter of this book, therefore, I shall then come on to assess the implications of this argument for the tasks of political theory as outlined in the introductory chapter, suggesting what modifications to them we now need to acknowledge. Finally, then, I shall look briefly at what the implications of these arguments might be for political science more generally, and sketch out what I take to be the most important and pressing areas where the argument needs further refinement.

## Notes

1 This point is made in Geoffery Bennington in *Legislations: The Politics of Deconstruction* (London: Verso, 1994), p. 172.
2 In this chapter, and indeed, for the rest of the book, I will use the terms 'modern' and 'postmodern' to refer to particular 'constellations of views' related to conceptions of modernity, especially modernity as mood as discussed in chapter 1 above. I do not suppose that these views are easily translatable into general views about art, literature, architecture etc., and I make no unstated assumptions about the relation between, for example, 'post-structuralism' and 'postmodernism' as 'isms'. Many (though not all) of those I shall be referring to as 'postmoderns' are also post-structuralists, but contra much recent writing, I believe that there is a very considerable difference between the two. Moreover, as we shall see, I shall argue that both moderns and postmoderns adopt an 'anti-foundational approach to questions of political theory that, at least in its current form, is damaging their own (variegated) projects, and that this shared 'anti-foundationalism' is largely independent of (for example) whether one is 'post-structuralist' or not. These questions are often highly individual. My characterization of the debate as being in important respects between 'moderns and postmoderns' should not be taken to imply that I think these are anything other than labels convenient for discussing my topic here.
3 See, for example, Michael Shanks and Christopher Tilly (eds), *Social Theory and Archaeology* (Cambridge: Polity Press, 1987).
4 A. Huyssens, 'Mapping the Postmodern', *New German Critique*, 33, 1984, pp. 5–52.
5 Michael Ryan, 'Postmodern Politics', in *Theory, Culture and Society*, 5, 2–3, June 1988, p. 559.
6 For representative samples of their œuvre see: Roland Barthes, *Mythologies* (London: Jonathan Cape, 1972); Michel Foucault, *The Order of Things* (London: Tavistock, 1970); Jacques Derrida, *De la Grammatologie* (Paris: Minuit, 1967); Paul de Man, *Blindness and Insight: Essays in the Rhetoric of Contemporary Criticism* (Minneapolis: University of Minnesota Press, 1983); Stanley Fish, *Doing What Comes Naturally* (New Haven: Yale University Press, 1989).
7 See, in addition to his novels *The Name of The Rose* and *Foucault's Pendulum*, Eco's more general writings, especially *Interpretation and Overinterpretation* (Cambridge: Cambridge University Press, 1992).
8 For a good discussion of this see Roy Boyne and Ali Rattansi (eds), *Postmodernism and Society* (London: Macmillan, 1990), introduction.
9 Rorty, *Essays on Heidegger and Others* (Cambridge: Cambridge University Press, 1991), p. 1.

10 Rorty, *Essays on Heidegger and Others*, p. 12.

11 See Jean-François Lyotard, *La Condition postmoderne* (Paris: Minuit, 1979).

12 Richard Rorty, *Philosophy and the Mirror of Nature* (Oxford: Blackwell, 1980). I would argue that this is so even if we assume the writings of Jacques Derrida should be included (as I think that they should) as displaying 'the postmodern mood'. Derrida's work, brilliant as it is, seems to me to fall largely under the general heading 'the interpretation of texts'. Moreover, deconstruction as a literary technique is very far from being equivalent to the postmodern mood. Derrida, it seems to me, is both a postmodern and a deconstructionist, but not either because of the other. While he is rightly seen as a brilliant exemplar of the postmodern mood on occasion, he has not (as far as I am aware) ever given as programmatic a reading of it as either Lyotard or Rorty in the books just cited.

13 Ludwig Wittgenstein, *Tractatus Logico-Philosophicus* (London: Routledge and Kegan Paul, 1961), proposition 6.43.

14 This is a point I take from Lyotard's arguments in *Au juste* [co-authored with J.-L. Thebaud] (Paris: Christian Bourgeois, 1979), and from his essay 'Réponse à la question: Qu'est-ce que le postmoderne?', included in his *Le Postmoderne expliqué aux enfants* (Paris: Galilée, 1986). In *Au juste*, Lyotard insists that 'postmodern' should not be taken in 'a periodizing sense' and in the later essay he remarks not only that 'the postmodern is part of the modern' but that it might be seen as being prior to the modern. An author who might be 'postmodern' in this sense is Montaigne, thus echoing Toulmin's sense of 'postmodernity' discussed in chapter 1. I shall return to the significance of all this later on in this chapter.

15 Boyne and Rattansi also talk of two 'sides' to postmodernism. My assumptions here, however, are rather different.

16 In her recent book, *Postmodernism and the Social Sciences: Insights, Inroads and Intrusions* (Princeton: Princeton University Press, 1991), Pauline Rosenau has also divided postmodern thought into two groups and has also used the term 'sceptical' to describe one group of postmodern writers (the other group she calls 'affirmative'). However, as with Boyne and Rattansi, my usage of the term differs somewhat from hers, and my assessment of the authors concerned differs very considerably. Just how different will become apparent later on in this chapter and in chapter 3.

17 The most exhaustive discussion so far of the ins and outs of the saga of Paul de Man, though clearly written as a case for the prosecution, is David Lehman, *Signs of The Times: Deconstruction and the Fall of Paul de Man* (London: André Deutsch, 1991).

18 The book that raised this controversy again was Victor Farias's *Heidegger et le Nazisme* (Paris: Legraffe, 1988), and the case against Heidegger has been prosecuted with devastating forensic skill by

Hugo Ott in *Martin Heidegger: A Political Life* (London: Fontana, 1993).

19 *Power/Knowledge* (New York: Pantheon, 1980), p. 131.

20 See Charles Taylor, 'Foucault on Freedom and Truth', in *Philosophy and The Human Sciences* (Cambridge: Cambridge University Press, 1985), p. 182.

21 See his paper 'Habermas and Lyotard on Postmodernity', in *Essays on Heidegger and Others* (Cambridge: Cambridge University Press, 1991), p. 173.

22 Richard Ashley, 'Living On Borderlines: Man, Poststructuralism and War', in James Der Derian and Michael Shapiro (eds), *International/ Intertextual Relations: Postmodern Readings of World Politics* (Lexington, Mass.: Lexington Books, 1989), p. 278.

23 Michel Foucault, *The Foucault Reader*, ed. Paul Rabinow (Harmondsworth: Penguin, 1984), p. 384.

24 Ibid., 375, 377.

25 I should emphasize that I do not at all mean to suggest that Lyotard's or Baudrillard's views are simply 'the same' in terms of their relation to modernity. This would clearly be wrong. I do think, however, that the reasons for their scepticism are very similar in so far as the issues that I am discussing here are concerned. Much the same is true about Derrida, I think, whom I would also term in this sense a 'hard sceptic'. However, I shall say more about Derrida a little later on.

26 This last point is particularly associated with Baudrillard. See, for example, William Stearns and William Haloupka (eds), *Jean Baudrillard: The Disappearence of Art and Politics* (London: Macmillan, 1992).

27 Jean-François Lyotard, *Driftworks* (New York: Semiotext(e), 1982).

28 See, for example, Jean-François Lyotard, *La Condition postmoderne: rapport sur le savoir* (Paris: Minuit, 1979). In English as *The Postmodern Condition: A Report on Knowledge*, trans. G. Bennington (Manchester: Manchester University Press, 1974).

29 A good selection of Baudrillard's writing can be found in English in Mark Poster (ed.), *Jean Baudrillard: Selected Writings* (Cambridge: Polity Press, 1988).

30 Jean Baudrillard, *Les Stratégies fatales* (Paris: Bernard Grasset, 1983).

31 Mark Poster, introduction to *Jean Baudrillard*, p. 7.

32 Ryan, 'Postmodern Politics', p. 565.

33 See Baudrillard, 'Revolution and the End of Utopia', in Stearns and Chaloupka (eds), *Jean Baudrillard*, p. 240.

34 See Homi K. Bhabha (ed.), *Nation and Narration* (London: Routledge, 1990).

35 Interesting pieces from these last four writers are included in Der Derian and Shapiro (eds), *International/Intertextual Relations*. See also William Connolly, *Political Theory and Modernity* (Oxford: Blackwell, 1988).

36 See Connolly, 'Identity and Difference in Global Politics', in Der Derian and Shapiro, *International/Intertextual Relations*.

37 William E. Connolly, *Identity/Difference: Democratic Negotiations of Political Paradox* (Ithaca: Cornell University Press, 1991).

38 Ibid., 1. My remarks on Connolly's arguments here draw partly on my review of Connolly's book (see *Millennium: Journal of International Studies*, 20, no. 3, winter 1991, pp. 531–4). I am also grateful to Bill Connolly for several helpful discussions.

39 Connolly's most recent book is in fact a treatment of what he calls the 'Augustinian imperative' that builds on this analysis. See William Connolly, *The Augustinian Imperative* (London: Sage, 1993).

40 See Connolly, *Identity/Difference*, p. 4.

41 Ibid., 8.

42 Ibid., 215.

43 I discuss this logic in much more detail in my forthcoming book, *Duties Beyond Orders* (London: Routledge, forthcoming 1996), ch. 5.

44 Bonnie Honig, *Political Theory and the Displacement of Politics* (Ithaca: Cornell University Press, 1993).

45 Ibid., 2.

46 Ibid., 6–7.

47 Judith Squires (ed.), *Principled Positions: Postmodernism and the Rediscovery of Value* (London: Lawrence and Wishart, 1993).

48 In this context, she is even kind enough to cite an article of mine where I outlined an earlier version of the distinction between hard- and soft-sceptical postmoderns (see N. J. Rengger, 'No Time Like The Present: Postmodernism and Political Theory', in *Political Studies*, 40, no. 3, Sept. 1992. The implication is that 'weak postmodernism' and the soft-sceptical stance I outline there are much the same. In essence, I think that this is so, except I would not want to include all of her 'weak postmoderns' as my soft-sceptical ones, and I think that my notion of the postmodern is far less tightly drawn than hers in the essay, as I explain above.

49 Squires, *Principled Positions*, pp. 3–4. Again, I would argue that there is a danger in running too much together here, though it is certainly true that most 'postmoderns' would share at least some of the views herein outlined.

50 This understanding will be seen by those interested in such things to have a very distinct Platonic tint. In that all of the Hellenistic schools saw themselves to a greater or lesser extent as 'Socratic' this is, of course, no accident. I shall come back to these linkages in chapter 3.

51 See, for example, Cornell West, *The American Evasion of Philosophy* (London: Macmillan, 1989), and Stanley Fish, *Doing What Comes Naturally* (Oxford: Oxford University Press, 1989).

52 See *Philosophy and The Mirror of Nature* (Oxford: Blackwell, 1980). *The Consequences of Pragmatism* (Minneapolis: University of Minnesota Press, 1982).

53 Richard Rorty, *Contingency, Irony and Solidarity* (Cambridge: Cambridge University Press, 1990). In ch. 2 he is explicitly critical of Epicurean themes; however, the similarity is still there, I think. See also

his two volumes of collected essays *Objectivity, Truth and Relativism* and *Essays on Heidegger and Others*, both published by Cambridge University Press in 1991. For his amnesty lecture, see Susan Hurley and Michael Shute (eds), *Human Rights* (Oxford: Oxford University Press, 1994).

54 See, for example, his remarks about 'Geistesgeschichte' as canon formation in 'The Historiography of Philosophy: Four Genres', in Richard Rorty, J. B. Schneewind and Quentin Skinner (eds), *Philosophy in History* (Cambridge: Cambridge University Press, 1984), where he argues that we need canons as long as we realize they are 'stories'.

55 Rorty *Essays on Heidegger and Others*, p. 176.

56 Rorty 'Solidarity or Objectivity', in *Objectivity, Truth and Relativism*.

57 Rorty 'Cosmopolitanism without Emancipation', in ibid.

58 See Bernard Yack, *The Longing for Total Revolution: Philosophical Sources of Social Discontent from Rousseau to Marx and Nietzsche* (Princeton: Princeton University Press, 1986).

59 Rorty, *Essays on Heidegger and Others*, p. 184.

60 A good example, discussed by Geoffery Bennington in *Legislations* (p. 47, n. 2), is Rorty's claim that Derrida should not be doing 'philosophy' but should just be telling stories, thus reifying that which Derrida (and Rorty in other moods) suggests should be 'problematized'.

61 See e.g. her *Rethinking The Political* (London: Verso, 1992).

62 Marshall Berman, *All that is Solid Melts into Air* (New York: Basic Books, 1982).

63 Ibid., 15.

64 See e.g. Robert Keohane's remark in his *International Institutions and State Power* (Boulder, Colo.: University of Colorado Press, 1989), p. 21.

65 He has elaborated this critique in a number of papers and books. See, most significantly, *Der philosophische Diskurs der Moderne: Zwölf Vorlesungen* (Frankfurt: Suhrkamp Verlag, 1985). An English version is *The Philosophical Discourse of Modernity* (Cambridge: Polity, 1990). See also his essays and reply to his critics in Richard J. Bernstein (ed.), *Habermas and Modernity* (Cambridge: Polity, 1985).

66 It is interesting and significant, I think, that Habermas singles out for criticism his old mentor Adorno. The connections between Adorno's thought and certain characteristics of deconstruction in literary theory are clear. They parallel, in certain respects, those of his friend and intellectual collaborator, Benjamin.

67 Habermas, *The Philosophical Discourse of Modernity*, p. 336.

68 Ibid., 337.

69 It is a concern, for example, in *Strukturwandel der Öffentlichkeit* (1962), is one still in *Der Philosophische Diskurs der Moderne* (1985) and remains one in *Faktizität und Geltung* (1992).

70 It is worth pointing out here the ease with which this view of modernity could be accommodated to that of Blumenberg discussed in the last

chapter. Of course, Habermas does not necessarily subscribe to this view; nor does he contradict it, at least in general outline. I shall return to this point in a moment.

71 Habermas, 'Left Hegelians, Right Hegelians and Nietzsche', in *The Philosophical Discourse of Modernity*, pp. 55–6.

72 Habermas, *Philosophical Discourse of Modernity*, p. 74.

73 See Martin Jay, *Fin de Siècle Socialism* (London: Routledge, 1988).

74 It is worth pointing out here that this term (i.e. 'differance') is at least as equally disputed between, for example, the likes of Derrida and Lyotard, as it is between (say) Habermas and Lyotard or Habermas and Derrida. It is one of a number of examples in Habermas's critique of the postmoderns where he simplifies the very real differences between those he is lumping together. As my concern is with the character of his critique and not, for the moment, its accuracy, I shall do no more than note this, however.

75 Jay, *Fin de Siècle Socialism*, p. 141.

76 This 'turn' is most obviously manifested, of course, in Adorno and Horkheimer's *Dialektik der Aufklarung* (Frankfurt: Suhrkamp Verlag, 1986 [1947]), trans. John Cumming, *Dialectic of Enlightenment* (London: Verso, 1979). Adorno remained for the rest of his life highly suspicious of the Enlightenment and its legacy and profoundly pessimistic (though certainly not despairing) of the possibility of positive social action. As has been pointed out by a number of writers, Adorno is also close to many of the assumptions of (for example) deconstruction in literary theory (largely due to his relationship to Walter Benjamin), and as such is very ambiguously related to the kind of defence of modernity offered by his pupil and one-time assistant, Habermas. For good general discussions of Adorno, though his thought is hardly susceptible of summary (quite intentionally), see Martin Jay, *Adorno* (Cambridge: Harvard University Press, 1984); Gillian Rose, *The Melancholy Science: An Introduction to the Thought of Theodor W. Adorno* (New York: Basil Blackwell, 1978); and Stephen Eric Bronner, 'Dialectics at a Standstill', in *Of Critical Theory and Its Theorists* (Oxford: Blackwell, 1994). I have explored the intellectual difficulties for critical theory in the differences between Horkheimer, Adorno and Habermas in more detail in a forthcoming paper, 'Critical Theory and Liberal Politics', which also relates their thought to the problems I take to be inherent in critical theory *tout court*.

77 For example, it is the theme of his inaugural lecture at Frankfurt in the mid sixties ('Erkentniss und Interesse'), as well as of his book of the same title published a few years later (English translation, *Knowledge and Human Interests* (Boston: Beacon Press, 1971)); and remains central to the endeavour outlined in *Theorie des Kommunikatives Handelns* (Frankfurt: Suhrkamp Verlag, 1981), 2 vols, trans. Thomas McCarthy, *The Theory of Communicative Action*, 2 vols (Cambridge: Polity Press, 1989).

78  Habermas, in *Habermas and Modernity*, p. 198, quoting Dewey.

79  Ibid., 197.

80  The elaboration of a 'discourse ethics' by Habermas and his Frankfurt colleague Karl-Otto Apel is the latest stage of the development of his reconstructed critical theory, and has strongly influenced a number of his followers, especially in the USA. See, for Habermas's elaboration of a discourse ethics, his *Moral Consciousness and Communicative Action* (Cambridge: MIT Press, 1992), and, especially, *Erlauterungen zur Diskursethik* (Frankfurt: Suhrkamp Verlag, 1992). A good elaboration of Apel's version is Karl-Otto Apel, *Diskurs und Veranwortung* (Frankfurt: Suhrkamp Verlag, 1988). A good discussion with both US and German participants and both for and against the Habermasian position is Seyla Benhabib and Fred Dallmayr (eds), *The Communicative Ethics Controversy* (Cambridge: MIT Press, 1990). For a use of it that shows how some of Habermas's US followers are adapting it see Jean Cohen and Andrew Arato, *Civil Society and Political Theory* (Cambridge: MIT Press, 1992).

81  For good examples of how Habermas thinks this is specifically so, see his very first book, *Strukturwandel der Öffentlichkeit: Untersuchungen zu einer Kategorie der bürgerlichen Gesellschaft* (Darmstadt und NeuWeid: 1971 [1962]). This was only translated into English in 1989 (as *The Structural Transformation of The Public Sphere* (Cambridge: MIT Press, 1989). For its continuing relevance for his theory see his 'Further Reflections on the Public Sphere', in Craig Calhoun (ed.), *Habermas and the Public Sphere* (Cambridge: MIT Press, 1989).

82  Charles Taylor, *Sources of the Self: The Making of the Modern Identity* (Cambridge: Cambridge University Press, 1989).

83  Taylor, *Sources of The Self*, p. xi. I should emphasize that those 'unconditional supporters' from whom modernity needs saving are, effectively, not the likes of Habermas (who is hardly an unconditional supporter anyway), but the positivists and those like them who see themselves as 'children of the enlightenment', but offer no defence and often misunderstand what it is they seek to emulate.

84  Ibid., 498.

85  This conflict is one he develops especially out of the tensions and debates that are associated with the rise of the romantic movement. His readings of this are found chiefly in chs 22 to 24 of *Sources of the Self*.

86  Ibid., 499.

87  Ibid.

88  His chief discussion of this can be found in ch. 21 of *Sources of the Self*.

89  Ibid., 383–4.

90  Ibid., 500.

91  Which he explicitly notes, ibid., 506.

92  Ibid., 509.

93  Though he does not, of course, agree with the manner of Habermas's claims about communicative rationality in detail. His own suggestions as

to how we constitute ourselves through language are chiefly explored in part one of *Sources of The Self.*

94 Ibid., 510.

95 Ibid., 518. It hardly needs emphasizing that on this point, Taylor is at one with moderns like Habermas and critics of modernity as different as Strauss and MacIntyre.

96 Ibid.

97 Ibid., 519.

98 This is quite compatible with some postmoderns (e.g. Lyotard) also believing that the reaction against the Enlightenment would effectively be one of 'returning', as it were, to earlier conceptions; although it would not simply be this, of course.

99 The phrase in quotation marks is from Bennington's essay, 'The Rationality of Postmodern Relativity', in *Legislations.*

100 Richard Bernstein, *The New Constellation: The Ethical-Political Horizons of Modernity/Postmodernity* (Cambridge: Polity Press, 1991), p. 9.

101 As always, the translation of the Greek word *nomos*, depends very much on the context. It can mean, for example, both 'law' and 'convention', though in Aristotle's *Nicomachean Ethics*, for example, 'law' also has a natural side and is therefore not simply 'conventional' (see e.g. the discussion of 'political' and 'absolute' justice in Book V). I shall assume (since he does not specify any particular usage) that Bernstein is using it to imply a range of meanings which can perhaps be summed up in the word 'conventional', or perhaps 'artificial'; thus implying the whole range of human-created resources for communal living.

102 Foucault, quoted in Rabinow (ed.), *The Foucault Reader*, pp. 375, 377.

103 Rorty, *Contingency, Irony and Solidarity*, p. 194.

104 The most honest and among the most interesting versions of the postmodern sceptical attitude to 'ethics' in this sense is, in fact, John D. Caputo's book, actually entitled *Against Ethics* (Bloomington: Indiana University Press, 1994). Caputo's subtitle is also significant ('Contributions to a Poetics of Obligation with Constant Reference to Deconstruction'), showing the influence of Heidegger and Derrida, on both of whom he has been such an acute commentator (see, e.g., *Demythologising Heidegger* (Indiana University Press, 1994)). However, other postmodern writers moving in this general direction (though they might prefer to call it a 'post-Nietzschean', indeed, post-Foucauldian direction, rather than a Heideggerean one) include, I think, Bill Connolly and Rob Walker. See, in addition to *Identity/Difference* and *The Augustinian Imperative* Connolly's recent article 'The Post-Nietzschean Ethics of Michel Foucault', in *Political Theory*, 21, no. 3, 1993; and R. B. J. Walker, *Inside/Outside: International Relations as Political Theory* (Cambridge: Cambridge University Press, 1992).

105 For example, I think this would be the view of Iris Marion Young both in her *Justice and the Politics of Difference* (Princeton: Princeton University Press, 1991) and in her contribution to Squires (ed.), *Principled*

*Positions*: 'Together in Difference: Transforming the Logic of Group Political Conflict'.

106 I am not especially concerned to deny this, though I think that it is certainly a minority view within postmodern reflections on politics. It does not, in any event, vitiate the main point of this argument, as we shall see.

107 Thomas McCarthy, *Ideals and Illusions: On Reconstruction and Deconstruction in Contemporary Critical Theory* (Cambridge: MIT Press, 1993), p. 181.

108 Habermas, *The Philosophical Discourse of Modernity*, p. 364.

109 Ibid., 365.

110 Taylor, *Sources of The Self*, p. 520.

111 Taylor and Amy Guttmann (eds), *Multiculturalism and the Politics of Recognition* (Princeton: Princeton University Press, 1992), p. 41.

112 Ibid., 32.

113 Most recently and interestingly by William Connolly, in ch. 1 of *The Augustinian Imperative*, where he discusses a case unearthed by Foucault from the Parisian archives, the case of Alex/ina.

114 For those who want to follow up the historical account of the Enlightenment given here see N. J. Rengger, *Reason, Scepticism and Politics: Theory and Practice in the Enlightenment's Politics* (Ph.D. thesis, Durham University, 1987).

115 Roy Porter and Miklaus Teich (eds), *The Enlightenment in National Context* (Cambridge: Cambridge University Press, 1981), p. 4.

116 For the two most exhaustive and, to my mind, satisfying overviews of the Enlightenment which take this view, see Ernst Cassirer, *Die Philosophie der Aufklärung* (Tübingen: JCB Mohr, 1932); and Peter Gay, *The Enlightenment: An Interpretation*, 2 vols (New York: Wildwood House, 1970).

117 Gay, *The Enlightenment*, vol. 2, p. 398.

118 Taylor, 'Cross Purposes: The Liberal–Communitarian Debate', in Nancy Rosenblum (ed.), *Liberalism and the Moral Life* (Cambridge: Harvard University Press, 1989).

119 Ibid., 159.

120 Bentham, cited in Rengger, *Reason, Scepticism and Politics*, p. 55.

121 For a fuller discussion of this see Rengger, *Reason, Scepticism and Politics*, ch. 3.

122 I shall return to it in ch. 3, however.

123 It is also worth pointing out that, in general terms, most of the 'advocacy' of moderns and postmoderns alike at the level of actual politics falls quite happily within an 'Enlightenment' frame, if that is interpreted broadly – as I think it should be. Very rarely, you get some writers – such as Nietzsche and Heidegger – who genuinely reject completely the 'Enlightenment' setting both in terms of ontology and advocacy. More frequently you get some 'anti-moderns' (note that I do not say just postmoderns) who reject a lot of the Enlightenment legacy in terms of both ontology and advocacy (for example, MacIntyre and Strauss).

124 The postmoderns I have in mind here are soft-sceptical postmoderns such as Connolly and Honig. It is no accident, I think, that on this point the influence of Hannah Arendt is quite explicit, especially on Honig. I shall return to Arendt on evil in chapter 3. Some moderns are not unaware of the problem I am discussing. It is clearly present in Charles Taylor's work, for example.

125 See Hannah Arendt, *Eichmann in Jerusalem: A Report on the Banality of Evil* (New York: The Viking Press, 1965).

# Part II:
# LIVING WITH/IN MODERNITIES

*Know yourself is a precept for those who, being manifold, have the task of appraising themselves so as to become aware of the number and nature of their constituents, some or all of which they ignore as they ignore their very principle and their manner of being.*

Plotinus, *Ennead* VI, 7, 41

# 3

# AN ETHICO-POLITICAL
# IMPERATIVE?

*On this account each of us must, to the neglect of other studies,
above all see to it that he is a seeker and student of that study by
which he might be able to learn and find out who will give him
the capacity and the knowledge to distinguish the good and the
bad life and so everywhere and always to choose the better from
among those that are possible.*

Plato, *The Republic*, 618c–d

This chapter seeks to argue, contrary to the assumptions of
both moderns and postmoderns as detailed above, that the
question of nature/convention is central to a proper understanding of both modernity and of how significant modernity is for
political theory. I shall try to show that by reconsidering this
question, the other two central aspects of 'the question of
modernity' discussed in chapter 1, i.e. rationality and temporality, attain a rather different and, at least in some respects, an
even more important significance, while at the same time the
three problematic aspects of the 'modernity debate' discussed at
the end of chapter 2 are rendered rather less problematic. Taken
together, these reflections can then, I suggest, help us to return
to the question of 'the tasks of political theory' by giving us a
better framework to support an investigation into the relationship between modernity as mood and modernity as socio-cultural form, a framework that I shall sketch towards the end of
this chapter. The more general implications of all of this for
political theory and, indeed, politics more generally will then
become the subject of chapter 4.

In the course of this argument, it will become apparent that like some others in contemporary political theory, I am suggesting that classical thought offers us a very helpful and potentially fruitful framework for reflecting upon the politics of our own time. It is very important, however, that my adherence to classical thought not be misunderstood, and so before I embark upon the long and rather tortuous journey that this chapter will perforce have to take, I want to make a few remarks about this aspect of it.

I shall argue that classical thought offers us ways of reading our ethico-political circumstances and most especially a framework *for* reading them significantly superior to most modern (or indeed postmodern) ones. However, this view is not meant as an antiquarian one. It does not suppose that we can therefore understand ethics and politics best by concentrating only on the interpretation and elucidation of the great works of classical philosophy and political theory, important though that is, nor does it suggest that we can afford the luxury of simply criticizing or abandoning 'modern' thinkers in favour of their classical forebears.[1] As Stanley Rosen, an author I shall be returning to several times in this chapter, has pointed out in a brilliant essay on Plato and Kant, both Plato and Kant are 'Platonists' and both are 'anti-Platonists', and in seeking to understand either we cannot avoid a real engagement with the text and its arguments.[2] It might be true in important ways (as we shall in fact see later on) that Plato is every bit as 'modern' as Kant or that Kant is as importantly 'ancient' as Plato.

Thus, emphasizing the value of ancient thought does not, for me at least, mean denigrating the value of modern thought, although it is unquestionably true that some aspects of modern thought would need to be revised or abandoned. Then again, I hardly endorse all aspects of ancient thought (Socrates, after all, disagreed with the sophists!). My point here, in short, is to draw a difference between the arguments I intend to make and those of thinkers such as Strauss or MacIntyre who also advocate classical themes. For Strauss and MacIntyre (though as we have seen in different ways) advocating the ancients seems to mean rejecting the moderns. For me, advocating an ancient frame means challenging that very distinction, at least in important ways, and using an unjustly neglected framework to help integrate aspects of modern (as well as ancient) thought.

Having said all this by way of preamble, let me start to consider the question of nature/convention in earnest.

## Nature/Convention

Before I can properly begin this argument, I must clarify the character of the question of 'nature/convention' with a view to pointing up why it might be significant for the overall inquiry. For, to begin with, it is an obvious fact that the question of 'nature' as such has hardly been absent from intellectual discussion in the nineteenth and twentieth centuries. As many have emphasized, one of the defining questions of contemporary intellectual life is the appropriate role of 'naturalistic' (i.e. scientific) explanation in social and political studies. To give just one very obvious example, the 'behavioural' or 'positivistic' turn in political and social science, discussed briefly in the introductory chapter, championed exactly the claim that the study of society should be properly scientific. A 'science of human behaviour' is obviously based on the assumption (however it is manifested) that there is some sort of a 'nature' which this 'science' might appropriately explain.

This is more generally observable in a good deal of contemporary philosophy and social science. It is true, I think, that a good deal of Anglo-American philosophy (especially philosophy of mind and language) as well as contemporary work in the social sciences is 'naturalistic' in this sense.[3] As I shall suggest later on, there is much that is of value in such an approach, and it is far from my intention to suggest otherwise. However, a problem about a good deal of this work is that it barely recognizes that there is a problem with modernity at all, and therein lies much of its danger. Without an awareness of the historical development and evolution of ideas about 'nature' – in all its varied sense – and the ways in which such ideas can be linked to other claims, naturalistic arguments couched in modern terms are easily pulled apart by those (both modern and postmodern) who are aware of this history and of the aporias and discontinuities within it, that contemporary naturalisms have often ignored.

It is, of course, against this model of 'scientific' explanation that many participants on both sides of the modernity debate – Lyotard, for example, and in a very different way, Habermas[4] – have defined themselves,[5] and in this they are following trajectories sketched out by many of their precursors in twentieth-century thought.[6]

In what follows, therefore, and in order to differentiate between those moderns who are concerned about modernity as such and those who are not, I shall designate as 'unreflective' moderns those moderns who do not really discuss modernity, and those who do as 'reflective' moderns. I do not mean to imply anything by this usage other than their decision to reflect upon 'modernity' (as a problem) or not. In respects other than this the unreflective moderns are undoubtedly as 'reflective' as anyone else.

The main point of the foregoing, however, was simply to emphasize that the question of 'nature', in this sense, has clearly not been ignored; indeed, it has been central to an enormous amount of contemporary thought, and especially to its most dominant modes. However, it is precisely the question as to whether we *should* see 'nature' in this sense that is the issue in what I want to look at now.

One way of beginning to look at this is to take the point, familiar enough to students of contemporary social theory (and indeed to students of the modernity debate), that this 'sense of nature' itself has a history, and if we take the trouble to briefly examine that history the assumptions implicit within it become both apparent and, in certain respects, highly questionable.[7] Many writers have, of course, discussed aspects of this history, and as I indicated above, it has been a central theme linking modern and postmodern accounts of the problems of modernity. However, I want to start the argument here by considering the views on this topic of one of the thinkers we have already had occasion to discuss – Leo Strauss.[8]

For Strauss, the general argument about science and its history is, of course, significant chiefly because of the implications it has for *political* science. Strauss draws a direct comparison between the 'new' political science,[9] based upon the conception of science that emerged in the seventeenth century, and the 'old' political science, the paradigm of which was Aristotle's conception of political science. The detailed argument does not concern me at the moment (though I shall return to it again later, especially in chapter 4), but the way in which Strauss structures it depends upon a central distinction which we need to consider. 'For Aristotle,' he points out, 'political science is identical with political philosophy because science is identical with philosophy . . . the distinction *between* philosophy and science . . . was a consequence of the revolution which occurred in the seventeenth century. This revolution was primarily not the victory of science over metaphysics but what one may call the victory of the new philosophy or science over Aristotelean philosophy or science'[10] (emphasis added).

Of course, the claim that 'science' underwent a 'revolution' during the seventeenth century is hardly a new one. In its specific connection with understandings of nature, writers as diverse as R. G. Collingwood and C. S. Lewis have discussed different aspects of the 'pre-modern' view of nature and science and its implications.[11] More directly relevant to my concern here is a central aspect of Stephen Toulmin's analysis of modernity sketched in chapter 1. For Toulmin, too, remember, it is the turn to a 'scientific' phase in the seventeenth century that is the mistake, in that it turned people away from the humanistic, literary concerns of the 'first phase of modernity' in the late Renaissance. It is also Toulmin's argument, however, that a good deal of the most recent scientific theorizing is, in fact, also turning its back on the seventeenth-century model, and coming round to a more humanistic (as he would put it) perspective,[12] a point also emphasized by some postmoderns, perhaps most notably Lyotard.

However, Strauss's point is much deeper than simply a (relatively uncontroversial) recognition of the differences between Greek science and modern science. As we saw earlier, at the root of his concern is a particular understanding of ancient Greek thought and its relation to modern thought. In Strauss's

thought, whatever he was nominally writing about, this relationship was at the centre of his concerns; most especially, it
lay at the heart of the new quarrel between the 'ancients and the
moderns' that was such a distinguishing mark of Strauss's
thought. How we should understand this quarrel is, therefore,
itself one of the most important aspects of Strauss's legacy, both
among his friends, students and disciples and among his
enemies and critics.[13]

As I indicated in chapter 1, in my view Strauss is among the
most interesting analysts and interpreters of modernity precisely
because of the very radicalism of his critique of modernity.
Given that one of the central aspects of this critique is Strauss's
understanding of nature,[14] conceived as the *reason* for the fundamental quarrel between 'ancient' and 'modern' thought, it is
likely that we will find his own interpretation of the question of
nature/convention an illuminating one for us, whether or not
we find that we can ultimately agree with it.

There is, however, another reason for supposing that
Strauss's 'quarrel between the ancients and the moderns' will be
of use to us in our attempt to understand the modernity debate.
This is because as Strauss himself and a number of commentators have made abundantly clear, the status and role of the
Enlightenment is absolutely central to this question. Stanley
Rosen, for example, in one of the most acute essays on Strauss's
*œuvre*, has even remarked that in important ways, Strauss's
'quarrel' underlies 'the Enlightenment'[15] itself. Given the centrality of the Enlightenment in the modernity debate, as we saw
in chapter 2, a consideration of this question will obviously
further our interpretation of modernity.

To set the scene for this discussion, however, I want first to
return to the way I originally raised the question of nature/
convention, for in doing this, we can begin to see the significance of the way in which Strauss answers it.

### Bernstein's argument: Greek thought about nature/convention

The question of nature and convention, it will be recalled, was
introduced through a discussion of Richard Bernstein's argu-

ment that '*nomos*' was the central link between ethics and politics for the ancient Greeks, and (he went on to suggest) the proper foundation for a practical philosophy that unites ethics and politics today. In chapter 2, I suggested that this claim needs to be modified to the extent that it was the *question of* nomos *and/or* physis (rather than the simple fact of *nomos*) that was central for the Greeks, not a specific (and conventional, in the literal sense) answer. To properly follow my meaning here and to provide an introduction to the argument which follows, let me briefly sketch in the background to the question in Greek thought itself.[16]

The question that we refer to as nature/convention had, in many respects, been a concern of Greek thinkers, certainly from the times of Hesiod and Heraclitus (and arguably, indeed, from Homer himself).[17] However, it is with the rise of the *sophistai* in the fifth century BC that the question is put in the form with which Bernstein (and, of course, Strauss) is concerned and on which I shall concentrate.

The fundamental question here arises in the context of ideas that had emerged as central to Greek thought during the sixth century BC and which, in their ethical and political form, might be best put as the question 'what is man?'[18] The answer given by many of the older writers – I shall call them, as they were often called in antiquity, the 'poets'[19] – was that man was a creature of divine justice.[20] This answer had a number of variations, of course. The Homeric and Hesiodic conceptions, for example, stressed DIKE, 'the right way and its divine authority', as Sinclair interprets it.[21] Heraclitus, too, held to a version of this, as is indicated by the well-known fragment which comments that 'all human laws are nourished by one divine law'.[22] Terence Irwin calls these writers 'the naturalists' in his excellent recent survey of classical thought, following Aristotle in this regard, who named them so because they asked questions about 'the nature of things'.[23]

By the fifth century, however, these views were widely challenged. Many of these challenges came from writers who were, in many ways, sympathetic to naturalism, such as Herodotus, Aeschylus, Democritus and Thucydides.[24] Others, however, and most importantly sophists like Protagoras and

Gorgias,[25] challenged naturalism *per se*. Their contention, by contrast, was that the polis determined morality, that it was the source of morality and law.[26]

It is in the context of this debate that the contributions of the three thinkers who were to decisively shape Greek thought (and also, of course, Western thought more generally[27]), Socrates, Plato and Aristotle, should be seen.[28] Of course, one should not assume that their answers (in so far as they provided them) were necessarily the same, and I shall suggest later on the respects in which at least the manner of presentation of the answers of Plato and Aristotle differed.

This point also raises a more general question which I shall address briefly here, before returning to it again later on. The difficulties of interpreting the thought of Ancient writers in general, and Socrates and Plato in particular, are well known. The dominant tradition in Plato interpretation, certainly recently – and in some ways since shortly after his own death – has been 'doctrinal and nondramatic'. As Gerald Press has pointed out, 'On the one hand, we are told about Plato's doctrines (e.g. the doctrine of ideas, of Two realms, of recollection, of Platonic love, the ideal state); and on the other hand, these doctrines are extracted from the dialogues with little or no attention to their literary and dramatic nature.'[29]

This view of how to interpret classical thought is one to which Strauss, for example (together with many of his followers), has been very hostile, a hostility that has been fully reciprocated by the predominant schools of thought in both classical studies and analytic philosophy.[30] Strauss is hardly alone in this, however. As Press also points out, over the last few years a wide range of challenges to this dominant approach have been developed.[31] Press suggests that one can find three broad approaches within them: classical philologists (e.g. Schleiermacher, Shorey, Scharer, Thesleff, Tigerstedt, Arieti);[32] a 'continental' existential–phenomenological (and essentially philosophical) approach (Friedlander and Gadamer – though Press includes both Strauss and Rosen here);[33] and an American pragmatic–naturalistic approach (Woodbridge, Randall, Eckstein, Tejera).[34] I would add at least two more; a 'deconstructionist approach' (Derrida, Irigaray, Kristeva)[35] and the Tübingen school (Gaiser, Kramer and some fellow travellers such as Findlay).[36]

The significance of this will become more apparent a little later on in the argument. However, it is worth bearing in mind that it is a version of Aristotle's answer to this question to which Bernstein is attracted. Significantly, it is also a version of Aristotelean political science which Strauss contrasts with 'the new, modern' political science: the 'ancient' answer to the specifically 'modern' problem that Strauss sketched in 'The Three Waves of Modernity'. I shall therefore have to come back to these different and in important respects contrasting neo-Aristoteleanisms a little later on. In attempting to suggest how we might resolve such interpretive differences my own predilections in the methodological debate just outlined will become apparent. There is no point in doing this, however, until we have finished our discussion of the debates over nature/convention, and so it is to this that I now return.

## Ancients and Moderns: Reinterpreting Nature/Convention

Strauss, as we saw in chapter 1, has a very particular view about the character and development of modernity, different from either moderns or postmoderns as discussed in chapter 2 above, and, indeed, very different from Bernstein. I want now to highlight the main aspects of Strauss's version of the quarrel between the ancients and the moderns as a way of reviewing the modernity debate from a perspective that emphasizes a (very particular) conception of nature. I shall suggest, in fact, that using Strauss's arguments (though without accepting all of them or the conclusions he thinks follows from them) we can rearticulate the question of nature/convention for modernity, and through such a rearticulation we can come to have both a much better understanding *of* modernity and a clearer framework *for* seeing its centrality for contemporary political theory.

Of course, in the space available to me here I cannot do justice to the rich and complex body of thought Strauss has left us. Instead, I want to focus on the claim that the central

aspect of Strauss's thought is his view of the relationship between 'philosophy' (which for Strauss is almost always personi-
fied by Socrates) and the city.[37] Most specifically, it is found
in Strauss's view that this relationship is *always* one of
ineliminable tension and that, as a result, 'philosophy' must
present itself in an accommodated manner.[38] As Strauss writes:

> In what then does philosophical politics consist? In satisfying the
> city that the philosophers are not aetheists, that they do not
> desecrate everything sacred to the city, that they reverence what
> the city reverences, that they are not subversives, in short that
> they are not irresponsible adventurers but good citizens and even
> the best of citizens. This is the defence of philosophy which was
> required always and everywhere, whatever the regime might
> have been . . . This defence of philosophy before the tribunal of
> the city was achieved by Plato with a resounding success
> (Plutarch, *Nicias*, ch. 23).[39]

However, Strauss argued not only that this was the 'natural'
condition of the relationship between philosophy and the city,
but that 'modern' philosophy (from Machiavelli onwards, that
is) had 'forgotten' this and in that act of forgetting lay its
greatest danger. 'Modern' philosophy, philosophy understood
in terms of the 'waves of modernity' thesis in other words,
believes *either* that philosophy and the city can be easily rec-
onciled, in that the one (philosophy) can prescribe to and for the
other (the city) – which is the view of Machiavelli and Hobbes
and, indeed, the mainstream Enlightenment and its legacy – *or*
that such a gambit is impossible and that, therefore 'philosophy'
has come to an end and all we are left with is the struggle for,
and in, the city (Nietzsche).

A second crucial aspect of this difference between 'modern'
and 'classical' philosophy is that, unlike classical philosophy,
modern philosophy, whatever its differences, is united in its
struggle against revealed religion.[40] For Strauss, as Stanley
Rosen has pointed out, the crucial step in the Enlightenment *is*
the struggle against revealed religion, and as a number of his
allies (as well as one or two of his sympathetic critics) have
pointed out, Strauss saw the quarrel between Athens and Jerusalem as at least as deep and profound as that between the
ancients and the moderns.[41] However, because of the necessity
of religion to the city and because of modern philosophy's

refusal to cloak itself in the manner of ancient philosophy, its attack on religion has become coeval with an attack on the city itself. It is this point that leads some, such as Rosen, to agree with Strauss (however much they might also disagree in detail) that this aspect of the 'quarrel' between the ancients and the moderns underlies the Enlightenment itself.

However, there are very considerable problems in properly interpreting Strauss's arguments here. The central problem, which has been well discussed by Rosen, consists in a seeming paradox present in Strauss's writings. On the one hand, he asserts that ancient philosophy masked its true meaning so as to continue to exist in the city, and his critique of modern philosophy clearly implies that he agrees with this claim; yet in the process of publically asserting it Strauss is surely engaging in 'open', exoteric philosophizing. As Rosen puts it, 'by publishing [his] observations, and indeed, by devoting virtually his entire professional career to an exposé of the political rhetoric of philosophers, or the distinction between their esoteric and exoteric teachings, Strauss tacitly but unmistakably identified himself as a modern and hence as a son, or stepson, of the Enlightenment'. Rosen concludes that, as a result, 'Strauss's . . . defence of the classics has to be understood *as a defence of the conservative dimension of the Enlightenment*' (emphasis added).[42]

Rosen goes on to suggest that, in fact, Strauss was practising what he preached; he was writing 'early' esoteric philosophy in the language of the Enlightenment, even perhaps the post-Enlightenment,[43] as the best way of 'adapting himself to his times'.[44] 'Early esotericism' here is taken from Strauss's view that pre-Enlightenment writers accepted 'as natural the distinction between the wise and the vulgar and denied the power of education to efface this distinction, or to overcome the hatred of the majority for philosophy. Accordingly they regarded concealment of genuine philosophical views as necessary "not only for the time being, but for all times".[45] This is in contrast to the Enlightenment writers who began to believe that an appropriate understanding of public education could, at least in principle, prepare all people for enlightenment. Strauss argued that these writers 'concealed their views only far enough to protect themselves as well as possible from persecution; had they been more subtle than that, they would have defeated their purpose, which was to enlighten an ever-increasing number of people who were not potential philosophers'.[46]

Rosen suggests that 'within his powers [Strauss] wished to create a world fit for the habitation of philosophers and non-philosophers alike ... this required an ingenious mixture of frankness as well as of devices to prepare ... a "pleiade" of disciples who would carry out the practical work ... The two questions that have to be raised concerning Leo Strauss's teaching ... are whether his intentions were sound and his rhetoric suitable to the task.'[47] Rosen's view is that, whatever might be said about the intentions, the rhetoric faced a nearly insuperable difficulty in that Strauss could hardly make an impression on twentieth-century intellectuals by speaking in the style of Xenophon or Maimonides; thus he adopted the relatively 'daring' strategy of (for example) publishing his arguments about esotericism.

However, such a strategy, Rosen suggests, also allows the very thoroughly *modern* roots of a good deal of Strauss's thinking to become visible; to 'flash up' (to use a phrase Strauss himself uses in connection with Maimonides) on the surface of his writings. Rosen, indeed, suggests that Strauss's thought has Nietzschean, even Kantian roots,[48] for all of Strauss's well-known identification with the ancients. In this, I agree with Rosen and I would argue further that the way in which the underlying tensions in Strauss's thought can best be seen lies in examining his interpretation of *physis*.

Of course, Strauss formulates this in a number of ways during his career, but I agree with Rosen that, fundamentally, the argument is that there is a 'pre-philosophical' understanding of nature upon which philosophical understanding rests. As Strauss says in *What is Political Philosophy?*, 'Classical philosophy originally acquired the fundamental concepts of political philosophy by starting from political phenomena as they present themselves to "the natural consciousness", which is a pre-philosophic consciousness.'[49] As Rosen points out, effectively this represents two different *senses* of 'nature', a 'philosophical' (hence questioning and necessarily masked) sense and a pre-philosophical (available to all) sense.

In the writings for which he is best known[50] Strauss adopts a political rhetoric dependent upon this distinction, and he is followed in this by many (if not all) of his best-known followers.[51] This rhetoric is what is usually cited to 'prove' that Strauss was a 'conservative'.[52] To all intents and purposes, it consisted in the assertion that an aristocracy of rural gentlemen is the political imitation of the rule of the philosophers, and that as a result some form of 'mixed regime, following Aristotle, is the best regime. Rosen's view with which (again) I agree, is that Strauss adopts this rhetoric at least in part because of the strong Nietzschean elements in his thought. To wit, while he agrees with much of the matter of Nietzsche's 'aristocratic' critique of modernity he does not agree with either the manner of its expression or its effects. Rosen suggests that as a result, 'the solution adopted by Strauss, in the light of the specific circumstances of mid-twentieth-century America was to effect a *rapprochement* with the "conservatives" who would be "habituated" to virtue by a special race of academic administrators, themselves acting under the impression that they are wise men'.[53]

The chief problem with this is that it elides a profound difference of opinion between Nietzsche on the one hand and Plato on the other, which threatens to tear Strauss's carefully balanced structure apart. Rosen puts it like this:

> Nietzsche [believed] that nature understood as the Greek Physis is not accessible to us . . . all theory, including the theory of nature, is a construction, the value or sense of the theoretical entities comes from the will . . . For Plato [however], the distinction between the constructive and preconstructive senses of theory is also the basis for the distinction between nature as the standard of legitimate volition and nature as the product of the will to constructive knowledge . . . In other words, esoteric as well as exoteric Platonism is grounded in the thesis that we have a satisfactory understanding of the natural articulation of life that is not the same as the assumption of the eternal order.[54]

While Strauss broadly agrees with the Platonic distinction, the Nietzschean aspects of his thought, most especially his view

that 'philosophy is an act of the will' (a view which, as Rosen
rightly points out, is in a sense both Nietzschean and Kantian),
pulls him in the opposite direction. His 'conservative' rhetoric
stems from the fear that philosophy (seen in this light) is *always*
dangerous, a realization the ancients possessed, but that the
moderns have forgotten and that, therefore, we need to 'habitu-
ate' people to both political order and to allowing space for
philosophy, which, however, must recover its 'ancient' (i.e.
esoteric, masked) nature.

Yet this view of the 'ancient' conception of philosophy is
itself by no means uncontroversial. If I return to the point I
made earlier about the different ways of interpreting Platonic
texts (for example), then I would argue that Strauss is quite
correct to emphasize the dialogic character of Plato's dialogues
and that his interpretations and theorizings are, therefore, often
an indispensable aid to reflecting on the similarities and differences of classical and modern thought. In this context, the
'dialogic' interpretation of Plato and, indeed, of much other
ancient writing can teach us a great deal. However, saying this
does not commit us to accepting the *particular* way in which
Strauss interprets the dialogic aspects of the dialogues. In my
view, he seriously underplays the significance of the tradition of
the unwritten doctrines[55] and what they might imply for the
interpretation of how Plato conceives philosophy, as well as the
significance of the relation of philosophy and the city.

In terms of my present argument, the point here cannot be
primarily exegetical. It is to say, however, that Strauss's arguments about the character of ancient philosophy should be seen
against a much wider interpretive background than they usually
are in discussions of his political thought. On many aspects of
interpretation he is indeed a far more reliable guide than his
critics are prepared to countenance. However, even recognizing
that the dialogic and dramatic aspects of the Platonic dialogues
are much more important than much traditional scholarship has
allowed does not mean, given the range of interpretive positions, that Strauss's interpretation is necessarily the one we
should follow. Equally, therefore, we should not be led to
assume that his presentation of the 'quarrel between the
ancients and the moderns' and his seeming espousal of 'the
ancient' side in the debate means that we are obliged to accept

the conclusions he derives from his interpretations, or that he is not himself in many ways a 'modern'.[56]

Despite the power and acuity of his readings of classical writers, then, there are many problems with his interpretation of them and to the extent that his case against modern philosophy – and modernity – rests upon that interpretation, there are therefore problems with that as well. Of course, it cannot be denied (and I, for one, would not wish to deny) that Strauss's readings are still enormously suggestive. Many of his critics (as well, or so it seems to me, as some of his pupils and allies) have grossly misunderstood what he was trying to teach, as well as how he was trying to teach it, and in this context it is worth remembering, I think, that Strauss's early training and studies were focused on medieval thought, especially medieval Jewish and Islamic thought. Allan Bloom has pointed out[57] that it was Strauss's immersion in these writers that led to his seeing the problems of classical and modern philosophy in the way that he did, in that it was the practice of medieval Jewish and Islamic esotericism that first alerted him to the question in classical thought. However, the practice in Jewish and Islamic medieval thinking was itself shaped by sets of circumstances that already distanced them from the ancients.[58] The problems that Strauss studied and reflected upon were real enough. His enormous erudition and hermeneutic sensitivity have been unjustly slighted by many of his critics (or misunderstood by some of his friends) who failed to see his true radicalism when they called him (either dismissively or as a term of praise) 'conservative'. However, the fact that esotericism was practiced (by the ancients or by anyone else) does not mean, of itself, either that they were right to do so or that they need always do so.

As Rosen emphasizes, for example, the publication of the Platonic dialogues given the circumstances of the time was 'a revolutionary act of extreme fearlessness . . . this is true *despite* the various accommodations to those circumstances that Strauss pointed out with so much acuity and hermeneutical sensitivity'.[59] In other words, even though the dialogues are, unquestionably, 'esoteric writings' in some form or other, they do not *always* 'mask' philosophy or 'hide' it from the city. Quite the contrary. Yet if this is so, then 'philosophy' might, at least sometimes and paradoxically, become most useful when it is (in

Strauss's terms) most dangerous, that is to say most 'unhidden'. It will surely depend upon the context.

It is here, however, that the question of nature and convention surfaces again. For the point of the Platonic distinction that I cited earlier is to suggest that it is our understanding of the 'two senses of nature' that helps us to understand the significance of any given context. However, it does not do so by enabling us to 'read off', as it were, a right or a wrong set of ideas or actions *from* nature. It is not that any given set of actions, institutions or patterns of behaviour are 'natural' and others 'unnatural'. Rosen rightly points out that in most respects classical (or at least Platonic/Aristotelean) thought did not attempt a theoretical defence of nature as opposed to convention. Rather it was recognized that 'theory' was a construction, but a construction which had to make sense in the light of the two senses of 'nature' just discussed. That is to say, in order to see whether or not a theoretical construction makes sense we need to see whether or not it is 'in harmony with our fundamental intentions or ends, which, of course, have their being in the "life world" or pre-theoretical horizon of constructive activity. But so are rival or contradictory ends. To use Strauss' terminology, baseness is as much in conformity with nature as is nobility.'[60]

This point is quite central to what I shall argue in more detail later in this chapter, and I want, therefore, to dwell on it for a moment. The assumption that Bernstein, and (I suggested in chapter 2) most moderns and postmoderns continue to make in this context is to assume that *nomos* – conventionalism, let us say here – is all that there is. At one level this is so, and born out even by thinkers such as Strauss who on the surface at least would seem to dispute it. However, an attentive reading of the Straussian texts which do dispute it, as well as to the context in which this dispute emerges, reveals a rather more complicated picture. A sense in which, while there is no fixed deployment of 'nature' or the 'natural', there is a recognition that 'conventionalism' takes place against the background of, and in the light of, pre-theoretical settings – let us call them lifeworlds – which, we might say, set the parameters for the possibilities of conventionalism. In terms of the argument I made towards the end of chapter 2: we might say that these 'lifeworlds' provide the *conditions*, within which both ontological theories and particular acts of advocacy can be articulated.

These 'conditions' are 'natural' in the way suggested by the first Platonic sense of nature discussed above. It is not supposed in this context that we can grasp the 'eternal order of things' through *this* understanding of nature – for this, as Plato suggests, 'divine madness' is required[61] – but we might suppose that we can use this understanding as a *base* for both 'theoria' and for 'phronesis', in their Aristotelean sense. As Roger Masters has put it:

> humans have a nature, but it is complex and changing. Societies are responses to the social and physical environment, but they are virtually never in stable equilibrium. Because the contradictory intentions and behaviours in any social group need to be reconciled, politics is natural to an animal using speech and language to supplement the genes as a means of encoding and transmitting information . . . [such an understanding] leads to a philosophical perspective remarkably like that of Aristotle . . . On the one hand, observation and explanation of the different political regimes are possible; on the other, ethical judgement of better and worse can be derived from theoretical reflection on the human condition.[62]

Of course, as Masters himself admits, this requires us to change our sense of what 'nature' means in this context. There is an argument I shall touch on later which suggests that ultimately we do indeed need to embark on some 'divine madness' to properly comprehend both our 'nature' and that of the world around us. What I want to look at now, however, is what the narrower sense of nature might be said to mean, and to imply for our ability to interpret and understand modernity and the debates to which it has given rise.

## Natural Conditions 1: Habits and Political Theory

I want to start here by suggesting that the most obvious initial focus for the sense of the natural discussed above is the notion of 'habit'. This idea has had a rather bad press in many of the human sciences of late,[63] and it is time it was rescued from such relative disuse. Let me begin, then, by offering a definition of what I mean by 'habit' in this context. The concept of habit has recently been defined as denoting 'something semi-permanent that is able to transmit social traits across generations without recourse to heredity or even the mind but through the medium of culture'.[64] In the terms I have been using in this book we might refigure this definition as follows: *habits are that part of the conditions of the lifeworld which shape the parameters of the meeting of ontology and advocacy generated by the specificities of the lifeworld or lifeworlds in question* (I shall come a little later on to how we might define the other parts of these conditions).

In other words, as Stjepan Mestrovic has argued, 'Habits refer to settled dispositions or tendencies to act in certain ways that are partly unconscious or otherwise involuntary ... *habits are second nature, all the things that are done as a matter of course and routinely, stereotypes that are fixed and rooted in one's social and individual character*. To act habitually is to act on the basis of the heart not the mind, to be ruled by the will, not by "rational social action" ... in a word habits are non-modern' (emphasis added).[65]

This last point requires a brief comment. It is worth pointing out that Mestrovic does not say that habits are '*anti*-modern' (either pre- or post-), merely that they are *non*-modern, meaning by this that they do not fit very well into modern thinking, which emphasizes certain (largely instrumental) conceptions of reason, downplays notions of 'nature' and, at least in a good deal of modern thinking, emphasizes known and 'rational' choices. His book can be read, at least in part, as an excellent account of how and why a good deal of twentieth-century social and political theory ignored or marginalized the concept of 'habit'. This is true of both moderns and, in large part, postmoderns, and the reasons are significant.

For the moderns, the central task of social and political theory is often seen as requiring some version of liberation from 'traditional' habits and the cultural and socio-political assumptions that go with them. Even where this is not explicitly the case, it is usually true that the perception is that what has to be explained in human behaviour are the reasons behind choice or reflective action, whether individual or collective. As James Bohman has recently argued, for example, many of the most interesting research programmes in the 'new' social science (he is discussing rational choice, Garfinkel's ethnomethodology and Habermas's theory of communicative action) all seek to 'resolve problems of the social indeterminacy of [social] causes and rules by giving a much fuller, theoretically embedded account of rational and meaningful action'.[66] Note that this is a description of those 'modern' thinkers that are aware of the problems of the 'old' social science (for example, the behaviouralism of the 1960s) and have sought to meet them. The emphasis is on choice and reflection, i.e. on 'rational' behaviour, thus behaviour that is in an important sense unchosen (because simply 'habitual') is unlikely to be taken as seriously as it warrants. Postmodern challenges to these modern understandings have themselves tended to problematize the concentration on reason (as we saw in chapter 2). They too, therefore, have tended to pay little attention to habits as such.

Those thinkers who have done or do, such as *fin-de-siècle* thinkers such as Thorstein Veblen (Mestrovic's book is also in large part an attempt to rescue these thinkers from what he considers undeserved oblivion), have themselves been marginalized from or homogenized within, the dominant forms of social and political theory. (If Veblen has been marginalized then a good example of someone who has been homogenized, for Mestrovic, is Durkheim.)

Habits are, of course, very complicated phenomena to use as a focus. To begin with, they are peculiarly resistant to positivistic forms of explanation. As Mestrovic has pointed out (though he is here drawing on a well-known body of work including, amongst others, Jung,[67] Waller,[68] Camic,[69] Lalande[70]): 'Habits cannot be "observed" by positivistic methods, because the moment that they are made self-conscious . . . they cease to be habits and become rationalisations . . . the actor who is asked to explain his or her habits would react incredulously.'[71]

Equally, however, habits are unlikely to be a part of the postmodern frame. Partly, as noted above, this is because postmoderns tend to problematize modern notions of reason while sharing the modern hostility to what is perceived as habitual or traditional behaviour. At the same time, however, the postmodern emphasis on the fragmented character of modern identities (for example) breaks up, or deconstructs the character of the habits that are in question, and in so doing they therefore often miss the character of the routinized behaviours 'we' (whoever the 'we' are in any given context), have come to accept as normal.[72]

Of course, to suggest that habits, in the manner used here, are a good place to start does not mean that they are all that a political theory of modernity should focus upon. They are the beginning of such enquiries, not a terminus for them. Before I can move on to this wider argument, however, I want to outline in general terms three particularly important implications of this focus on habits.

## Classical retrieval

The first implication, and one to which I have already had occasion to refer a number of times in this book, is that those thinkers who have suggested that classical philosophy offers us a good starting point in attempting to understand modernity are right, though one does not need to agree with any or all of their specific reasons for saying this. The reason is that classical thought in general (and Plato and Aristotle in particular) made habits in the sense discussed above a central plank of their ethico-political theory. One of Socrates' best known criticisms of the sophists, for example, was that they claimed to be able to teach virtue. In the sense in which it was meant, however, virtue could not be 'taught', it is matter of character and character is developed, shaped and tested through habitual action. Habits are acquired; they can therefore be learnt. In a very important sense, however, they cannot be taught.

Of course, this argument should not be taken to imply that reason is inoperative in human affairs. Few thinkers have as much general faith in the power of reason (properly understood) as Plato or Aristotle. Habits are *part* of our understanding in this context, not the whole of it. As was pointed out above, *both* nobility and baseness are located in the lifeworld and *both* will be manifested in habitual action. The point is to understand the character of such habitual action, and in so doing widen the scope of self-reflection, and therefore also of the possibilities of rational (but not just instrumental) choice.

If this is so, however, then the fundamental question becomes: what social and political conditions are most favourable for the development of virtuous habits and the supression of vicious ones? This question, the real question of nature and convention in post-Socratic Greek thought, is where the classical thinkers begin themselves to divide. Plato's treatment of these issues (I do not think he provided answers) in the *Republic* and the *Laws*, for example, are subtly different from Aristotle's more programmatic suggestions in the *Nicomachean Ethics*, the *Eudemian Ethics* and the *Politics*. The centrality of this question, however, is what gives classical thought much of its overall pattern and many of its characteristic themes.

It is here that the significance of the interpretive debates I mentioned earlier becomes most apparent. As is obvious, the extant works we have from Plato and Aristotle differ markedly in temper and tone. We have largely fictional dialogues from Plato and an intriguing mixture of treatises and lecture notes from Aristotle. Perhaps more important still, we have Plato's 'divine madness' (what P. Christopher Smith has called his 'mythical, metaphorical way of putting things'[73]), contrasted with Aristotle's balanced, rational conceptualizations and categorizations. Hans-Georg Gadamer, in an important book,[74] has argued that the key to understanding both thinkers is to look at the general context out of which their thought emerges, and that if this context is taken seriously then the differences between them (he does not suggest that there are none) become far less significant than the areas of agreement.

In particular, Gadamer suggests that Plato's starting point in all of his work is what Plato perceives as a 'near total moral dissolution in his society',[75] represented by the advent of the *sophistai*. Aristotle, by contrast, already enjoys the fruit of Socrates' and Plato's response to the sophists. He inhabits a moral universe where such near total dissolution has been decisively opposed, and his philosophical thinking is prompted by *thaumazein* – wonder – rather than by existential political crisis.

For both Plato and Aristotle, however, the idea of the good is central, and broadly speaking it is much the same. The difference lies in this different orientation. For Gadamer, Aristotle did subject Plato's teachings to radical critique but in the process remained 'Platonic' (and, indeed, Socratic).

> There are basic truths that the Socratic Plato did not lose sight of any more than did the Platonic Aristotle: in human actions the good we project as *hou heneka* (that for the sake of which) is concretised and defined only by our practical reason – in the *euboulia* (well-advisedness) of phronesis. Furthermore, every existent thing is good when it fulfills its telos ... Plato ... anticipated in his number doctrine[76] what the good in such a universal sense actually means. Aristotle found conceptual answers to this question ... the idea of the good ... is formulated only metaphorically in Plato's dialogues ... in Aristotle's thought, what Plato intended is transferred to the cautious and tentative language of philosophical concepts.[77]

The character of the critique, however, given this similarity is also significant. For both Plato and Aristotle, the good must function as both an ontological and a practical concept. The problem, as Aristotle sees it, is that whereas (as the *Phaedo* makes clear) natural processes should be understood as purposive – as tending towards the good, specific examples of goods are inevitably bound up with the conditions of particular human practices. This distinction is not clear in Plato; Gadamer uses a nice example to illustrate his point: 'according to Aristotle, we would have to clearly differentiate between "good snow" in so far as it approaches the ontological good of pure whiteness – perfect snow as snow, as what it means to be snow – and "good" snow in practice, snow that is "good" for skiing, for instance. The ontological sense is wholly irrelevant when there is a question of what ought to be done ... of whether one ought to go skiing given the snow conditions.'[78]

This argument shows both the constancy of the Platonic–Aristotelean tradition as well as instructive differences within this tradition. In a moment I shall want to add a qualification to

Gadamer's argument (though I accept it in broad terms) which will have considerable implications for the conclusion of my argument in chapter 4. However, let me just point out that, in the context of the applicability of this argument to questions about modernity and political theory, the themes of the character of habitual action, the role of rationality in the light of this and the character and significance of regime type (which provides the setting and conditions for habitual action and which needs therefore to be considered in the light of what we think is necessary to promote virtuous habits or discourage or eliminate vicious ones) are once more clearly central. As Aristotle says, at a key point in the *Politics*, 'The Law has no strength to exact obedience other than habit and this does not come into being except through lengthy passage of time.'[79] In my view, this recognition of the applicability of classical thought for discussing central questions of modern political theory of science is among the most obvious lessons of the modernity debate.

## Material conditions

A second implication is that the sense of nature/convention I have been using here has to address material conditions as well as what we might call cultural ones. If we assume that these latter are what we have referred to here as habits, then there remains the former to be dealt with. In this context we can see that modernity as socio-cultural form is itself something of a hybrid notion. As was suggested at the end of chapter 2 and as has been amplified here, the conditional aspect of the understanding of modernity must be part of what comprises the sense of modernity referred to in chapter 1 as modernity as socio-cultural form. Yet this sense consists both of habits and more obviously naturalistic phenomena such as biological and ethnographic aspects of human existence. What is necessary as well, of course, is the material and structural settings of and for those habits and other forms of action and behaviour. These material conditions are also central for a proper understanding of modernity as socio-cultural form, and I shall say something more about them a little later on.

It is clear, however, that through our rearticulated sense of the natural, we can find a bridge for the conceptions of modernity as mood and modernity as socio-cultural form.

## Temporality again: history, memory and practices

A third implication is more problematic. Because habits are things which are, so to speak, culturally generated and sustained in the context of specific forms of socio-economic and historical associations and communities, they of course last across time and span generations. Understanding habits is, therefore, at least minimally an historical task. We understand habits, therefore, not by 'observing behaviour' but by interpreting practices and telling historical (and other) stories. As J. G. A. Pocock has said,

> Societies exist in time and conserve images of themselves as continuously so existing. It follows that the consciousness of time acquired by the individual as a social animal is in large measure consciousness of his society's continuity and of the image of its continuity which that society possesses; and the understanding of time, and of human life as experienced in time, disseminated in a society, is an important part of that society's understanding of itself – of its structure and what legitimates it, of the modes of action which are possible to it and in it.[80]

This aspect of the focus on habits has not, of course, entirely escaped the notice of political and social theorists. Michael Oakeshott, for example, has made such notions (under the guise of terms like 'custom' and the pursuit of intimations) central to his portrayal of politics.[81] Not unrelated themes are found in Gadamer's work, whose hermeneutic sensitivity to the customary and the traditional are well known and well displayed, both in his *magnum opus* and in shorter writings.[82] The same is true of Hannah Arendt, whose concern for memory, especially memory of and about political foundings, is equally well known.[83] More recently, a number of scholars have discussed the importance, indeed the centrality, of memory to politics, or at least to certain forms of politics.[84] Finally, of course, it plays a role, though in a slightly different form, in Alasdair

MacIntyre's preferred solution to the dilemmas of modernity that we discussed in chapter 1.

I said then that we would have to return to his prognosis and this is the moment to do so. For, of course, as Strauss would certainly have warned us, history is the route that modernity has usually taken at the expense of nature. To make my own deployment of the notion of habit and its implications clearer, then; to show how it is centrally related to conceptions of nature that are not historicist and to prepare the ground for the wider sense of the natural I want to discuss in a moment, it is useful to compare it briefly with MacIntyre's discussion of practices.

## Habits or practices?

MacIntyre's whole approach in *After Virtue* is built on a three-tiered argument, amended somewhat in his later work but essentially remaining at the core of his moral philosophy. He outlines it thus:

> The first stage requires a background account of what I shall call a practice, the second of what I have already characterised as the narrative order of a single human life and the third an account . . . of what constitutes a moral tradition. Each later stage presupposes the earlier but not vice versa.[85]

He then goes on to define a practice as 'a coherent and complex form of socially established human activity through which goods internal to the form of activity are realized in the course of trying to achieve those standards of excellence which are appropriate to, and partially definitive of, that form of activity, with the result that human powers to achieve excellence and human conceptions of ends and goods involved are systematically extended'.[86] As Peter McMylor has rightly commented, therefore, 'a practice is above all else, for MacIntyre, the social background within which a coherent practice of the virtues is intelligible'.[87]

This definition itself builds on MacIntyre's conception of a human virtue as 'an acquired human quality the possession and exchange of which tends to enable us to achieve those goods which are internal to practices and the lack of which effectively prevents us from achieving any such goods'.[88] He goes on to argue that this argument further requires a conception of the good life for human beings as such and defines it (somewhat vacuously, it must be admitted) as the search for the good life for human beings as such.[89] He completes this argument by pointing out that, given all of the above, we function within and gain our identity through communities which have histories and develop traditions into which our histories can be fitted (and, indeed, outside which our histories may not make any sense). Of such traditions, vital and alive traditions, MacIntyre says that 'the virtues find their point and purpose not only in sustaining those relationships necessary if the variety of goods internal to practices are to be achieved and not only in sustaining the form of an individual life in which that individual may seek out his or her good as the good of his or her whole life, but also in sustaining those traditions which provide practices and individual lives with their necessary historical context'.[90]

Let me pause now and try to put this conception next to the one I discussed above. To begin with it is clear that there are some similarities. Both MacIntyre and I want to suggest that we are embedded in lifeworlds and that our being in these worlds should be taken much more seriously than both moderns and postmoderns usually do. Equally, we both suggest that alternative ways of viewing politics, ethics and society that take their bearings from classical thought can help to correct this mistake. However, there are also very considerable problems with MacIntyre's arguments.

To begin with there is a serious problem with MacIntyre's notion of a 'tradition'. It seems very unclear how we might actually define a tradition, in MacIntyre's terms. In his Gifford lectures, for example,[91] MacIntyre effectively identifies what he terms 'genealogy' and 'encyclopedism' as two rival world views, 'traditions', counterposed to the 'tradition' of Thomism. Yet within all three of these are surely views which might defensibly self-identify as a tradition themselves. Liberal and Marxist views, for example, would presumably both be part of the 'encyclopedist' position as MacIntyre sketches it, and yet each would in its own right be clearly identifiable as a tradition on MacIntyre's premisses as sketched earlier.[92] What makes the encyclopedist view a 'tradition' that, in some sense, encapsulates the other traditions? What about Western philosophy itself, in which all three rival views of MacIntyre's would fit. Is not this a 'tradition' in his sense?

By attempting to suggest that 'traditions' constitute practices and virtues, therefore, MacIntyre, it seems to me, weakens rather than strengthens his case by making incoherent what it could mean to talk of a 'practice' within a tradition. The understanding of the role of habits that I gave above, however, is not guilty of this. Habits are part of the routinized, unreflective part of individual or communal actions, and as such are not self-consciously part of any 'tradition' in a MacIntyrean sense which, very explicitly, is a self-conscious, and very reflective enterprise. As McMylor says, 'a [MacIntyrean] tradition to be meaningful must involve debate about what constitutes itself as a tradition'.[93] Habitual behaviour is the antithesis of this, and by ignoring it, MacIntyre weakens his case.

Thus, although 'habits' may arise out of 'practices', broadly understood as MacIntyre might, practices of the MacIntyrean sort are too self-conscious to ground 'habits' in the sense that, say, Mestrovic means. The significance of this is simply that whatever appeal MacIntyre's account of practices may have, it can only be a partial one, in that it largely ignores those sorts of actions that are not in a very obvious sense 'reflective', and it fails therefore to ask the very important question 'how can we derive the latter from the former?' In passing I should also remark that while MacIntyre (at least in *After Virtue*) appeals to Aristotelean authority for his account of practices and traditions, it was one of Aristotle's most salient points that virtuous actions stem from a virtuous character which is virtuous because its actions are of a certain type *habitually*, not (or at least not usually) reflectively.[94]

This brings me to another problem with MacIntyre's argument, one which has been well highlighted by Richard Bernstein.[95] Here the argument is that in his attack on the Enlightenment, MacIntyre reveals himself to be a child of the Enlightenment. In particular, Bernstein argues, MacIntyre appropriates, perhaps without fully realizing it, the Kantian principle of 'always acting so as to treat humanity, whether in your own person or that of another, as an end and not as a means'. This principle, says Bernstein, is effectively central to MacIntyre's project in *After Virtue* (though perhaps not as obviously central in later revisions of MacIntyre's thesis), because a good deal of MacIntyre's reconstruction of the Aristotelean virtues consists in rejecting the idea of exclusion, that principle on which, historically the tradition of the virtues had been based. MacIntyre denies this principle, saying in a partial defence of Aristotle's subscription to it, 'this blindness of Aristotle's was not, of course, private to Aristotle; it was part of the general, although not universal, blindness of his culture'.[96] For MacIntyre, any adequate conception of the good life should not exclude in principle any member of the human species, and while MacIntyre might claim to be simply 'strengthening' the tradition of the virtues, it seems unavoidably true that, as Bernstein remarks, he 'universalizes the tradition of the virtues on the basis of principles which were hammered out in the Enlightenment'.[97] After all, Aristotle is only 'blind' by the lights of a culture that has already decided that a principle of exclusion is partly constitutive of moral or conceptual blindness. Largely as a result of shifts brought about in liberal thinking by philosophers of the Enlightenment, our culture has done this (at least in principle), and MacIntyre is a child of that shift, and hence is not rejecting the Enlightenment: rather he is reconfiguring aspects of the Enlightenment project so as to criticize other aspects. Many of his criticisms are, I would argue, well made. In making them, however, he is not rejecting 'the Enlightenment'; he is rebuilding parts of it, with material excavated from the mines of classical antiquity.[98]

This, too, is a point to which I shall have to return in a moment, but, again in contrast to MacIntyre, the argument I have been outlining does not need to assert that certain types of argument are necessarily specific to a particular time, place or intellectual milieu. Rather it accepts that 'baseness' and 'nobility' will be found in all such milieux, and the task of differentiating one from the other will be begun when a grasp of the habits that govern the regimes of those milieux (whether intellectual, political or of any other kind) has been achieved.

## *Habits, desire and human nature: eros and* physis?

To conclude this section of my argument, I want to take up this point in the context of a focus on the relationship between how the understanding of habits contributes to an understanding of the 'natural conditions' of politics. To begin with I want to return to an argument I have already briefly mentioned, that of Stjepan Mestrovic.

Mestrovic's argument is long and complex but at its heart is the contention that the most fashionable social and political theories of our day (effectively what I have called the modern and the postmodern moods) cannot properly understand the character of our lives or our societies because they fail to understand that 'the human animal cannot be tamed by civilisation'. This raises the question of 'how one should teach virtue or achieve the good society . . . From the Final Solution to the Gulag, to Hiroshima to the Gulf War and now the cruel war in former Yugoslavia – how long can social scientists pretend that humanity is becoming less barbaric?'[99] Mestrovic attempts to construct what he calls a 'postmodern critical theory' in order to understand this problem and account for it (he does not suggest that he can answer it). In doing so he draws support from a wide range of thinkers and writers including (most especially) Veblen, Baudrillard, Horkheimer, Sorokin, Durkheim, Simmel and Freud. Lying behind a good deal of this is also a considerable affection for Schopenhauer.

As we have already seen, a major plank of Mestrovic's argument is a focus on cultural habits, derived from Veblen but, as he asserts, possessed of a long history going back to classical thought. The major point of this, for Mestrovic, is that 'for Veblen, as for many of his contemporaries, the drama of social life is to be explained on the basis of the interplay between peaceable versus barbaric cultural habits . . . Veblen believes that Western civilisation is fundamentally peaceable *as well as* barbaric and that this dualism will never be resolved completely' (emphasis in original).[100]

As the argument progresses we come to see how Mestrovic combines philosophical and sociological analysis in an attempt to formulate his account, and we can see the centrality of Schopenhauer for it. Most especially he relies on Schopenhauer's analysis of desire, which he argues deeply influenced both Freud and Durkheim, and was explicitly picked up by thinkers like Simmel.[101] 'Schopenhauer opens the possibility that humans can be bound to each other on the basis of desire, including compassion, sympathy, and various derivatives of love . . . [however] the imperious will is Janus-faced; evil and benign, destructive and constructive.'[102]

In many ways, Mestrovic's argument here is certainly a powerful one and it is not necessary to agree with everything he says, nor (necessarily) share his enthusiasm for Freud and Durkheim to accept this. As he rightly points out, I think, the sense that human beings are what Durkheim called *homo duplex*, both individuals *and* creations of that 'everything in us that expresses something other than ourselves',[103] is something that modern social and political theory has had tremendous difficulty dealing with. Both moderns and postmoderns have been especially suspicious of dualisms, at least those that might be suspected of metaphysical tendencies. The accompanying sense that human societies are, at least in a certain sense, always to be seen as riven by competing drives and characters is equally problematic in that it is often mistaken for the belief (assumed to be the view of the dreaded 'conservatives' and, often, indeed, shared by them) that human society cannot, therefore, get any better or improve in anything other than the most superficial ways.

Some of the time, Mestrovic's arguments lend some support to this view, though I think it is far from his intention and I do not think that it at all follows from his argument as such. That he can be read in this way, however, is partly due to his hostility to our old friend, the 'Enlightenment'. For Mestrovic, the key aspect of the Enlightenment (as we saw for many moderns and postmoderns in chapter 2) is its emphasis on reason. Throughout his argument, the Enlightenment's tendency to rely on reason and its denigration of passion (usually referred to as desire, eros, etc.) is a common theme, and one which Mestrovic criticizes bitterly. Yet, as we saw in the case of MacIntyre, this is a gross caricature of the Enlightenment. Is it really plausible to suggest that Hume (for example) or Rousseau 'denigrated passion'? Again, in an attempt to produce a unified 'Enlightenment' suitable for attack, an author has mistaken *aspects of* the Enlightenment for the whole of it. Mestrovic's argument is left seeming to be a 'conservative' attack on the 'Enlightenment' disguised, perhaps even from Mestrovic, by the language of sociology and the frame of reference involved. In trying to create a 'postmodern critical theory' Mestrovic runs the risk, or so it seems to me, of making the errors of each and having the focus of neither.

The best example of the problems this leads Mestrovic into is observable in his concluding section. Here, Mestrovic argues that the central insight to be gained from a study of the *fin-de-siècle* thinkers on whom he chiefly relies is

> the horrifying idea that enlightenment cannot contain the forces of barbarism – that the will is stronger than rationality. If that is true then all utopian schemes and efforts at social engineering are suspect. Modernity cannot tame nature once and for all. Rather, human societies and culture are a part of nature. If anything like a cosmopolitan humanity is to emerge, one that is mindful of the planet and of the human rights of all its citizens, it must learn to balance its barbaric tendencies with peaceable habits that have been ignored for too long. Veblen and his colleagues offered no blueprint for this balancing act, no utopian promises, and neither do we.[104]

The problem with this is that its arguments run in a bewildering variety of directions. On the one hand we are told that all utopian schemes are suspect, on the other it is implied that we should try and encourage the emergence of 'a cosmopolitan humanity mindful of the planet and of the rights of all its citizens', which sounds about as utopian as it is possible to get. At the same time we are told that modernity – by which it is clear Mestrovic means the 'Enlightenment' and its legacy – cannot 'tame' nature once and for all *and* that human beings and their societies are part of nature, as though these two statements were somehow contradictory, which, as far as I can see, they are not. Very few Enlightenment thinkers would ever have suggested that we could 'tame nature once and for all'. The whole cast of mind of the mainstream Enlightenment was alien to such an ambition.[105] In part, this error is caused by an overestimation of the views of the mainstream Enlightenment on reason.

As we have seen in Part I, the Enlightenment's views on reason are castigated at every turn. But beyond the obvious fact that there were a number of different conceptions of reason operative in the Enlightenment (think of Rousseau again and contrast him with Hume or Kant), it is also true, I think, that the mainstream Enlightenment's conception of reason actually represented a humbler conception of reason than did the great metaphysical systems of (say) the seventeenth century. As Ernst Cassirer has said, 'What reason is and what it can do [for the Enlightenment] can never be known by its results but only by and through its function.'[106] It is this conception of reason that is the hallmark of most of the mainstream Enlightenment and which has led some scholars of the Enlightenment to use terms startlingly reminiscent of Bennington's phrase that I cited in chapter 2: the Enlightenment is a revolt against rationalism, though not against rationality. The effects of this view, however, imply that the claim that the Enlightenment believed that humankind would 'tame nature once and for all' is a gross exaggeration. Hume, as so often, spoke in the authentic accents of the mainstream Enlightenment when he has his character Palamedes remark, in *A Dialogue*, 'what rule shall we establish for the many different, very contrary sentiments of mankind?'[107] and when as related by Adam Smith, Hume acknowledged the hardiness of the very things he himself was most critical of, in the wry excuse he imagined himself giving to Charon to avoid passage to the underworld: 'I have been endeavouring to open the eyes of the public,' Hume imagines himself saying, 'If I live a few years longer, I may have the satisfaction of seeing the downfall of some of the prevailing systems of superstition'. Charon, however, would have none of this. 'You loitering rogue,' he replies, 'Do you fancy I will give you lease for so long a term?'[108] Hume was well aware that nature, like superstition, was unlikely ever to be 'tamed, once and for all'.

Perhaps the most problematic aspect of all, however, is that Mestrovic seems unable or unwilling to discuss just how we might integrate his insights (it is only fair to say, I think, that his book contains many) into an understanding of politics that is both 'natural' – in the sense in which we have been using the term here – *and* can help us evaluate regimes, characters and actions. In certain respects, the problems with Mestrovic's arguments are almost the mirror image of those we saw when discussing MacIntyre. If MacIntyre presents us with an understanding of 'practices' that is unconvincing because too intellectualized and 'reflective', Mestrovic gives us a view of habits which is not reflective enough, hence unable to yield any discussion of how we might live as *homo duplex*, how we might evaluate and judge and thus act, politically and ethically.

While I agree with part of Mestrovic's case, therefore, I most certainly do not accept all of it. I agree that habits should be central to our understanding of politics, and for very similar reasons to Mestrovic, but in saying this one is not abandoning 'the Enlightenment' (for there would have been many a philosophe or *Aufklärer* who would have agreed with that proposition) nor is one abandoning 'reason' in emphasizing desire or eros (can anyone imagine Plato suggesting that we abandon reason?). The error here seems to be that, in addition to caricaturing the Enlightenment, Mestrovic does not pay close enough attention to the classical roots of the arguments he is citing. Strange as it seems, however, I think that in one respect at least the same is true of MacIntyre and even of Strauss, whose reliance on classical models is so intense and clear that it has not sometimes been examined with the care it deserves. As Rosen has put it, though in a rather different context, 'what we need to learn from the ancients is not prudence or the superiority of temperance to courage [or, he might have added, the role and significance of esoteric writing, important though that might be in other contexts] but the *intimate connection between reason and the good*'[109] (emphasis added).

The most important question, then, lies in how we can combine reason *and* desire, nature *and* convention, and in doing so provide a framework for understanding and evaluating the complex matrix that we can call modernity, thence properly performing the tasks of political theory. To develop this argument, however, requires that I must now turn briefly to the second understanding of nature I mentioned above and relate it to the first.

## Natural Conditions 2: 'Divine Madness' and Political Theory

The first sense of nature derived from the Platonic distinction I gave above was, you will recall, that we can have 'a satisfactory understanding of the natural articulation of life that is not the same as the assumption of the eternal order'.[110] In the argument I made above, I emphasized both the obviously natural elements of human individual and social life (biological and ethnographic, for example, which the more conventional 'naturalistic' explanations in the social sciences would also emphasize) and the complex cultural matrix which unreflective modern, self-consciously modern and postmodern thinking often ignores or marginalizes.

For Plato, however, the assumption is clearly present – though the manner of its presence and indeed its content is justly a matter of heated debate – that there is also an 'assumption of the eternal order' which we can achieve and which is also central to our overall understanding of ourselves and our societies. I want to dwell, for a moment, on how we might understand this and what its implications would be for my overall project.

The first point that needs to be made in this context is that a full exploration of this issue would take (at least) a book in itself. However it is interpreted, it implies that a proper understanding of society and self requires relating political philosophy and ethics to the philosophy of mind and metaphysics at the very least, and quite possibly to theology as well. I do not pretend that I am going to attempt that task here, it will have to await another occasion. However, it is worth pointing out that such a task can be conceived of in very different ways. The Aristotelean injunction that the student of politics must study the soul[111] is one, for example, that guides Susan Hurley's massive and impressive *Natural Reasons*,[112] whose opening sentence states that it 'is about the rationality of the decisions and actions of persons and illustrates the continuity of philosophy of mind, on the one hand, and ethics and jurisprudence on the other'.[113] Her approach largely draws on the philosophies of Wittgenstein and Davidson, which would not be my choice, but it is unquestionably true that the agenda she lays out in the book is both interesting and fruitful in terms of the sort of naturalism I was outlining above – especially the first aspect of it – though it is concerned with a rather different set of problems which fit quite obviously into the 'Anglo-American' political theory that I discussed briefly in the introductory chapter.

In exploring my own agenda here, however, I want to focus on a rather different way of drawing on the classical – that is to say Platonic–Aristotlean – tradition, to discuss the interdependence of these themes: to wit, Stephen R. L. Clark's three-volume study *Limits and Renewals*.[114] I choose Clark partly because I strongly agree with some (though certainly not all) aspects of his argument but also because he provides me with the best way I can think of to bring out the significance for political theory and modernity of that wider sense of 'nature' that I suggested above would be necessary.

Clark's trilogy of books is an attempt, to use his own words, 'to restate theocentric traditionalism as the one true rival of "modernist error".' However, he significantly adds, 'that although I often use the terms "liberal" and "modernist" pejoratively, it should not be assumed that I therefore disapprove of all "liberal" actions. On the contrary, my complaint is often that fashionably *liberal theories are inadequate to defend really liberal institutions and policies*'[115] (emphasis added).

In order to begin this task, however, Clark seeks to illuminate certain assumptions which, he suggests, are now so deeply embedded in Western culture that 'we hardly notice them'; they are in other words – though Clark does not use the phrase – almost 'habitual', at least among certain groups within Western societies. These assumptions give rise to nine doctrines or dogmas that Clark thinks are definitive of 'liberal modernism'. In shortened form they are as follows:

1 No-one ought to believe . . . anything more than she can her-self demonstrate on the basis of her own personal knowledge.
2 No-one ought to believe . . . anything that will be believed to be incompatible with 'modern knowledge' or fashionable opinion.
3 No-one ought to believe any positive doctrine that cannot be verified by the 'scientific method', though it is obligatory to believe all opposing negative doctrines.
4 Long-established beliefs and practices have no greater claim on our practical and theoretical allegiance than newly minted ones and may be properly dismissed as obsolete.
5 No-one can be obliged to do or to believe anything that she herself can at the moment see no reason to do or to believe.
6 No-one should believe that there are any obligations 'laid down from above', except perhaps an obligation to be 'sin-cere', and no-one ought ever to advance her own moral opin-ions to another.
7 All modern persons must acknowledge that the body of genu-inely true propositions is entirely value free . . .
8 No modern person should think anything more important than 'personal relationships'.
9 No modern person should think anything more important than 'this-worldly' ties or give credence to 'dualistic' or 'other-worldly' philosophies.[116]

Of course, Clark does not suggest that all of these beliefs are held all at once by the 'liberal moderns' he is criticizing (he refers to them at one point as the 'pontificating classes') but in some form or another he thinks that versions of them go to-gether to form what we might call a 'nested set' of beliefs constitutive of 'liberal modernism'. It is worth adding, I think, that it looks suspiciously likely that lurking in the background of these ideas and, indeed, in the very notion of 'liberal modern-ism', is that caricature of the Enlightenment that we have be-come so familar with by now. However, Clark does not make the error some others do and suppose that there is some essen-tial category called 'the Enlightenment' which believes these things. Many Enlightenment thinkers, as he well knows, would not believe them, or would do so only in a partial or attenuated way. In this respect his argument is less vulnerable than some of the others we have seen.

It is worth adding also, however, that Clark's nine dogmas do seem to be constitutive of at least aspects of 'the modern' position as I outlined it in the first section, though they are rather less applicable to the postmodern one. However, postmodern thinking fares little better in Clark's schema and he does, in any case, still think that the two are inextricably yoked together in ways which parallel my point in chapter 2 about their shared hostility to 'nature'.

> Some moderns, or 'postmodernists' who have acknowledged the social context of rational inquiry have gone to the other, irrationalist, extreme. In place of the impossible demand that we should prove our beliefs to be logically indisputable, they have set up the claim that all relevant criticism of a thought world must be internal, that either there is no reality outside consensus reality or at the least we can have no access to it as a criterion against which to measure received opinion . . . I share Duerr's opinion that too many of those who have criticised modernist dogma have done so by adopting a limply contrived relativism . . . forgetting that they thereby make it impossible to criticise the very modernist doctrines they disdain.[117]

This characterization of the postmodern mood is undoubtedly rather crude, as we can see from chapter 2, none the less it retains a certain bite, certainly for the hard sceptics and, more interestingly, for the Epicureans. As I shall suggest a little later on, however, I think at least some soft sceptics are rather less vulnerable. As far as the nine dogmas of 'liberal modernism' are concerned, however, they certainly do represent, or so it seems to me, a good many of the assumptions that are made by (how shall we put it?) 'unreflective' moderns, positivists and empiricists, liberals and others. As far as the reflective moderns (such as Habermas and Taylor) are concerned, it seems rather less fair (especially dogmas 2, 3, 6 and 7), though certainly still relevant. For my purposes here, in any case, I want to concentrate on dogmas 1, 4, 6 and 7 – with a small excursus on dogma 9! The reason is relatively simple. These dogmas contain within them those aspects of the modernity debate which I picked out in chapters 1 and 2 as especially problematic: to wit, rationality, temporality and – of course – nature/convention. In discussing Clark's treatment of these dogmas we will be able to see more clearly, or at least so I hope, the relevance of the 'second sense of nature' for the modernity debate and how we can relate it to the first.

Clark begins his account by disagreeing sharply with the first of his dogmas, that we must only believe what we can prove to ourselves to be true: 'We live within a sea of testimony: everything that we normally count upon has been handed down to us; the very possibility of demonstrating anything itself rests upon our having been initiated into the techniques and the presuppositions of the testifying community ... the onus of proof ... must in most cases be on those who wish to subvert received wisdom, the testimony of the ages ... [though this] in no way implies that such disputation is impossible or irrational.'[118]

On this point it seems to me that Clark is absolutely right. We do indeed rely, every day, on an enormous matrix of assumptions for which we have very little assurance. Postmoderns, of course, have also sometimes made this point, but their reaction to it varies. Hard sceptics, like Baudrillard, for example, seem to use it simply as one more piece of evidence for the emergence of 'hyperreality' where truth and falsehood, knowledge and opinion all merge and become indistinguishable. Postmodern Epicureans such as Rorty claim that they are not worried by it and simply say that we just have to learn to get used to living with such epistemological uncertainty. Some soft sceptics again, however, are rather more sensitive to this issue, and I shall take up their response a little later on.

The biggest question here, however, and it is one put by moderns to postmoderns in the modernity debate very frequently and in a variety of ways, is how, if this is true, you can decide between one claim and another. In other words, the argument runs, surely this claim leads to a sapping and ultimately sterile relativism.

For some postmoderns, I think it often does. However, as I suggested earlier, I do not think this is unique to postmoderns (many moderns can be relativists); and in any case, the framework that Clark adopts allows him an option that is not thought to be open to either moderns or postmoderns (at least by themselves). What follows for Clark is that, contrary to the fourth dogma, long-standing beliefs and practices have a status that should not be lightly or easily set aside. 'Old doctines are not true merely because they are old, any more than new ones are true because they are new; but it is not absurd to suggest that the old ones have our prior allegiance, that they do not need to establish themselves on just the same terms as new theories, that they have, as it were, the benefit of the doubt.'[119]

It is important to see, I think, that Clark is here not necessarily endorsing political conservatism in the sense I briefly explored earlier, for all that he cites well-known political conservatives such as Burke and Gadamer in making his point. His point is rather that it is surely enormously arrogant to suppose that 'we' liberal moderns have suddenly thought of something unforeseen or unknown to our ancestors in anything other than the most obviously technical sense. 'Can there really be many serious and important truths about life, the universe and everything,' he remarks (with I assume conscious irony), 'that have been noticed literally for the first time in the last hundred years of a thousand million years of growth and evolution?'[120]

These arguments then give rise to Clark's reason for rejecting dogmas 6 and 7. As he says, a common response to his views would undoubtedly be to say that, whatever might be the case in 'factual' areas (electrical engineering, medicine, etc.), there can be no such expertise in matters moral or political and no higher understanding than the preferences of those compelled to decide what to do, and these decisions must be transparent in a way that epistemological decisions (about what to believe or take on trust) need not be. Although Clark does not discuss it, such responses are very familiar in political theory, as those that would be made by a wide range of political scientists influenced by economic models of reasoning such as rational choice. However, it would also be a response that would be made by some postmoderns.

It is very important, of course, to stress that the unreflective modern responses and the postmodern responses would be very different in terms of content, though formally – and this is the point – very similar. For example, rational-choice theorists would unquestionably emphasize the facts that most people most of the time seem to work according to certain sets of preferences and that many of the problems of politics emerge from the difficulties of collective action, i.e. decisions about (1) whose preferences to satisfy or (2) how to aggregate such preferences. In terms of the analysis of contemporary advanced industrial states, for example, this may well be true (indeed, I think it is true), but it is, in any case, largely irrelevant to the point being made since it has nothing to say to the claim (which I shall examine in a moment) that such behaviour, in so far as it is simply appetitive, is problematic simply as a result of that fact.

This would leave such theories with two choices. Either they could refuse to engage with discussions as to whether such preferences were right or wrong (for a variety of reasons) or they could claim that such preferences were indeed appropriate (or inappropriate) and give reasons for this judgement. However, once this kind of argument is embarked upon then the question becomes one of ethics in the sense implied by Clark (and that I shall discuss in a moment) and not one that can simply be settled by an appeal to the alleged 'facts' that people have certain preferences or manifest certain sorts of behaviour.[121]

The postmodern response (an example would be that of Chantal Mouffe[122]) would be put very differently, of course. Here the argument is predicated upon the assumption that people have conflicting 'preferences' which manifest themselves in the diversity of ways of life and ethical assumptions; this diversity (though the word used would probably be 'difference') is not resolvable in terms of one way of life, set of wants, or assumptions becoming shared by all others; and the consequence is that a radical and plural democracy is the only way in which such 'irresolvable' differences can be contained and managed. For all the differences in terminology and assumptions, the link between these two views is the assumption that there are only competing 'conventions', i.e. what people actually want (in terms of preferences) or how they actually live (in terms of difference) – and that these conventions are what structure and orient our politics. There is nothing, in other words, which needs to be acknowledged and accommodated, to the effect that there is something that people *should* want, or do, or be.

Clark's response is to point out that 'Ancient philosophers would have replied that our decision to act or to pursue a certain goal, is only a truly moral or human decision if we prefer the action as being *right*, the goal as being *good*. If our preference is merely appetitive, it does not differ in kind from animal or infantile or slavish behaviour.'[123] This view has the corollary, Clark thinks, that the way we seek to understand is itself deeply value laden, and hence the modern assumption that science (and indeed that social science) is 'value free' is not only mistaken but a perversion of the fact that 'the truth is made known to those who approach the world with a kind of love, love purged of concupiscence, and who are moved to admire the real form of things, a form certainly obscured by our particular prejudice and perhaps by real failures to live up to the norm'.[124]

Of course, many writers of all persuasions would accept that the social sciences – and even perhaps science as such – cannot in any meaningful sense be 'value free'. However, this recognition needs to be carefully hedged about with qualifications if it is not to collapse into, on the one hand, a kind of inchoate relativism, on the other, a kind of unacknowledged ideological warfare; or possibly even both. To return to one of our earlier themes, Strauss's famous critique of modern social, specifically political, science, ends up by accusing it of both. In certain respects it mirrors the argument I just gave above. 'The new political science leaves the justification of values or of preferences . . . to ideology on the ground that any justification of preferences would have to derive values from facts and such derivation is not legitimately possible. Preferences are not, strictly speaking, opinions, and hence cannot be true or false.'[125] In this respect, I think that Strauss is correct. However, as my earlier argument suggested, Strauss himself was guilty of at least the latter activity. He does not give us *arguments* to display the nobility or correctness of the ancients, what he gives us is a carefully designed and (in my view at least) enormously interesting body of political rhetoric that *shows* us – if we have eyes to see – their nobility. However much we might agree that Strauss's readings of ancient authors are powerful and suggestive (and I would), we have also seen that even those ancient authors most attracted to the 'truth that loves to hide' (as Heraclitus put it) did make arguments and did not suppose that these arguments could not be evaluated.

Of course, for Clark, all of the above points are part of an argument designed to challenge the ninth and last dogma. As Clark says from the outset, his aim is to restate traditional theism in its relation to Society, Soul and the Universe. Such an undertaking seems to me at least as serious an activity at outlining modern or postmodern ontology, and every bit as relevant.[126] However, in so far as the political philosophy he outlines in *Civil Peace and Sacred Order* is concerned, it is important to note that it is not *dependent* on any particular theistic system, as Clark himself emphasizes. In his concluding chapter he provides a convenient summary of his overall argument which is worth quoting at length, as I shall be returning to it in chapter 4.

> I have been . . . pointing out that we all live within networks of familial and friendly relationships, that states gain such authority as they have only by embodying moral and sacred values that transcend the merely economic and contractual, that business, sects and nations all have a part to play in a civilised world order whose lineaments are visible in times of war as well as in times of peace. I have also insisted that we human beings live within and upon a world whose ecosystemic health is essential to any purposes we might have for the future, that the beauty of the whole earth is a sacred value, something that any world order must recognise and serve if it is to deserve our loyalty . . . the world of our human experience . . . is still structured by familial affection, sexual desire and trade, by the demands of hospitality and word once given, by the spirits of our different nations, by war and innocence and the world's beauty.[127]

As he points out, in outlining this argument he has written as an educated philosophical pagan.[128] He believes that this is a preliminary to writing as a convinced Christian,[129] but he also implies that the general arguments he has outlined here stand independently of this. Philosophical paganism, as Clark understands it, 'is the celebration of the human world within which we grow to virtue . . . we find ourselves within a life world that already contains the natural universe'.[130]

This view, I submit, has a good deal to offer us in terms of a way of linking the two senses of nature I discussed above, and thereby both looking at the question of nature/convention and at reconceiving the modernity debate. It also suggests some interesting arguments to which I want to return in chapter 4. Of course, as I suggested earlier, there are also points where I would disagree with Clark. He is unfairly general in his treatment of the postmoderns, his critique of 'liberal modernism' is rather too sweeping for my taste as well as too entwined with questionable readings of some aspects of the Enlightenment and its legacy, and the most noticeable absence from his argument is any real consideration of modernity as socio-cultural form.

I shall seek to remedy these latter defects in my final chapter; for now let me close this section by suggesting how it might link to the earlier discussion of nature/convention which hinged on the notion of habit as a central feature of social existence, a notion that had been ignored by a good deal of modern social theory. I pointed out here that classical thought, on the other hand, did pay attention to questions of 'habit'. We can now supplement this claim by pointing up one of the aspects that Clark rightly stresses, to wit, the extent to which classical thought emphasized that habitual behaviour was not *of itself* good. It required a *setting* which allowed virtue to develop; and this, of necessity, carried with it certain assumptions about the character of the setting and, indeed, of virtuous action within it. Our 'natures' in this sense must be held to include the 'conventions' we generate to ensure such settings are in place or, if they are not, the ways in which we go about attempting to create them. These conventions must in the first instance be reflective ones, however much they might also then become 'traditional' – habitual – ones over time.

A second assumption that flows from this, one which I shall take up in much more detail in the next chapter, is that many of the distinctions drawn up in, and by, contemporary thought hinder, rather than help, the performance of this task, and must therefore be eradicated and overcome, if the task is to be properly performed at all, both theoretically or philosophically and practically, as we shall see.

Putting the two senses of 'nature' together also acknowledges that philosophical 'divine madness' may be necessary to attempt to understand at least some aspects of this (greatly expanded) arena of ethical and political theory on at least some occasions. As I suggested in my discussion of Gadamer's argument about the idea of the good in Platonic–Aristotelean philosophy, and as can also be inferred from my discussion of Strauss and Rosen earlier, there would be settings, contexts or conditions, wherein philosophical rhetoric would need to take the shape of (for example) the Platonic dialogues or even (to give a different example) the novels of Dostoevsky. However, these settings or conditions will not occur in the same way. It is thus a central part of the practice of political philosophy that we come to see how to judge the conditions or settings,[131] and therefore shape our philosophical rhetoric accordingly.

This is a fact which (some) postmoderns seem to have understood rather better than many moderns.[132] However, it means neither that there is only one path to proper knowledge of the political and ethical phenomena with which we must inevitably be concerned, nor that any path will do. To use the language that Clark uses, the ancients taught that all the wise were friends and the wise, in this tradition, 'are identified by their devotion to the laws of God and nature and by their recognition of wisdom wherever it may be found, in whatever race, or creed or country'.[133] Or, one might add, in whatever methodological stance or epistemological frame. Of course, it takes a considerable feat of the imagination to see the modern academy as, in any respect, even a pale imitation of the city of the wise; yet if it is not, what (noble) purpose can it possibly serve?

Thirdly, the argument implies that 'nature' – understood as we have described it here – that is to say as a 'philosophical pagan' would understand it – is at least as important as 'convention', in that without seeing 'nature' in this way we will be unable to make much sense of the conventions that are, unquestionably, the most important aspect of politics as such. As such the argument agrees with Bernstein (and many others) that political theory really must include ethics, for if we seek to separate the two neither can be properly understood; but it agrees in ways that can incorporate aspects of our situation and character that a purely 'conventional' (or narrowly naturalistic) understanding would fail to properly discuss or possibly even see.

Thus, our rearticulation of the question of nature/convention comes down to a reaffirmation of what ancient thought felt was central to the task of understanding as such. It is unquestionably true that this is much wider than a good deal of contemporary political theory, methodologically far less tightly focused than many would like, and potentially very damaging for the assumption that the modern academy can be usefully split up into different disciplines with their own methods and clearly demarcated subject matters. It is also true, or so it seems to me, that it is only if we make these assumptions – or something very like them – that we can make real sense out of our political and ethical situations at all.

## Reconceiving the Modernity Debate

There remains, then, the task of relating all of this to the modernity debate itself. It is only once we have done this that we can then go on and take another look at the tasks of political theory in the light of the discussion as a whole. I shall follow a three-stage strategy here. To begin with I want to recall the analysis of the modernity debate offered in Part I and relate it to the arguments I have just outlined, in the process making good on my earlier comment that reconceiving the question of nature/convention could help us to move beyond 'enlightenment and critique' and thus beyond the modernity debate in its present form. This will result in seeing aspects of both modern and postmodern positions in a new, and I hope fruitful, way. It will also give rise, however, to a question about the character of the 'ethics' that we seek to relate to political theory and so, secondly, I shall address some arguments in postmodern ethics, especially those of Zygmunt Bauman and William Connolly. I shall then be able to conclude by outlining the sense of the ethico-political imperative that I take my argument in this chapter to sustain. This in turn will provide the framework for the reconsideration of the tasks of political theory that I shall offer in my final chapter.

## Beyond the modernity debate

At the end of chapter 2, it will be recalled, I outlined three problems internal, as it were, to the structure of the modernity debate. The first of these was the question of the Enlightenment as such, subdivided into two questions: the problem of defining the Enlightenment in the way that seemed to be required by both moderns and postmoderns and, secondly, the question which we have seen dogging the modernity debate in all its various permuations, the question I referred to in chapter 1 as 'temporality'. The sense, in other words, that there is in some way a 'break', a 'discontinuity' in history associated with modernity.

Following the argument of the last two chapters, however, it is possible to suggest a way round both these problems. Firstly, it is both impossible and unhelpful to see the Enlightenment as the sort of 'unity' that one can be 'for' or 'against'. Enlightenment thinkers such as Kant are too complex for such stereotyping. In so far as Enlightenment thinkers advocate or can be plausibly presented as advocating arguments that have given rise to an unreflective acceptance of modernity (for example) then they can certainly be criticized for that, as many moderns and postmoderns have done and as I would do, following the argument of this chapter. However, this is largely incidental to their being Enlightenment thinkers. There are thinkers from the ancient world (or the Renaissance or, indeed, any other given historical period) who would be equally vulnerable to similar sorts of objections or criticisms.

This also leads to a rather different way of seeing the question of temporality. 'Modernity as mood', in the sense implied here, has more to do with the growing dominance of certain ways of thinking and certain sets of assumptions than it does with discrete historical periods which are themselves usually only obvious (if at all) after the event. These assumptions are not necessarily, therefore, rooted in the 'Enlightenment' (or indeed, 'the Renaissance'), though they may certainly be given particularly important or significant formulations during particular periods. In this sense we can agree with scholars as different as Blumenberg, Connolly and perhaps even with Strauss, that 'modernity *as mood*' is a mood that we can see in many different historical periods, though unquestionably it has been given a particularly influential elaboration over the last couple of hundred years.

This observation, however, brings us to the second problem we identified at the end of chapter 2 which had to do with the way in which modernity as mood and modernity as socio-cultural form were related by the most prominent authors within the modernity debate. Specifically, I suggested that there was a sense in which we needed a third element as a bridge between modernity as mood and modernity as socio-cultural form, which I called the 'conditions' of modernity.

Modernity as socio-cultural form must be seen as a complex matrix of forces (cultural ones such as habits, and biological or ethnographic ones as well as material ones such as economic and social structures). There is no sense in which we can necessarily say one of these is causally prior to the others. Understanding modernity as socio-cultural form means understanding this matrix *and its contextuality*. Sometimes material forces will be more powerful than cultural factors; at other times not. However, in the current context of the relationship between modernity as mood and modernity as socio-cultural form, it seems fair to assume that the conditions of the last two hundred years (in terms of the economic and social structures that we usually identify as distinctively modern) have been both encouraged by and supportive of those elements of modernity as mood that have been most obviously criticized by the postmoderns and by the more reflective moderns in the modernity debate. These elements include instrumental rationality (of which more in a moment) and, indeed, the whole set of dogmas of 'liberal modernism' outlined by Clark.

Thus, when modernity as socio-cultural form is seen as (for

example) equivalent to a capitalist world economy, this expresses, I submit, a truth, though a very partial one. In so far as contemporary world politics is shaped in large part by the workings of a capitalist, global economy, the assumptions that most happily sit with it – assumptions that have perhaps by now become 'habits', and often, therefore, are not examined or even recognized as choices that might be changed – are among the most important parameters of political action and understanding. Certainly this is what 'modernity' is, at least in part. However, we need also to bear in mind that both the structures and the assumptions are increasingly fragmented and that this fragmentation – most obviously picked up and elaborated by postmoderns – equally expresses a (partial) truth about contemporary politics. I shall take up the implications of this more thoroughly in the next chapter.

However, it brings me to the third problem I mentioned at the end of chapter 2. This was that which, drawing on Connolly and Blumenberg, I called the problem of the two senses of evil (i.e. 'evil' meaning willed human action and its consequences, and 'Evil' meaning the problem of evil as such). Connolly's argument, with which I agreed without (at that stage) giving any reasons, was that the first sense of evil moved 'silently' within the latter. I now want to suggest why this might be so and look briefly at its implications. Let us use, for a moment, terms less loaded than the notion of 'evil'. Earlier in this chapter I pointed out that focusing on 'habits' did not mean we avoided the task of trying to choose what was good and what was not. Moreover, I argued that the classical (largely Platonic/Aristotelean) framework I was adopting *required* us to make that choice as the hallmark of truly human, truly ethical action.

However, as has also been indicated, such a possibility assumes that the context exists in which such choices are possible and make sense. If our social conditions are such that our habits have become, so to speak, impregnated with forms of action that we might in other contexts wish to term 'evil', then our actions will be, so to speak, routinely 'evil' inside a setting in which no real answer to the question of 'Evil' is possible. Only if we have the possibility of answering the question of 'Evil' by confronting it and holding out the possibility that 'Evil' can be denied (perhaps 'negated' would be better) can 'evil' also be properly understood and come to terms with.

So far this has all been rather unhelpfully abstract. To explain what I mean here, therefore, I want to dwell on a concrete example. I take this from Hannah Arendt's magnificent *Eichmann in Jerusalem*.[134] As is well known, this book continued Arendt's searching examination of the experience of totalitarian politics in the twentieth century.[135] Of the many aspects of this that Arendt touches on in the course of the book I want to focus on one, the reason for the book's famous subtitle, *A Report on the Banality of Evil*. As a number of writers have made clear, I think,[136] Arendt was astonished during Eichmann's trial by that part of his defence that relied upon an explicit reference to Kantian philosophy and by no means an inaccurate one. 'I meant by my remark,' he stated on being questioned, 'that the principle of my will must always be such that it can become the principle of general laws.'[137]

Of course, Arendt scorned the notion that Eichmann was in any way a Kantian, and provided a coruscating critique of his use of Kantian terminology. However, as Philip Hansen suggests, 'to hear the precepts of a giant of German humanist philosophy quoted with considerable accuracy and with no hint of hypocrisy [by a leading Nazi] left an impression on her that profoundly affected her'.[138]

Her explanation of this claim is that Eichmann, and by implication many millions of others in Nazi Germany, fastened on to one aspect of Kantian thinking – that is, the commitment to enforce the law universally – and came to assume that doing this – often against one's inclinations, whether these were base or noble – was *in itself* moral action. Thus, for Arendt, Eichmann was neither stupid nor conventionally 'immoral', but literally 'thoughtless' in that he did not 'think' about the laws he was 'morally' enforcing. Thus his evil actions were in that sense 'banal'. A good deal of Arendt's subsequent work went in to attempting to explain how this could come about and, most especially, how we might prevent it, through developing an account of 'judging'.[139]

Let me now look at this example from the perspective I have been developing here. One way of reading Arendt's analysis is to suggest that what she was tracing in the behaviour Eichmann was the lineaments of a cultural matrix that generated certain 'habits' that had become 'routinized' – and hence unquestioned – in such a way that the wider ethico-political framework (the web on which we are all nodes, according to Clark) has become effectively meaningless in this context. Of course, in order to fully understand this cultural matrix we must abstract from the particular manifestations of any given individual (Eichmann, for example) and look at the origin of how this matrix came about, ask what sustained it, how it evolved and what material conditions encouraged it to flourish.[140] In doing this we are asking questions about (and at least implying answers to) 'evil' *and also* – or so I want to suggest – providing a way of dealing with the question of 'Evil' that accepts Blumenberg's portrayal of it as a central question of modernity, without supposing that it is likely to be 'overcome' or permanently resolved. In this process we would have to provide an understanding of modernity as mood and an understanding of modernity as socio-cultural form, and would relate them together in a way that accepted that neither could be privileged over the other if we hoped to have the fullest possible understanding of the phenomena that we are seeking to understand and, as a corollary, evaluate.

Both moderns and postmoderns, of course, have sought to provide understandings of such phenomena and have often been extremely insightful about them. I do not want to suggest that we either can or should attempt to comprehend modernity without, say, Adorno and Horkheimer's elucidation of the 'dark side' of the Enlightenment, Habermas's superb evocation of the rise and decline of the public sphere, Lyotard's dissection of the postmodern condition or Foucault's many-sided analysis of power in all its forms. My point is that in an important sense understanding modernity means understanding all of these, for in some form all of them are part of that complex matrix (mood *and* socio-cultural form) that shapes and constrains modernity. Of course, one might take issue with any or all of the ways in which they make their case, but in taking the stance they have on the question of nature/convention they have failed to see one of the ways in which their multifarious insights might indeed be put together in such a way as to provide ways of understanding modernity that neither could achieve alone. Moving beyond

'Enlightenment and critique' is not just a rather flaccid attempt to put epistemological, ontological and practical political questions on hold and adopt the maxim that 'every dog should have its day'; it is to say, firstly that we *have* to move beyond them, for the good historical reasons already identified; but that, secondly, if we fail to move beyond the rather sterile oppositional readings of modernity then we are unlikely to come to a rich enough or full enough understanding of that phenomenon to enable us to properly come to terms with it. It is, therefore, both an ethical and a political imperative of the first order.

### Postmodern ethics and evaluation: a short excursus on Connolly and Bauman

A moment ago, I pointed out that the analysis of modernity must of necessity involve evaluation as well as understanding. On the basis of the arguments I have put forward in this book, it is a requirement of ethico-political theory as such that it ask whether certain actions or communities or practices are right or good. Many moderns (non-relativist ones at least) would have little problem with that as an aim, even if they probably would be very hostile to my chosen method of approaching it.

With the postmoderns, however, this could not be – if I am forgiven the word – true. From across the wide range of postmodern thinking as discussed in chapter 2, one of the most insistent messages is that no such evaluations could be made. However, at this point the postmoderns themselves divide. The fact that evaluations of this sort cannot be made does not mean that evaluations as such are impossible. Most postmoderns are at pains to argue that they do not suggest that no evaluation is possible, only that it cannot take certain forms. This is so across the spectrum of postmodern thinking as I have already shown, from Baudrillard to Rorty to Connolly.

However, I have several times in this chapter suggested that the 'soft-sceptical' postmoderns are particularly interesting in this regard, and so in order to address this issue of evaluation and assess its implications, I want to turn briefly to two authors whom I would include under that rubric, William Connolly and Zygmunt Bauman.[141]

Let me look at Bauman first. Already known as one of the most interesting and widely cited analysts of modernity in his previous work,[142] in his recent book *Postmodern Ethics* Bauman engages in a wide-ranging and challenging attempt to refute the claim that 'postmodern ethics' is a contradiction in terms. Indeed, for Bauman a proper understanding of the postmodern represents the beginning and not the end for a truly human ethics. He is sharply critical of those 'hard-sceptical' postmoderns – he singles out Gilles Lipovetsky[143] – who seem to be arguing for a kind of 'anything goes' philosophy. Lipovetsky, writes Bauman, 'suggests we have finally entered the epoch of *l'après-devoir*, a post-deontic epoch, where our conduct has been freed from the last vestiges of oppressive "infinite duties", "commandments" and "absolute obligations" . . . the "after-duty" era can admit of only a most vestigial, minimalistic morality: a totally new situation, according to Lipovetsky – and he counsels us to applaud its advent and rejoice in the freedom it has brought in its wake'.[144]

For Bauman, Lipovetsky commits 'the twin errors of representing the topic of investigation as an investigative resource, that which should be explained as that which explains. To describe prevalent behaviour does not mean making a moral statement: the two procedures are as different in postmodern times as they used to be in pre-postmodern.'[145] Bauman then goes on to articulate what he thinks the postmodern perspective on ethics is:

> The postmodern perspective to which this study refers means above all the tearing off of the mask of illusions: the recognition of certain pretences as false and certain objectives as neither attainable nor, for that matter desirable . . . I suggest that the novelty of the postmodern approach to ethics consists first and foremost not in the abandoning of characteristically modern moral concerns, but in the rejection of the typically modern ways of going about its moral problems (that is, responding to moral challenges with coercive normative regulation in political practice) and the philosophical search for absolutes, universals and foundations in theory.[146]

Bauman then looks at what the implications of this perspective are. He locates them in the claim that modernity has consistently refused to admit that it exists in an aporetic situation, i.e. in a situation of irresolvable conflict or contradiction. Modernity was about conflict *resolution* and could not accept the thought that such resolutions could never come:

> Modern ethical thought in co-operation with modern legislative practice fought its way through to [this] 'solution' under the twin banners of universality and foundation . . . The right design and final argument can be, must be and will be found . . . any allegedly 'foolproof' recipe could be proved wrong, disavowed and rejected but not the very search for a truly foolproof recipe . . . the moral thought of and practice of modernity was animated by the belief in the possibility of a non-ambivalent, non-aporetic ethical code. . . . It is the disbelief in such a possibility that is postmodern – post not in the chronological sense . . . but in the sense of implying . . . that the long and earnest efforts of modernity have been misguided, undertaken under false pretences and bound to – sooner or later – run their course.[147]

This basic assumption about what the postmodern perspective yields for ethics is, interestingly, one that Bauman shares with William Connolly.[148] In his *Identity/Difference*, Connolly suggests that 'engaging the paradox of ethicality by cultivating the experience of contingency does not entail the celebration of any and every identity. It does not open itself to a politics of racism or genocide, for instance. For identities that must define what deviates from them as intrinsically evil (or one of its modern surrogates) in order to establish their own self-certainty are defined as paradigm instances to counter and contest. They stifle cultivation of care for the ambiguous relations of identity/difference through the way they constitute good and evil.'[149]

Of course, by drawing attention to the fact that they share a view of the perspective I do not mean to suggest that they do not differ on where the perspective takes them, though there are several points of contact here too. Bauman suggests seven broad marks of the 'moral condition' as seen from a postmodern perspective:

1 Humans are morally ambivalent: both good and bad and therefore moral conduct cannot be guaranteed, we need to learn to live without such guarantees.

2 Moral phenomena are inherently non-rational (by which he means instrumental, means-end rationality).
3 Morality is incurably aporetic.
4 Morality is non-universalizable, taken not as endorsing moral relativism but as opposing moral imperialism.
5 For the purpose of the 'rational order', morality is and is bound to remain irrational.
6 Given the ambiguous impact of the societal efforts at ethical legislation, one must assume that moral responsibility – being *for* the Other before one can be *with* the Other – is the first reality of the self, a starting point rather than a product of society.
7 The claim (again) that the postmodern perspective does not reveal the relativism of morality. On the contrary it is ethical codes which are plagued with relativism, that plague being but a reflection or a sediment of tribal parochialism of institutional powers that usurp ethical authority. This kind of understanding, Bauman concludes, is unlikely to make moral life easier, but might make it a bit more moral.[150]

Connolly's vision is rather less programmatically formulated. For him, his perspective yields 'an ethical sensibility, anchored in an ontological problematic, rendered through genealogies of the possible, cultivated through tactics applied by the self to itself, embodied as care for an enlarged diversity of life in which plural communities co-exist in more creative ways than those simply sustained by a communitarian idea of harmony or a liberal idea of tolerance, politicised through a series of critical engagements with established dualities of good/evil, normal/abnormal, guilt/innocence, rationality/irrationality, autonomy/dependence, security/insecurity.'[151] Such a view requires, he thinks a genealogical method combined with what, in *Identity/Difference*, he called agonistic democracy.[152]

Of course, there is much that is similar here, as well as a good deal that is not. I shall not follow either author deeper into their arguments, for my own purpose is not to assess those arguments as such,[153] but rather to look at how the framework compares with my own and what its implications are for the modernity debate more generally.

The first point to note is the similarity between this soft-sceptical postmodern ethical sensibility and the one I have outlined in this chapter. Like me, both Bauman and Connolly question many of the assumptions of 'liberal modernism' (particularly its assumptions about rationality); like me, Bauman (in particular) suggests that human beings are 'ambivalent' (*homo duplex*), and Connolly suggests that engagement with politics necessarily involves constant engagement with ethics. Like them, I suggest that diversity is a good and we should recognize it as one, though not all diversity and not all the time. Finally, like them, I do not suggest that postmoderns cannot have a real concern for (and contribution to make to) ethics and, as we shall see in the next and final chapter, their political ethics is important as well.

However, *unlike* them I do not suppose that any of this implies that all good actions *always* include elements of bad actions with them, nor do I suppose that the recognition of this fragmentary, often (at least) aporetic character of human ethical choices and the lack of universal purchase of instrumental rationality means that we cannot make judgements about the right and the good. We can and we must. Of course, such judgements are never final. Given this, of course, we have to have political arrangements for acknowledging and dealing with errors and mistakes. It was Hannah Arendt who insisted on the political importance of forgiveness for the good city, but the point is implicit in a good deal of classical thought of the Platonic–Aristotelean type. This aspect of the Platonic–Aristotelean tradition was most fully developed, I think, in the Neo-Platonic school most strongly developed by Plotinus and which exerted so powerful an influence on early Christianity.[154] Ultimately the differences between my arguments and those of soft-sceptical postmoderns like Bauman and Connolly rest not in the details of ethics but in the framework into which such judgements can be best put. The postmodern frame, as I see it, is too narrow a frame to bear the ethical weight that postmoderns like Connolly and Bauman want to put on it. However, it is far preferable to either the arid rationalizations of many unreflective moderns or the triumphalist and (Bauman is quite right) false 'relativism' of some (perhaps equally unreflective) postmoderns.

## Towards a political imperative?

I have reached the end of this long and rather tortuous journey. I have outlined what I hope is a relatively clear framework into which we can put much of the modernity debate, retaining much of its vitality and insights but losing those aspects of it that are becoming increasingly sterile and pointless, a seemingly endless parade of criticisms and counter-criticisms. The ethico-political nexus which has been rearticulated in the process has been shown to have points of contact with both modern and postmodern agendas, and I have suggested that as a result the debates that will undoubtedly follow are likely to be far more beneficial than before. However, the proof of the pudding is in the eating. It is time to return to the task that I set myself at the outset and consider the implications of all of this for the tasks of political theory as such.

### Notes

1 This charge, often laid at the door of Leo Strauss and his friends and followers, cannot I think be sustained in this instance. One need only think of the work of Strauss himself on Hobbes and Spinoza, Allan Bloom on Rousseau, Thomas Pangle on Montesquieu, Locke and the Founding Fathers or Harvey Mansfield, Jun. on Machiavelli (as well as a host of others) to see that an assertion of the priority of ancient virtue does not mean a denigration of modern thought. As will be seen later, I am critical of Strauss and his allies on a number of points, but not on this one. See e.g. Leo Strauss, *Die Religionskritik Spinozas als Grundlage seiner Bibelwissenschaft: Unteruschungen zu Spinozas Theologisch-politischen Traktat* (Berlin: Akademie-Verlag, 1930); and *The Political Philosophy of Hobbes: Its Basis and Genesis* (Oxford: The Clarendon Press, 1936). Allan Bloom, trans. and introd. to Jean Jacques Rousseau, *Emile* (Harmondsworth: Penguin, 1979); Thomas Pangle, *Montesquieu's Philosophy of Liberalism: A Commentary on the Spirit of the Laws* (Chicago: University of Chicago Press, 1973), and *The Spirit of Modern Republicanism: The Moral Vision of the American Founders and the Philosophy of Locke* (Chicago: University of Chicago Press, 1988); and Harvey Mansfield Jun., *Machiavelli's New Modes and Orders: A Study of the Discourses on Livy* (Ithaca, NY: Cornell University Press, 1979).
2 Stanley Rosen, *The Ancients and the Moderns: Rethinking Modernity* (New Haven: Yale University Press, 1989), ch. 3, 'Anti-Platonism; A Case Study'.

3  This is true of, e.g., the work of philosophers such as Daniel Dennett in the philosophy of mind (see his *Brainstorms* (Brighton: Harvester, 1981)), as well as a good deal of general work in the social sciences, such as that of Jon Elster and Clifford Geertz.

4  *La Condition postmoderne*, after all, is subtitled 'a report on knowledge', and is often concerned with questions of scientific, naturalistic explanation. Habermas's critique of instrumental rationality in *Erkenntnis und Interesse* and *Theorie des Kommunikativen Handelns* are both intimately bound up with a critique of a good deal of contemporary models of the social and natural sciences.

5  Of course, it is also worth pointing out here both that there are many different types of 'science' that might serve as a model and that 'science' itself hardly stands still. The implication is clear. The notion popular in the 1950s and 1960s among self-conscious 'behaviouralists', that all one needed to do was to apply 'scientific' method to social phenomena in order to acquire cumulative knowledge of said phenomena, will simply not stand up to much scrutiny any more. To their credit, most 'Social Scientists' (and I capitalize them deliberately) would no longer argue this. Whether what they have substituted for this assumption is any better is a different matter. As I indicated in chapter 1 and as I shall take up again in chapter 4, my general answer to that question would be in the negative.

6  It is, for example, a commonplace now that, for all their differences, Heidegger and Adorno were each highly critical of the character of twentieth-century science. See e.g. Theodor Adorno, *Zur Metakritik der Erkenntnistheorie* (Frankfurt: Suhrkamp, 1971); Martin Heidegger, *Vortrage und Aufsätze* (Pfullingen: Neske, 1967). The best general treatment of the commonalities between Heidegger and Adorno, beneath the very real and deeply felt differences, as it were, is Hermann Morchen, *Adorno und Heidegger: Untersuchung einer philosophischen Kommunikationsverweigerung* (Stuttgart: Klett-Cotta, 1981).

7  It is related to e.g. the old question of the 'scientific' status of the social sciences, around which there has been an avalanche of comment over the last thirty or so years. For a general discussion of the competing claims of the 'old' and 'new' philosophies of social science, see especially James Bohman, *The New Philosophy of Social Science* (Cambridge: Polity, 1991).

8  See e.g. 'An Epilogue', included in *Liberalism, Ancient and Modern* (Cornell University Press, 1989 [1968]); 'Social Science and Humanism', in Thomas Pangle (ed.), *The Rebirth of Classical Political Rationalism* (Chicago: University of Chicago Press, 1989); and ch. 2 ('Natural Right and the Distinction between Facts and Values') of *Natural Right and History* (Chicago: University of Chicago Press, 1950). The question is also touched on frequently in Strauss's voluminous correspondence with, e.g., Alexander Kojève and Eric Voeglin. See Leo Strauss, *On Tyranny; Including the Strauss–Kojève Correspondence*, eds

Victor Gourevitch and Michael S. Roth (New York: The Free Press, 1991), and Peter Emberly and Barry Cooper (eds), *Faith and Political Philosophy: The Correspondence between Leo Strauss and Eric Voeglin 1934–64* (Pennsylvania: Pennsylvania State University Press, 1993).

9　By which he means 'behaviouralism', 'positivism', etc. It should be remembered that the book was originally published in 1968.

10　Strauss, 'An Epilogue', p. 205.

11　See e.g. R. G. Collingwood, *The Idea of Nature* (New York: Oxford University Press, 1960 [1945]); and C. S. Lewis, *The Discarded Image* (Cambridge: Cambridge University Press, 1964).

12　See Stephen Toulmin, *Cosmopolis: The Hidden Agenda of Modernity* (Chicago: University of Chicago Press, 1990), p. 84.

13　See e.g. the discussion in Luc Ferry, *Philosophie politique 1. Le Droit: la nouvelle querelle des Anciens et des Modernes* (Paris: Presses Universitaires de France, 1984); Robert B. Pippen, 'The Modern World of Leo Strauss', in *Political Theory*, 20, no. 3, Aug. 1992, 448–72; M. F. Burnyeat, 'Sphinx Without A Secret', *New York Review of Books*, 32 (30 May 1985), 30–6; Richard Kennington, 'Strauss' Natural Right and History', in *The Review of Metaphysics*, 25 (1974).

14　A focus that can have a wide variety of offshoots even among Strauss's self-confessed pupils or followers. While many of the best known of these (such as Bloom or Pangle) speak of nature after the manner of Strauss, some other former pupils of his have taken a 'naturalistic' approach to politics in a very different direction. Perhaps most interesting among these is Roger Masters, known as a very considerable Rousseau scholar, who, in *The Nature of Politics* (New Haven: Yale University Press, 1989), offers an interpretation of politics derived from a thorough knowledge of modern work in biology and related life sciences. Masters' book is dedicated to Strauss, and in the preface he emphasizes the centrality for Strauss of the question of the relation between the study of human politics and the natural sciences (properly understood, of course) and the importance for him (Masters) of the question to which he was introduced by Strauss. I shall return to Masters' argument a little later on. The best general treatment of Strauss's views on the question of nature rather more narrowly conceived than my conception here is Kennington, 'Strauss' Natural Right and History'.

15　This point is made by Stanley Rosen in *Hermeneutics as Politics* (Oxford: Oxford University Press, 1987), to which I shall return later.

16　The argument of the following few paragraphs is drawn from more detailed considerations in two unpublished papers of mine; 'Rhetoric and Philosophy: Gorgias and Socrates on Ethics and Politics' and 'Plato's Metaphysical Politics: The Tübingen School and the Interpretation of Political Thought'.

17　Among excellent general discussions of this topic are F. Heinemann, *Nomos and Physis* (Basel, 1945), and T. A. Sinclair, *A History of Greek Political Thought* (London: Routledge and Kegan Paul, 1951). Hesiod's

*Works and Days* and *Theogony* are easily available in a Penguin translation. Heraclitus's writings are available, of course, only in fragments.
The standard collection is H. Diels, *Die Fragmente der Vorsokratiker*,
6th edn, revised by W. Kranz (Berlin: Wiedmann, 1952). A modern
reading of the fragments is brilliantly offered in Charles Kahn, *The Art
and Thought of Heraclitus* (Princeton: Princeton University Press, 1983).

18  Meaning, of course, 'what is humanity?' though it is also unquestionably
the case that most Greek thinkers were really concerned with man in a
less general sense (i.e. with males).

19  They include some, for example Herodotus, who is clearly not a 'poet' in
the modern sense. However, I shall follow Plato, who saw a link between
the poets of Greek tradition and the *sophistai*, a link he draws attention
to in the *Protagoras*, where Protagoras is proud to call himself 'a teacher
of mankind, a Sophist, like the Poets of old' (see *Protagoras*, 316 D-317
C).

20  Of course, it is important to bear in mind that the link just mentioned
was the claim to be a teacher of mankind, not the argument about divine
justice, about which the Sophists were extremely sceptical.

21  See Sinclair, *A History of Greek Political Thought*, p. 48.

22  See Kirk and Raven, *The Pre-Socratic Philosophers*, pp. 202 and 205.

23  See Irwin, *Classical Thought*, p. 20. For Aristotle's accounts of the
history of Philosophy see the *Metaphysics*, 1000a9–20, and 983b20–1.
The accounts of naturalism by Aristotle's pupil Theophrastus are also
central.

24  These writers were all critical of naturalism in different ways and supportive of it in different ways. Irwin calls them, collectively, 'critical
naturalists'. For Herodotus, see *The Histories* (an easily available translation is Aubrey de Selincourt's for Penguin. Harmondsworth: Penguin,
1954). For Aeschylus, see *The Oresteia* trilogy of plays (well translated
by David Grene for the University of Chicago Press). Discussions of and
quotations from Democritus can be found in Sextus Empiricus, *Outlines
of Pyrrhonism* (trans. R. G. Bury, London: Loeb, 1933–49, 4 vols), and
he is well discussed in C. Bailey's *The Greek Atomists and Epicurus*
(Oxford: Oxford University Press, 1928) and Edward Hussey, *The Pre-
Socratics* (London: Duckworth, 1972). For Thucydides, see, of course,
the *History of the Peloponnesian War*. There are many available translations of this; in my own view the best is still that of Hobbes. A good
recent edition, with an excellent introduction by David Grene, was
published by the University of Chicago Press in 1989.

25  For Protagoras (of Abdera), it is perhaps unfortunate that our best source
is also his most profound critic, i.e. Plato. See the *Protagoras* and the
*Theaetetus*, for Plato's presentation of Protagoras. Fragments of
Protagoras's work are preserved, however, and can be found in Diels and
Kranz, *Fragmente der Vorsokratiker*. Much the same is true of Gorgias
(of Leontini), whose fleeting appearance in the Platonic dialogue named
after him (the *Gorgias*) sets the scene for the political ideas of Callicles,

widely supposed to have been a pupil of Gorgias but about whom virtually nothing else is known. Fragments of Gorgias's most famous treatises, such as the *Treatise on Not Being* and the *Encomium on Helen*, are included in Diels and Kranz.

26 It is important in this context to bear in mind, of course, that sophists like Protagoras and Gorgias were by no means carbon copies of one another. The extant works of Gorgias we have, for example, show that he differed considerably from Protagoras on many points, especially on epistemological issues and also on the question of whether virtue could be taught, a characteristic sophistic claim that Gorgias, apparently alone among the major sophists, refused to endorse. It is also significant that in his major dialogues dealing with these two sophists (*Protagoras*, *Theaetetus* and *Gorgias*) Plato presents a by no means unflattering portrait of them that does not disguise their differences but equally does not suggest that they were in themselves men of no moral fibre. In the *Gorgias*, it is Callicles who presents doctrines designed to be shocking, not Gorgias himself, and we are left to infer that Callicles is indeed the logical extension of Gorgias's own philosophy, but nowhere does Plato suggest that Gorgias himself would endorse Callicles' ideas.

27 Not just 'Western' thought either, of course. Jewish and Islamic thought was at least as powerfully affected by Platonic and Aristotelean thought. For discussions see Ralph Lerner and Muslim Mahdi (eds), *Medieval Political Thought: A Sourcebook* (Ithaca: Cornell University Press, 1966).

28 Note that I say 'thinkers' here not writers. Socrates, of course, did not write anything. None the less he was hugely influential.

29 Gerald A. Press (ed.), *Plato's Dialogues: New Studies and Interpretations* (Maryland: Rowen and Littlefield, 1993), p. vii.

30 For a particularly good account of the hostility as it applies to Strauss's own writings on classical thought, see Miles F. Burnyeat, 'Sphinx Without A Secret', in *The New York Review of Books*, 32 (30 May 1985), and the exchange in vol. 32 (10 Oct. 1985) of the same publication, 'The Studies of Leo Strauss: An Exchange'.

31 Along with Press, a good collection that highlights some of them is Charles Griswold (ed.), *Platonic Writings, Platonic Readings* (London: Routledge, 1988).

32 See, for good examples, Holger Thesleff, 'Studies in the Styles of Plato', *Acta Philosophica Fennica* 20 (Helsinki, 1967); J. A. Arieti, 'A Dramatic Interpretation of Plato's Phaedo', *Illinois Classical Studies* 2 (1986), 129–42; E. N. Tigerstadt, *The Decline and Fall of the Neo-Platonic Interpretation of Plato* (Helsinki: Soc. Scientarum Fennica, 1974).

33 See Paul Friedlander, *Platon* (Berlin: De Gruyter, 1954); Hans-Georg Gadamer, *Dialogue and Dialectic* (New Haven: Yale University Press, 1982), *The Idea of the Good in Platonic-Aristotelean Philosophy* and *Plato's Dialectical Ethics* (New Haven: Yale University Press, 1989); Leo Strauss, *The City and Man* (Chicago: University of Chicago Press, 1963),

and *Studies in Platonic Political Philosophy* (Chicago: University of Chicago Press, 1963); Stanley Rosen, *Plato's Sophist: The Drama of Orginal and Image* (New Haven: Yale University Press, 1983), *Hermeneutics as Politics* (Oxford: Oxford University Press, 1987), esp. ch. 2, and *The Question of Being: A Reversal of Heidegger* (New Haven: Yale University Press, 1992).

34  See e.g. J. E. Woodbridge, *The Son of Apollo: Themes of Plato* (New York: Houghton-Mifflin, 1929); John Hermann Randall, Jun., *Plato: Dramatist of the Life of Reason* (New York: Columbia University Press, 1970); Victorino Tejera, *Modes of Greek Thought* (New York: Appleton Century, 1971) and *Plato's Dialogues One by One* (New York: Irvington, 1984).

35  The crucial essay here is 'La pharmacie de Platon', in Jacques Derrida, *La Dissemination* (Paris: Editions du Seuil, 1972).

36  The most comprehensive statement is Hans-Joachim Kramer, *Plato and The Foundations of Metaphysics*, trans. John A. Caton (New York: State University of New York Press, 1990). See also Kurt Gaiser, 'Plato's Enigmatic Lecture "On the Good"', *Phronesis*, 25 (1980), 5–37; Thomas A. Szlezack, *Platon und die Schriftlichkeit der Philosophie* (Berlin: De Gruyter, 1985); Giovanni Reale, *Per una nuova interpretazione di Platone: Rilletura della metafisica dei grandi dialoghi alla luce delle 'Dottrine non scritte'* (Milan: Vita e Pensiero, 1987); Marie-Dominique Richard, *L'enseignement oral de Platon. Une nouvelle interpretation du platonisme* (Paris: Editions du Cerf, 1986); and John Findlay, *The Written and Unwritten Doctrines of Plato* (London: Routledge and Kegan Paul, 1974).

37  This point is, I think, widely accepted among those who have studied Strauss's writings, whether they be friend, admirer, critic or (as I would wish to see myself) friendly (and admiring) critic. Of course, there are other very important features of Strauss's thought. As Thomas Pangle in particular has stressed (see his introduction to *Studies in Platonic Political Philosophy*), an almost equally important aspect of Strauss's thought is the quarrel between Athens and Jerusalem. However, this quarrel has to be seen, I think, in the light of the other: to wit, the view that there is a fundamental disjunction between faith and reason.

38  This general view, that is to say that the tradition of philosophy in Western, Judaic and Islamic thought at least up to the end of the Western Middle Ages was an esoteric one (i.e. that philosophers hid their meanings), was largely responsible for the enormous hostility and ridicule that Strauss and some of his followers have attracted in the Anglo-American academic world. For his fullest discussion of this see his *Persecution and the Art of Writing* (Glencoe Ill.: The Free Press, 1952).

39  See Leo Strauss, 'Restatement of Xenophon's Hiero', in Victor Gourevitch and Michael Roth (eds), *Leo Strauss On Tyranny, revised and expanded edition, including the Strauss–Kojève Correspondence* (New York: The Free Press, 1991), pp. 205–6. The reference to

Plutarch's *Nicias* is to a passage wherein Plutarch details the hostility of the city to philosophy, particularly of the 'naturalist' sort but encompassing even non-naturalists like Protagoras (who was exiled) and, of course, Socrates (who was executed). Plutarch is clear that it was Plato's achievement, both by the manner of his life and by his writings and teachings, to reverse this hostility; and it is to this, of course, that Strauss refers.

40  This aspect of Strauss's thought is stressed by a number of commentators, friendly, hostile and neutral. See e.g. Thomas Pangle's Introduction to Leo Strauss, *Studies in Platonic Political Philosophy* (Chicago: University of Chicago Press, 1983); Stephen Holmes, *The Anatomy of Anti-Liberalism* (Cambridge: Harvard University Press, 1993), esp. ch. 3; and Stanley Rosen, *Hermeneutics as Politics*, ch. 3.

41  For Strauss's discussion of this in some detail, see 'Jerusalem and Athens: Some Preliminary Reflections', in *Studies in Platonic Political Philosophy*.

42  See Rosen, *Hermeneutics as Politics*, pp. 112–13. The notion of the 'conservative dimension of the Enlightenment' is, unfortunately, left rather under-explained in Rosen's book. That some members of the philosophical flock were, at least at times, 'conservative' in terms of disposition (think of Hume, for example) is, I think, true. However, as I shall suggest a little later on (ch. 3, n. 52), 'conservatism' as a political doctrine requires rather more than this. I assume that Rosen is referring to those elements of the Enlightenment that were shared between the philosophes and, for example, Burke, and even on occasion Kant (think of his acceptance of state power over his views of religion, for example, and his famous phrase from the *Opus Postumum*, 'Think as much as you like, argue as much as you like, but obey' (*Opus Postumum*, in *Kant-Studien*, supplementary volume, 1920)). This would link up with the claim, which I shall discuss in a moment, that Strauss's thought had Kantian roots.

43  It is worth pointing out here that Rosen suggests that in his very last books, where 'the style of Al-Farabi comes to the fore' (Rosen, *Hermeneutics as Politics*, p. 117), Strauss probably abandons this practice. This might account for the almost total bafflement Strauss's last books have met with in the vast majority of their readers.

44  Of course, Rosen is not the only person who has suggested this. Shadia Drury, in her *The Political Ideas of Leo Strauss* (London: Macmillan, 1988) has a different and, in my opinion at least, rather overstated version of a similar case.

45  Rosen, *Hermeneutics as Politics*, p. 113.

46  Strauss, *Persecution and the Art of Writing*, pp. 33–4.

47  Rosen, *Hermeneutics as Politics*, p. 125.

48  I have to say that on this point I suspect that Rosen and I would differ substantially on Kantian interpretation. However, let this be, for the moment.

49  Strauss, *What is Political Philosophy?*, p. 75.

50  I assume that these are chiefly *Natural Right and History*, and *The City and Man*, closely followed by *What is Political Philosophy?* and *Liberalism, Ancient and Modern*.

51  Most obviously Allan Bloom and Harvey Mansfield, Jun. See Bloom's *The Closing of The American Mind* (London: Penguin, 1987) and Mansfield's *The Spirit of Liberalism* (Cambridge: Harvard University Press, 1978).

52  The very notion of 'conservatism' in this context is a rather curious one, I think. I would see conservatism as a distinct *political* outlook generated by a certain set of events and reactions to these events (the most important of which is undoubtedly the French Revolution). I would also accept the related but still distinct sense of a 'conservative disposition' (made much of by Michael Oakeshott, for example). Seeing Strauss in either of these terms, however, has always struck me as very odd. An interesting recent and explicit attempt to link Oakeshottian and Straussian thinking and contemporary conservatism and the new Right has recently been essayed by Robert Levigne in *Conservativism Recast: Oakeshott, Strauss and the Response to Postmodernism* (New Haven: Yale University Press, 1994). Ingenious though it is, I do not find it convincing as an account of either thinker, though there is some truth, I think, in the general presentation of the way in which some of their explicit followers have attempted to act in politics in the US and the UK. Michael Oakeshott's 'On being Conservative', included in his *Rationalism in Politics and Other Essays* (London: Methuen, 1962) cannot, I believe, be bettered as a general statement of the conservative disposition. Noel O'Sullivan's *Conservatism* (London: J. M. Dent, 1976) is about as good a general survey of conservatism as has been written, and includes the argument, with which I would agree, that conservatism as such has to be seen in political terms as a reaction to the French Revolution and what was associated with it. Philip Thody's *The Conservative Imagination* (London: Francis Pinter, 1993) is another very good general book that explores this theme.

   A related point is visible in the critique levelled at Strauss by Stephen Holmes in *The Anatomy of Anti-Liberalism* (Cambridge: Harvard University Press, 1994). Holmes suggests that Strauss is both a conservative and an elitist; Holmes also emphasizes his links to avowedly anti-liberal thinkers such as Heidegger and Carl Schmitt as well as his esotericism. I agree with Pippin ('The Modern World of Leo Strauss', p. 467 n. 6) when he says that the best judgement about Strauss's contemporary political opinions and intentions is that they are deeply ambiguous, 'but they are at least ambiguous, something often ignored in complaints about his elitism and inegalitarianism'.

53  Rosen, *Hermeneutics as Politics*, p. 137. It is significant, in the light of what I shall argue later on, that the term 'habituated' is employed here. I agree with Rosen that this is how Strauss saw his enterprise and think, further, that he was, in at least one very important sense, right to

conceive of it in this way. However, I believe that much of the associated ideas as to whom should be habituated, how and in what respect, are wrong.

54  Rosen, *Hermeneutics as Politics*, p. 126.

55  The rehabilitation of these have been primarily the work of the so-called Tübingen school of Plato interpretation headed by Konrad Geiser and Hans Joachim Kramer. I have discussed this thesis in much greater detail in 'Plato's Metaphysical Politics'.

56  In fairness to Strauss, he himself many times made the point that we cannot be anything other than moderns (see, e.g., *Liberalism, Ancient and Modern*, pp. 4–5, 10, 23, 207–8, *What is Political Philosophy?*, pp. 27–8, 78–87), a point that is seemingly forgotten by a good many of his critics.

57  *Giants and Dwarfs* (New York: Simon and Schuster, 1990), pp. 242–5.

58  For a discussion of Islamic thought in the key period, as far as Strauss is concerned, that is both scholarly and balanced and which gives a rather different interpretation to that of Strauss, see Ian Richard Netton, *Al-Farabi and His School* (London: Routledge, 1992). A representative selection of Strauss's own writings on medieval Islamic and Jewish philosophy would include 'Quelques remarques sur la science politique de Maimonide et de Farabi', in *Revue des etudes juives*, 100 (1936), pp. 1–37; 'Eine vermisste Schrift Farabis', *Monatsschrift für Geschichte und Wissenschaft des Judentums*, 80 (1936), pp. 96–106; most famously, *Persecution and the Art of Writing* and various essays in *What is Political Philosophy?*.

59  Rosen, *Hermeneutics as Politics*, p. 137.

60  Ibid., 133.

61  This phrase, used equally by Strauss and Rosen, seems to be an appropriate phrase to use when referring to Plato's conception of philosophy as such. Plato's famous discussion in the Seventh Letter of how knowledge 'flashes forth as when a fire is kindled', how it is 'born in the soul and immediately nourishes itself', indicates this too, I think (see Plato, *Seventh Letter*, 341D).

62  Masters, *The Nature of Politics*, pp. 245–6.

63  Of course, as with nature in general, this is not to say that it has been completely ignored. Some work in psychology, anthropology and sociology has focused on certain aspects of it. Moreover, certain movements in European social thought – especially philosophical anthropology – have picked up some similar themes to those I am advancing here, though not usually in the same context. Philosophers in English-speaking countries sympathetic to these approaches (e.g., Charles Taylor) have also touched on some of the same topics. I am happy to acknowledge the stimulus I have received from a good deal of this work. However, the use I make of the notion here is rather different than the vast majority of this work, for reasons that will become apparent later on. For interesting discussions see e.g. Hans Joas and Axel Honneth, *Soziales Handeln und*

*menschliche Natür* (Frankfurt: Campus Verlag GmbH, 1980); Charles Taylor, *Human Agency and Language* and *Philosophy and the Human Sciences* (2 volumes of philosophical papers (Cambridge: Cambridge University Press, 1985)).

64  Stjepan G. Mestrovic, *The Barbarian Temperament: Towards a Postmodern Critical Theory* (London: Routledge, 1993), pp. 5–6. I shall return to Mestrovic's argument, which has influenced my thinking on these points, several times in this chapter. Where we agree and where we disagree will, I hope, become apparent by the end of it.

65  Mestrovic, *Barbarian Temperament*, p. 14.

66  Bohman, *The New Philosophy of Social Science*, p. 58.

67  Carl Gustav Jung, *Four Archetypes* (Princeton: Princeton University Press, 1959).

68  W. T. Waller, 'The Concept of Habit in Economic Analysis', *Journal of Economic Issues*, 22 (1988), pp. 113–26.

69  C. Camic, 'The Matter of Habit', *American Journal of Sociology*, 91 (1986), pp. 1039–87.

70  A. Lalande, *Vocabulaire technique et critique de la philosophie* (Paris: Presses Universitaires de France, 1980 [1926]).

71  Mestrovic, *The Barbarian Temperament*, pp. 18–19.

72  Of course, this is not entirely true. Some postmoderns, perhaps most obviously Foucault, are very aware that the character of 'normality' is itself a creation and needs to be investigated. The emphasis, however, is on the fragmenting and deconstruction of these norms rather than on bringing the norms themselves to the surface.

73  P. Christopher Smith, Introduction to his translation of Hans-Georg Gadamer, *Die Idee des Guten zwischen Plato und Aristoteles* (Heidelberg: J. C. B. Mohr, 1978) (English title, *The Idea of the Good in Platonic–Aristotelean Philosophy*) (New Haven: Yale University Press, 1986), p. x. I owe a good deal to Gadamer's interpretation here and am happy to acknowledge it. Our differences will become apparent later on.

74  Gadamer, *The Idea of the Good*.

75  The phrase is Smith's. See *The Idea of the Good*, p. xiii.

76  Significantly (though Gadamer does not mention it here) the subject, apparently, of his famous (and only indirectly reported) lecture 'On the Good'. See e.g. Simplicius's comments on Aristotle's *Physics*, discussed in Kramer, *Plato and the Foundations of Metaphysics*, p. 203.

77  Gadamer, *The Idea of the Good*, pp. 177–8.

78  This is an example Gadamer used in conversation with Smith. Smith quotes it in his introduction, *The Idea of the Good*, p. xxvi.

79  Aristotle, *Politics*, 1268b22–1269a28.

80  J. G. A. Pocock, *Politics, Language and Time* (New York: Athenaeum Press, 1973), p. 233.

81  See Michael Oakeshott, *Rationalism in Politics* and, *inter alia, On Human Conduct* (Oxford: Clarendon Press, 1975).

82  See Hans-Georg Gadamer, *Wahrheit und Methode*, 4th edn (Tübingen:

J. C. B. Mohr, 1975 [1960]). See also English translations of some of the essays collected in his *Kleine Schriften*. See especially *Reason in The Age of Science*, trans. F. Lawrence (Cambridge: MIT Press, 1981) and *Philosophical Hermeneutics*, trans. D. E. Linge (Berkeley: University of California Press, 1976). A very good discussion of Gadamer's views on tradition, custom and habit can be found in Georgia Warnke's excellent *Gadamer: Hermeneutics, Tradition and Reason* (Cambridge: Polity Press, 1987). See esp. chs. 3 and 4.

83 See Hannah Arendt, *The Human Condition* (Chicago: University of Chicago Press, 1958). Good treatments of this aspect of Arendt's thought can be found in Bonnie Honig, 'Declarations of Independence: Arendt and Derrida on the Problem of Founding a Republic', in *The American Political Science Review*, 85 (1991), pp. 97–113; and Maurizio Passerein D'Entreves, *The Political Philosophy of Hannah Arendt* (London: Routledge, 1994), esp. ch. 2. Similar themes also occur in the work of such thinkers as Bertrand De Jouvenal and (rather more problematically and much more weakly) Walter Lippman. In my submission neither De Jouvenal nor Lippman can be compared to the other writings that I have just mentioned, and I shall not discuss them further here. See, however, Bertrand De Jouvenal, *On Power: Its Nature and the History of Its Growth* (New York: The Viking Press, 1949), and *Sovereignty: An Inquiry into the Political Good* (Chicago: University of Chicago Press, 1957). See also Walter Lippman, *The Public Philosophy* (New York: New American Library, 1975).

84 Most notable in this context in recent political thought is Bruce James Smith's excellent *Politics and Remembrance: Republican Themes in Machiavelli, Burke and Tocqueville* (Princeton: Princeton University Press, 1985). Other books that touch on this theme include Norman Jacobson's *Pride and Solace* (Berkeley: University of California Press, 1978), Sheldon Wolin's classic book for all seasons, *Politics and Vision: Continuity and Innovation in Western Political Thought* (London: George Allen and Unwin, 1960), and Janet Coleman's magisterial *Ancient and Medieval Memories* (Cambridge: Cambridge University Press, 1992).

85 Alisdair MacIntyre, *After Virtue* (London: Duckworth, 1981), p. 174.

86 Ibid., 175.

87 Peter McMylor, *Alisdair MacIntyre: Critic of Modernity* (London: Routledge, 1994), p. 149.

88 MacIntyre, *After Virtue*, p. 178.

89 In fact, MacIntyre actually says that 'the good life for man is the life spent in seeking the good life for man'. I assume, however (perhaps charitably), that by 'man' he implies humankind as such.

90 Ibid., 207.

91 MacIntyre, *Three Rival Versions of Moral Enquiry* (Lodon: Duckworth, 1990).

92 Other problematic aspects of MacIntyre's presentation of the liberal

'tradition' have been highlighted in essays by Stephen Pettit, Stephen Mullhall and Andrew Mason, in Susan Mendus and John Horton (eds), *After MacIntyre: Critical Perspectives on the Work of Alisdair MacIntyre* (Cambridge: Polity Press, 1994).

93  McMylor, *Alisdair MacIntyre*, p. 160.

94  A similar point is contained in Peter Johnson's essay, 'Reclaiming the Aristotelean Ruler', in Mendus and Horton (eds), *After MacIntyre*. I do, however, disagree quite strongly with one aspect of Johnson's argument, to which I shall return in ch. 4.

95  See Richard Bernstein, *Philosophical Profiles* (Cambridge: Polity Press, 1986).

96  MacIntyre, *After Virtue*, p. 149.

97  Bernstein, *Philosophical Profiles*, p. 137.

98  I have addressed MacIntyre's general position more fully in an unpublished paper, 'No Flowers, by Request: Alisdair MacIntyre and the Strange Death of Liberal Political Theory'.

99  Mestrovic, *The Barbarian Temperament*, pp. x–xi.

100  Ibid., 21.

101  Ibid., 248–9. Mestrovic is referring here especially to Simmel's essay 'Eros, Platonic and Modern', in D. Levine (ed.), *On Individuality and Its Social Forms* (Chicago: University of Chicago Press, 1971 [1921]). In this context it is perhaps worth pointing out that over the last few years there has been a gradual reassertion of the centrality of Simmel in both sociological and philosophical traditions. He figures prominently, for example, in Lawrence A. Scaff's superb study of the *fin-de-siècle* circle around Weber, *Fleeing the Iron Cage: Culture, Politics and Modernity in the Thought of Max Weber* (Berkeley: University of California Press, 1991) and many of his works have been re-translated into English. See e.g. *The Philosophy of Money*, trans. David Frisby (London: Routledge, 1978). See also Frisby, *Sociological Impressionism: A Reassessment of Georg Simmel's Social Theory* (London: Heinemann, 1981).

102  Mestrovic, *The Barbarian Temperament*, p. 247.

103  Durkheim, 'The Dualism of Human Nature and its Social Conditions', in *Emile Durkheim on Morality and Society* (Chicago: University of Chicago Press, 1973) ed. R. Bellah. See also Mestrovic, *The Barbarian Temperament*, p. 167.

104  Mestrovic, *The Barbarian Temperament*, p. 276.

105  In what follows here I am paraphrasing the argument of the central parts of my *Reason, Scepticism and Politics*, which goes into the historical and textual evidence for this in much greater detail.

106  Ernst Cassirer, *Die Philosophie der Aufklarung* (Tübingen: J. C. B. Mohr, 1932). The passage quoted is taken from Fritz Koellen's and James Pettegrove's English translation, *The Philosophy of the Enlightenment* (Princeton: Princeton University Press, 1951), p. 13. I have amended the translation slightly to point up the argument.

107  David Hume, *A Dialogue* in L. A. Selby-Bigge (ed.), *The Enquiries*

(Oxford: Clarendon Press, 1975), p. 343.

108 This account is taken from Smith's letter to the publisher Strahan, a friend of both him and Hume. See Ernest Mossner, *The Life of David Hume* (Oxford: Clarendon Press, 1980), p. 601.

109 Rosen, *The Ancients and the Moderns*, p. 20.

110 The words are Rosen's, *Hermeneutics as Politics*, p. 126.

111 Aristotle, *Nicomachean Ethics*, I.13.

112 S. L. Hurley, *Natural Reasons: Personality and Polity* (Oxford: Oxford University Press, 1989).

113 Ibid., 3.

114 See Stephen R. L. Clark, *Civil Peace and Sacred Order* (*Limits and Renewals*, vol. 1), *A Parliament of Souls* (*Limits and Renewals*, vol. 2) and *God's World and the Great Awakening* (*Limits and Renewals*, vol. 3). All published by the Clarendon Press, Oxford, 1989, 1990, 1991 respectively.

115 Clark, *Civil Peace and Sacred Order*, p. 4.

116 Ibid., 5–6.

117 Ibid., 9–10. Clark is here referring to H. P. Duerr's illuminating book, *Dreamtime: Concerning the Boundary between Wilderness and Civilisation* (Oxford: Blackwell, 1985).

118 Clark, *Civil Peace and Sacred Order*, pp. 7–9.

119 Ibid., 14.

120 Ibid., 16. It is worthwhile pointing out that this is a point that might be made, almost equally, against Strauss. Can Strauss really suppose that he, alone among investigators, has realized what has escaped all others over the last (at least) five hundred years? What reason do we have for supposing that? What reason do we have, moreover, for supposing, even if it is wholly or partially true, that it matters? Strauss gives us few, if any, reasons for believing that Plato (for example) is correct to think as he did, and that it is therefore central to understand Plato. As it happens I agree with Strauss that Plato (and classical thought more generally) has insights that are quite central to contemporary ethics and politics, but I at least have reasons for this view that I am happy to give and to defend, as, I believe, Plato did also. Strauss is correct to see Plato as writing the dialogues as dramas designed to hide some things and point the way to others, but Plato also did give lectures (in the Academy) directly focusing on issues, and clearly felt that such issues were central to the task of philosophy as he conceived it. Esoteric writing is part of the task of philosophy, that is true. However, it is not the whole of it. I have elaborated this case in greater detail in 'Plato's Metaphysical Politics: The Tübingen School and Plato's Political Thought'.

121 See e.g. some of the arguments put forward in Iain Maclean, *Public Choice: An Introduction* (Oxford: Blackwell, 1987).

122 See e.g. the argument in Chantal Mouffe, *The Return of the Political* (London: Verso, 1992).

123 Clark, *Civil Peace and Sacred Order*, p. 19.

124 Ibid., 24.

125 Strauss, *Liberalism, Ancient and Modern*, p. 220.

126 I hope on a subsequent occasion to outline some of my own ideas on the more obviously metaphysical and theological presuppositions of my argument. While I am obviously in considerable sympathy with Clark's general approach, I would differ from him substantially on aspects of the metaphysics and theology outlined especially in *God's World and the Great Awakening*.

127 Clark, *Civil Peace and Sacred Order*, p. 159.

128 Ibid., 160.

129 Or indeed as a convinced Jew or Muslim. I would broadly accept this claim as well, though I shall not elaborate upon it here.

130 Clark, *Civil Peace and Sacred Order*, pp. 163–4.

131 This suggests that the task of political judgement and practical reason is every bit as central as Aristotle thought it was. I shall return to this towards the end of my last chapter.

132 Though there are exceptions; e.g. Taylor.

133 Clark, *Civil Peace and Sacred Order*, p. 153.

134 See Hannah Arendt, *Eichmann In Jerusalem: A Report on the Banality of Evil* (New York: Viking Press, 1965).

135 Begun, of course, in *The Origins of Totalitarianism* (Cleveland: Meridian Books, 1951; 2nd edn, 1958).

136 For good discussions see Philip Hansen, *Hannah Arendt: Politics, History and Citizenship* (Cambridge: Polity Press, 1993); Margaret Canovan, *Hannah Arendt* (Cambridge: Cambridge University Press, 1993); Passerein D'Entreves, *The Political Philosophy of Hannah Arendt* (London: Routledge, 1994); Elisabeth Young-Breuhl, *Hannah Arendt: For Love of the World* (New Haven: Yale University Press, 1982). This is also as good a time as any to acknowledge my considerable debts to Maurizio Passerein D'Entreves, Judith Squires and Bonnie Honig for many (and continuing) discussions on Arendt.

137 *Eichmann in Jerusalem*, p. 136. See also Hansen, *Hannah Arendt*, p. 167.

138 Hansen, *Hannah Arendt*, p. 167.

139 As Hansen points out, this concern dominated her last, unfinished book *The Life of the Mind* (New York: Harcourt, Brace Janovitch, 1978), 2 vols. ('Thinking' and 'Willing'; there was to have been a third, 'Judging', but she died before she could finish it). Some ideas as to how she might have finished it can be found in her *Lectures on Kant's Political Philosophy*, ed. Ronald Beiner (Chicago: University of Chicago Press, 1982). See Hansen, *Hannah Arendt*, pp. 167–9.

140 In part, of course, this is indeed the task that Arendt performs (brilliantly) in *The Origins of Totalitarianism*. However, I would argue that there were parts of the story that Arendt herself missed or failed to discuss adequately.

141 I shall refer to William Connolly, *Identity/Difference: Democratic Negotiations of Political Paradox* (Ithaca: Cornell University Press, 1991); *The*

*Augustinian Imperative* (London: Sage, 1993); and 'Beyond Good and Evil: The Ethical Sensibility of Michel Foucault', in *Political Theory*, 21, no. 3 (Aug. 1993). Zygmunt Bauman, *Postmodern Ethics* (Oxford: Blackwell, 1993).

142 See especially *Modernity and the Holocaust* (Cambridge: Polity Press, 1989); *Intimations of Postmodernity* (London: Routledge, 1992); and *Modernity and Ambivalence* (Cambridge: Polity Press, 1991). It might be asked why, if Bauman is (as I agree he is) so good an analyst of modernity, I have not had occasion to discuss him so far. The answer is simply that, as I read him, he most obviously fits into chapter 4, where I shall be discussing 'postmodernity'. *Postmodern Ethics* is more usefully discussed here.

143 G. Lipovetsky, *Le Crépuscule du devoir* (Paris: Gallimard, 1992).

144 Bauman, *Postmodern Ethics*, pp. 2–3.

145 Ibid., 3.

146 Ibid., 3–4.

147 Ibid., 9–10. Note the similarity to Mestrovic's argument discussed above.

148 Also with some others. For example, Bonnie Honig, as we saw earlier, shares this view, as do – at least to some extent – Fred Dallmayr and Chantal Mouffe. For Dallmayr, see *Life World, Modernity and Critique: Paths between Heidegger and the Frankfurt School* (Cambridge: Polity Press, 1991).

149 Connolly, *Identity/Difference*, pp. 14–15.

150 Bauman, *Postmodern Ethics*, abstracted with some direct quotation from pp. 10–15.

151 Connolly, *The Augustinian Imperative*, pp. 151–2.

152 Connolly, *Identity/Difference*, p. x.

153 I hope to do so in the future, however.

154 For an account of modern social and political theory which seeks to develop a neo-Platonic (and Christian) 'postmodern theology' see John Milbank's enormously interesting *Theology and Social Theory: Beyond Secular Reason* (Oxford: Blackwell, 1990). Milbank's argument, which seeks to establish a neo-Augustinian framework for a social and political theory 'beyond secular reason', is an enormously interesting one which shares a good deal with the project outlined here. Although I disagree with aspects of his argument, he, like me, would emphasize the centrality of 'forgiveness' for a political theory that advocates practices that can create loyalty and obligation – the 'other city', as he would call it.

# 4

# TOWARDS A *POLITICAL* THEORY

*Every art we follow and every inquiry we make . . . may be held
to aim at some good or end . . . actions, arts and sciences are
manifold . . . If there is some end of the things done by us which
we desire for its own sake . . . then we must try to comprehend,
at any rate in outline, the nature of this master end and to
discover which is the science that has it for its object . . . the
political science appears to be of this nature.*

Aristotle, *The Nicomachean Ethics*, 1094a–b.

We have come full circle. The main aim in this chapter will
be to reassess the tasks of political theory discussed in the
introduction in the light of the discussion of the modernity
debate and its reformulation. Before I can do this, however,
there is one piece of unfinished business that I must clear up.
Sharp-eyed readers will have noticed that, so far, I have only
discussed two of the subjects flagged in the title of this book,
political theory and modernity. What, then, of postmodernity?
I have discussed postmoderns, certainly, but not postmodernity
in any detail. Before I return to the tasks of political theory,
then, I want to say something about this term and its
connotations.

## Post(?)-Modernities

Postmodernity, I shall seek to argue, needs to be differentiated
from the 'postmodern' mood, as I discussed it in chapters 2 and
3 above. In this respect I differ somewhat from those like

Zygmunt Bauman, who sees 'postmodernity' as largely a state of mind, marked by 'its all-deriding, all-eroding, all-dissolving destructiveness',[1] the view of what postmodernity brings with it which leads Bauman to outline the ethical paradox of postmodernity that I briefly outlined at the end of chapter 3.

Of course, Bauman also accepts that postmodernity can mean many different things to different people, and somewhat in the same vein David Lyon, in a short and well-written book, has suggested that we see postmodernity as a confluence of phenomena, social, philosophical and cultural.[2] Since we have taken modernity to be such a complex interweaving of different features there would be some logic to seeing 'postmodernity' in this way as well. My earlier argument suggested that understanding 'modernity' meant seeing it as a complex matrix of mood and socio-cultural form; and therefore we might see 'postmodernity' as that complex matrix of mood and socio-cultural form to which 'modernity' is giving way.

However, I want to suggest that it is perhaps more helpful to insist on a slight difference between modernity and post-modernity in this context. Not simply the obvious difference that one is supposed (in whatever sense) to be 'post' the other, but because it seems to me that 'postmodernity' (as opposed to 'the postmodern') is better seen as a short-hand term to describe a social and intellectual *condition* (in the sense I have used that term above), rather than simply or largely a mood or a state of mind together with a socio-cultural condition.

I should explain that what I have in mind here is that, as I have discussed it, the postmodern mood is a mood *within modernity*; it is indeed a reaction to or perhaps a dissolution of modern moods and intellectual categories. However, as we have seen, as such it is not necessarily temporally located in (for example) the 'post-Enlightenment' period. Moreover the postmodern mood can exist (as in certain respects it does in Heidegger and even Nietzsche, for example) in the absence of a corresponding socio-cultural form. Thus, it seems to me that if 'postmodernity' (as the complex matrix that Bauman and Lyon suggest that it is) is plausible at all, it is the socio-cultural aspects of it that are central; the socio-cultural form that perhaps best fits the postmodern mood, which, however, is conceivable (to some extent) without it.

Thus, as I shall use the term here, 'postmodernity' can be taken as the *hypothesis* that there are certain changes in our socio-cultural-political condition that are bringing forth or reinforcing intellectual and cultural changes that the postmodern mood has delineated. In other words, *'postmodernity' should be seen as a description of the current state of modernity as sociocultural form and what follows from that.* Given this understanding of postmodernity, then, the discussion of it properly belongs in this chapter, concerned with the political implications of the preceding arguments.

There are three general questions that follow from this. Firstly, what can the constituent elements of postmodernity be said to be? Secondly, is this a plausible description of the current and evolving socio-cultural form of modernity? Thirdly, what are the implications of the answers given to the first two questions for the modernity debate and for our subsequent discussion of the tasks of political theory?

## *Elements of postmodernity*

In this first section, then, I want to try to trace the parameters we might set for arguments about what constitutes postmodernity. In the first place, I shall look at that network of claims that are associated with terms like 'post-industrialism', as perhaps the most obvious starting point for a consideration of postmodernity as such, and then, secondly, I shall return to Bauman's argument and focus on his claim that postmodernity is 'modernity conscious of its true nature'.[3] I do not suggest that these discussions exhaust the sense that can be given to postmodernity, but for my purposes here they are the best place to start.

Let me begin, then, with post-industrialism and its correlates. Post-industrialism is, of course, not a new idea. It has been around at least since the early 1970s[4] and has had a number of different formulations, together with a large number of parallel or supplementary theories or hypotheses.[5] In addition, along the way a good deal of work that has focused on social transformation more generally has become associated with it.[6]

At its root, of course, post-industrialism simply suggests that the (so-called) 'advanced', 'industrial' societies are changing in very profound ways. The characteristic modes of production, consumption and exchange are shifting and new forms emerging. In particular, it has been suggested that the rise of new forms of technology, especially computers, informational technologies, and (in the 1990s especially) multi-media technologies, are producing axial shifts in the material basis of such societies.[7]

Lyon suggests that a good many of these arguments, especially early on, retained key modern aspects, most especially a theory of, or at least an assumption of, progress.[8] However, since Lyotard took up these sorts of themes and portrayed them in the context of a 'world beyond progress',[9] a formulation which has had a powerful influence on the ways in which postmoderns (especially of the hard-sceptical sort) view postmodernity, this feature of the discussion has largely disappeared.

This has had the effect, as both Lyon and Barry Smart have noted,[10] that the concern with post-industrialism has become increasingly bound up with the more general phenomenon of postmodernity, seen as a change in 'the character of Western civilisation itself'. As was suggested above, this change has been most usually associated with the enormous technological advances in communications, information technology and computing. As Mark Poster has pointed out, 'the solid institutional routines that have characterized modern society for some two hundred years are being shaken by the earthquake of electronically mediated communication and recomposed into new routines whose outlines are as yet by no means clear'.[11] Many other writers sympathetic to the postmodern mood have stressed similar issues.[12]

From these changes a whole host of others are held to follow and, in anticipation of something that I shall argue later, it is worth bearing in mind that the range of these changes is now seen to have global reach and reference rather than simply affecting the 'advanced industrial countries'. Thus, the

globalization of financial markets and the transformation of the
global political economy, the transformation of tourism, accelerating changes in consumerism, the development of worldwide computer networks, the spatial and temporal shrinking of
the globe; all have been discussed as aspects of the new situation
that we find ourselves in.[13] As we saw in chapter 2, much of this
has found its way into the postmodern mood, especially into the
work of hard-sceptical postmoderns such as Baudrillard, Virilio
and Vattimo,[14] and of course it has become a very influential
aspect of contemporary literature, film and art, activities
which, not accidentally, have more than their fair share of
'postmodern' participants.[15]

I shall come on in a moment to assess what we should make
of all this. Beforehand, however, I want to go back to Bauman's
argument. In his book *Intimations of Postmodernity*, he pre-
figures the argument he offers in *Postmodern Ethics*, but his
focus is on postmodernity as such, rather than on the ethical
paradoxes it raises. As I briefly mentioned earlier, he defines
postmodernity as follows:

> Postmodernity may be interpreted as fully developed modernity
> taking a full measure of the anticipated consequences of its
> historical work. . . . modernity concious of its true nature – mod-
> ernity for itself. The most conspicuous features of the
> postmodern condition: institutionalized pluralism, variety, con-
> tingency and ambivalence – have all been turned out by modern
> society in ever increasing volumes; yet they were seen as signs of
> failure rather than success . . . the postmodern condition can be
> therefore described, *on the one hand* as modernity emancipated
> from false consciousness, *on the other*, as a new type of social
> condition marked by the overt institutionalization of the charac-
> teristics which modernity – in its designs and managerial prac-
> tices – set out to eliminate and, failing that, to conceal.[16]

Let us, for the moment, assume that the first half of his either/
or refers effectively to the postmodern mood as I have described
it, and put it to one side. That leaves his claim that
'postmodernity' is characterized by a 'new type of social condition'. This, it seems to me, is effectively where all of the
arguments about postmodernity that I have been highlight-
ing are pointing. They suggest that these features of our

contemporary situation are *not* divorceable from it, indeed, they are specific to it. Thus in this respect, then, 'postmodernity' cannot be understood in the same way as we have understood modernity as mood (as simply a 'frame' that does not – necessarily – have any specific temporal location). Bauman's formulation makes it unambiguously clear that 'postmodernity' as such is dependent upon the changes that contemporary – not just advanced industrial – societies are currently undergoing being *both* correctly analysed *and* having the implications that the analysts think follow from them in terms of politics.

Before we can assess the plausibility of these arguments, however, it is necessary to see what its advocates *do* think follows from it. Again, I shall start with Bauman, who is, as always, extremely perceptive about this aspect of the argument as well. Bauman's view is that postmodernity is both a recognition of, and a contribution to, the scrambling of the traditional (i.e. modern) distinction between theory and practice which for him was itself dependent upon the activity of the modern national state. This, Bauman argues, was

> arguably the only social formation in history with pretensions to and ambitions of administering a global order and of maintaining a total monopoly of rule-setting and rule-execution. Equally policy was to be the state's monopoly and the procedure for its formulation had to be made separate and independent from the procedure legitimising an accceptable theory and, more generally, intellectual work modelled after the latter procedure. The gradual, yet relentless erosion of the national state's monopoly (undermined simultaneously from above and from below . . .) ended the plausibility of theoretical segregation . . . policy shifts away from the state . . . it dissipates, it splits into a plethora of localised or partial policies.[17]

This gives rise to a curious mixture of 'old' (modern) and new (postmodern) politics, argues Bauman. The old politics of inequality and redistribution, though displaced from its previous dominance, will remain a central issue, as will issues such as human rights, a sub-category of inequality and redistribution. However, alongside these survivals, new forms of politics will increasingly appear, or increase in significance where they have perhaps already been present. Bauman gives four named forms of 'new' postmodern politics, though they are not mutually exclusive. The first, which he calls 'tribal politics' he sees as 'entailing the creation of tribes as imagined communities' existing in no other form but the 'symbolically manifested commitment of their members'. He also stresses that they are fundamentally deterritorialized. The second form is what he terms 'the politics of desire', whose overall effect, he suggests, will be the heteronomy of choice over the relevance of certain types of conduct, supported by and in its turn sustaining the autonomy of the choosing agents. The third form he terms the politics of fear; it is, in a sense, a complement and a counterweight to the politics of desire in that it seeks to draw boundaries to heteronomy. These fears may crystallize, he suggests, around such issues as pollution, risk and bodily contamination. His final form he calls the politics of certainty, and it entails the vehement search for social confirmation of choice which emphasizes the centrality of trust for postmodern politics, as people need to feel that their choices are sensible given the plurality of other choices.[18]

These claims about what follows from postmodernity find their echoes in many other writers. Stephen White, for example, also dwells upon issues like informational technologies and suggests that 'new social movements' are forming an important new political sector[19] ('new tribes', perhaps, in Bauman's sense, engaged in the politics of fear, desire and certainty); a point which is picked up by many others, in different ways and to different degrees.[20] James Der Derian, for example, in a series of studies of issues like diplomacy, terrorism, and the spatial and temporal changes of 'late modernity' (as he, following Connolly, chooses to call it) has emphasized that (post)modern international (and intertextual) politics are marked by a 'chronopolitical' and 'technostrategic' discourse, in place of the spatially oriented and geostrategic one of traditional (modern) international relations.[21] A number of other postmoderns have ventured to hope that one of the most powerful implications of postmodernity will be both an increasing sense of personal responsibility for the possibility of choice and the kinds of choices made (this is stressed by both White and Bauman, for example), and an extending recognition that democracy in more radical forms than is currently the case anywhere, is the best way of managing the combination of the 'old' and 'new' politics.[22]

Postmodernity, then, will be an exciting time, a dangerous time, a liberating time and a repressive time. In short, it will be the best of times and the worst of times. Putting it like that, however, raises an obvious question; is it really likely to be very different from what has gone before? To begin to answer this question, then, let me turn to an interpretation of just how plausible 'postmodernity' – in the sense described above – is as a description of our here and now.

## Late modernity?

It is unquestionably true that many of the changes emphasized by the advocates of 'postmodernity' are real ones. Contemporary societies certainly are experiencing, at a rapid and accelerating pace, technological change, especially in the fields of informational technologies; they certainly do have globalized financial markets and, indeed, globalization (in various forms) is an undoubted feature of many other aspects of contemporary politics.[23] The problem, however, is how to interpret these developments and therefore how to assess how radical the changes that they are leading to might be said to be.[24]

A number of alternative ways of reading this situation are possible, of course. 'Postmodernity' is certainly one, but it is hardly the only one. The writings of scholars such as Ulrich Beck, Anthony Giddens, and Scott Lash and John Urry have equally emphasized the very real changes going on in contemporary societies without, however, wishing to see it as 'postmodernity'. Rather they see it as a process of (in their words) 'reflexive modernization'.[25] Quite explicitly they understand by this term a set of related themes that, as they put it, 'breaks the stranglehold which [debates about modernity versus postmodernity] have tended to place on conceptual innovation'.[26] They go on to suggest that one other common theme is what they term 'de-traditionalization', understood as the 'routine' subjection of traditions – and especially what they term traditions from the 'hidden substratum' of modernity (i.e.

traditions affecting gender, the family and so on) – to critical interrogation. A third common concern, they argue, lies in the ecological sphere, and they suggest that what is 'natural' is now so thoroughly entangled with what is social that nothing can be taken for granted any more.

From this analysis, they make a number of interesting and significant arguments. However, I shall choose to focus largely on one. They suggest that the notion of 'risk' is quite central to reflexively modern culture, because so much of our thinking is of an 'as-if' kind. 'In most aspects of our lives, individual and collective, we have regularly to construct potential futures, knowing that such very construction may in fact prevent them coming about. New areas of unpredictability are created quite often by the very attempts to seek to control them.'[27]

I do not want to delve further into the specifics of their argument here. I have said enough, I hope, to indicate both the similarities and differences between their approach and that of somebody like Bauman or Lyon. While they take the changes seriously they see them as part of a *continuous evolution of modernity as socio-cultural form*, and do not suppose that it is necessary to posit a completely new 'type' of socio-cultural form to either account *for* them or make interpretations *of* them.

In part, of course, the difference is perhaps semantic. The differences between do not really appear to be all that great. However, the difference that *does* exist implies something significant, I think: to wit, that the claim that there are many profound and accelerating social changes in the contemporary world does not mean that we *have* to see that world in ways completely new. We must adjust out vision, certainly; we do not (necessarily) need to presuppose an entirely altered landscape.

## Modernity in question

Let me now suggest what I take the implications of all of this to be. To begin with I think that it is useful to highlight three issues touched on by all our interpreters of late/post/reflexive modernity. In no order of preference these are the question of trust (and the concomitant question of risk); secondly, the question of nature and convention – again – and its scrambling or

ambivalence; and thirdly, the question of the globalized character of the changes which are significant for how we perceive late/
post/reflexive modernity.

In a moment, I shall turn to the discussion of the tasks of
political theory that I began in the introductory chapter, and
will want to relate the above three issues to those tasks, in the
light of the discussion of the modernity debate that was the
focus of chapters 2 and 3. However, before I move on to this, I
want to elaborate a little on these three issues, since all will play
a significant part in what follows.

Globalization is perhaps the most obvious issue that links all
the above thinkers. In each case, whatever they want to call the
phenomenon, they emphasize the fact that its range is now
global (though, of course, they differ in their accounts of exactly
*how* it is global). In one sense, again, this simply differentiates
late/post/reflexive modernity from the 'postmodern mood' as
such – this, as we saw in chapters 2 and 3, was very much a
product of a particular intellectual tradition and set of debates
(to wit, the 'Western' one).[28] That other – 'non-Westerners' –
are now involved in it is itself a reflection of the 'globalization'
process to which we refer.[29] However, this 'globalization' is
itself hugely problematic. Writers such as Bauman and
Connolly suggest that it implies the at least gradual diminution
in the power of the most formidable modern political unit, the
nation state, and there is a good deal of fashionable unreflective
modern writing that would concur (especially in areas such as
international economics).

For many, however, it seems likely that such a set of conditions are likely to increase the power of state forms (at least
certain state forms) in that it will make accountability and
responsible government much harder (some could see Giddens'
arguments in this way, for example), and this aspect of the
argument is supported by a good deal of recent writing on the
state which emphasizes its still formidable arsenal of weapons
aimed at control, coercion or even, perhaps, succour, welfare
and liberation.

It is also important, of course, to remember that amidst all
the discussion (whether that is positive or negative) of the 'new
tribalism' (I borrow the phrase from Michael Walzer), 'peoples',

'nations' or whatever you want to call them have always been, are, and will remain, a central aspect of politics whether or not the 'state' – the 'military–political–bureaucratic' state of the nineteenth and twentieth centuries – remains, evolves or declines. Given the argument of this book, it is easy to see why. It is 'peoples', 'nations', 'ethnicities' (and so on) that have the strongest sense of history, of continuity, of transmission from generation to generation and, therefore, of the habitual practices that these create. 'States' in their modern forms, for all their powers (and I, for one, still think them mightily formidable) do not have and cannot generate, at least by themselves, this kind of practice.[30]

The issue of ambivalence and nature and convention is also one which has a good deal of emphasis in much writing unconnected with modernity as such. The issue also highlights aspects of new technologies (genetic engineering, foetal research, etc.). It links in with risk – new technologies might easily create new risks – and also has profound implications for ethics and politics in terms of regulation and control (or, perhaps, the lack of regulation and control). Note also that, in and of themselves, these issues are ones that are recognized as significant in a way that is entirely disconnected to the modernity debate as I have discussed it here.

Finally, the issue of trust is unquestionably very important, about that Dunn is quite right. Whatever new technologies can do, and whatever problems they pose, it is clear that many of them are currently dependent upon 'experts' who must be seen to be accountable for what they do and how they do it. 'Trust' in the processes of accountability are surely central if societies are to manage these enormously complex technologies without building up huge resentments and storing up very real dangers for themselves and their futures.

I mention these considerations not because I think they are exhaustive (they are clearly not), but as an indication of some of the sorts of issues that arise out of considerations of late/post/reflexive modernity. However, as I have also pointed out, each of these issues is touched on (in different ways, to be sure) by writers, scholars and thinkers entirely unconcerned with modernity as such. The question must be asked, then, how does a consideration of modernity help us in considering these questions? and in order to answer this point, I must return to my original discussion of the tasks of political theory.

## Reprising the Tasks of Political Theory

At the end of the introductory chapter of this study, I outlined a possible way in which the consideration of modernity could, in fact, help resolve some of the problems I identified in both Anglo-American political theory and the history of political thought associated with the Cambridge School. I also referred to John Dunn's three tasks of political theory. Let me restate them here.

> Firstly, [political theory] needs to train us in ascertaining how the social, political and economic setting of our lives now is and in understanding why it is as it is; secondly, in working through for ourselves how we could coherently and justifiably wish that world to be or become; and thirdly, in judging how far, and through what actions, and at what risk, we can realistically hope to move this world as it now stands towards the way we might excusably wish it to be.[31]

In that first chapter, I suggested that illuminating as this presentation of Dunn's undoubtedly is, he himself fails to properly elucidate what these tasks require, partly because his concern is to elaborate a theory of prudence that oscillates between a strong conception (prudence as a *prerequisite* for dealing with the dilemmas of modern politics) and a weak conception (prudence as a central aspect of the *process* whereby trust – and hence political legitimacy and accountability – is sustained). Moreover, I suggested, that in part at least this problem is generated by Dunn's Lockean framework. I emphasized also the links one might draw between Dunn's account, the account of the problems of modern liberalism outlined by Richard Bellamy, and the attempt to revive and elaborate the civic republican tradition, in opposition to the 'dominant ideology' of modern Europe, that we find in the work of Quentin Skinner and some of his colleagues.

## *Risk and prudence*

The links between these three very different accounts of our modern situation crystallize, I think, around the desire to have active, responsible, citizens as a counterweight to overweening governments or political problems that dwarf the capacity of governments to deal with them.[32] In this respect, it touches quite clearly on some of the concerns that we have just seen manifested by writers such as Bauman, Connolly, Beck, Giddens and Lash. They, too, seek an active, engaged body of political agents, because only with such a body can the aporias of modernity (as Bauman might put it) be managed and lived with continually. Like Dunn, they emphasize those elements of modern society that create a problem of trust and, like them, he insists that the fundamental modern problematic is, in some sense or other, the risks that our modern societies are prone to, create and cannot escape. It is this, after all, that necessitates a theory of prudence 'adequate to the historical world in which we have to live'.[33] This point is echoed by Richard Bellamy, whose explicit acknowledgement of the stimulus his ideas have received from hard-sceptical postmoderns like Lyotard and Epicurean postmoderns like Rorty merely serves to point up the links that might be made here. For Bellamy, remember, contemporary liberalism (especially 'ethical' liberalism) is problematic because it 'flies in the face of a changing social reality' – hence his appeal to a 'political' democratic liberalism.[34]

I suggested, in the light of these arguments, that one of the problems with seeing the dilemmas of modern politics in this way, for all its power (and indeed, its prescience) is that it fails adequately to distinguish between modernity as mood and modernity as socio-cultural form and, as a result, fails to choose (for example) between different senses of prudence. I now want to pursue this argument in greater detail.

Briefly, it seems to me that the arguments that Dunn and Bellamy make are too heavily dependent on claims about the changing character of 'social reality' (Bellamy's term), without a corresponding sense of the contrasting 'moods' to which, and in which, that 'social reality' adheres. In other words, it is a recognition that there is something that is going on at the level of socio-cultural form that has real implications for the character of our politics and societies – let us call it modernity as socio-cultural form. However, Dunn and Bellamy also display a reluctance to discuss (at least overtly) what that might mean in ontological terms. As a result the account of the socio-cultural changes themselves remains curiously one dimensional.

Most importantly, however, the way the argument is allowed to rest at this point, gives us no chance of realistically performing the second of Dunn's tasks of political theory and, as a direct consequence, the third. Simply to claim that this is where prudence (on the one hand) or 'democratic liberalism' (on the other) come in will surely not do. We need to know what *kind* of prudence and under what circumstances it should operate. Equally we would need to have some way of judging in a 'democratically liberal society' when certain ways of living together or living apart were perceived to be damaging or destructive. Of course, Bellamy could justly say that this sort of decision is precisely the sort of thing that democratic liberalism is designed to decide, and it is certainly true that such a procedure would be a potentially endless one (in this respect, again, Bellamy shares a good deal with the likes of Connolly and Honig). However, even if this is granted, I (and you) would need to have ways of *making* those sorts of judgements that could properly assess the advantages and disadvantages of particular courses of action.

This is where the rearticulation of the modernity debate outlined in chapter 3 begins to become directly relevant. It has shown how necessary it is that the two senses of modernity be related to one another if we are to have a chance of even beginning to understand either. Moreover, understanding the 'social reality', the conditional aspect of modernity as socio-cultural form as I would have it, requires us trying to grasp the sense of the 'routinised', 'habitual' forms of behaviour that are, so to speak, 'givens' in the particular context as much as it requires us to examine the reflective, self-aware legitimations and justifications that ideologies and political languages will offer. In order to do this, however, I suggested that we needed to see the question of nature/convention in ways that echoed the usage of the Platonic–Aristotelean tradition, for only then would we have the resources to properly begin to answer the questions that such a procedure would inevitably raise about evaluation and judgement.

For example, in trying to understand what it might mean to have a workable conception of prudential behaviour, behaviour that can offset the risks of modern politics, we would need more than simply its 'democratization' (one of the things that Dunn puts the greatest store by). We would need to have a sense of the limits of that prudence, of when, indeed, we would need *not* to be prudent. At one level it almost seems that Dunn is making a similar mistake to Strauss (a thinker with whom in most respects, I should think, he would see himself being considerably at odds) in that he appears to be saying that we *always* need to be prudent, as Strauss seemed to be saying that philosophy *always* needed to cloak itself. Yet, surely we can only make that kind of judgement if we have a sufficient grasp not just of the 'risks' that exist but a full understanding of all the contexts, the conditions, in which those risks might occur.

This raises another point. If we are to know how to be 'prudent', we will also need to be able to weigh and assess *different* risks; we will need to know how to compare them against one another and how to go about making a judgement about which of the risks is the greater and which the lesser. For we must assume that there will be occasions when whatever we do will entail risks and, as Dunn himself has pointed out, the usual way that (Anglo-American) political theory tries to work out such an assessment (some version of economic models of reasoning) is highly restrictive in the sorts of risk it can helpfully compare.

To do such comparisons seriously over the range of issues that the modernity debate suggests will be – indeed already is – necessary; we surely require some form of understanding resembling the framework that I outlined in chapter 3. One, in other words, that is sensitive to our embeddedness in the web on which we are all nodes, to the dual character of our impulses, the deeply contextual character of our circumstances – and, therefore, our appropriate responses – and one that can at least attempt judgements of the good and the right, judgements which, as Rosen emphasized in the phrase I cited in chapter 3, made clear the intimate links between reason and the good. Inevitably, therefore, such an understanding requires as good an interpretation as we can manage of modernity – as mood and socio-cultural form and of the relations between them – for without that, our grasp of the sorts of risks and their consequences is likely to be dangerously incomplete, and our capacity to begin to make links between reason and the good fatally impoverished.

It does not really matter, of course, what such a matrix is called; 'modernity', as I also suggested earlier, is perhaps best seen as simply a shorthand term for a confluence of assumptions and conditions that is not limited to the 'modern world' in a strictly temporal sense, at least in terms of its ontological aspects. It *does* matter that the sorts of reflections engaged in by the participants in the modernity debate are awarded their due as contributions to the understanding of the matrix without which the sort of theory called for by Dunn or the kinds of institutions or policies called for by Bellamy could not, I think, be fully conceptualized let alone enacted.

## Language and history

The reconceptualization I offered in chapter 3 also offers another possible way of integrating the modernity debate into the sorts of concerns flagged by Dunn and Bellamy. I want to suggest that some participants in the modernity debate can play a much more important role in the first of Dunn's tasks of political theory than might at first seem to be the case.

The first task, of course, was to attempt to understand how the social, intellectual and political setting of our lives now is and how it became what it is. Part of this is obviously what the Cambridge School themselves seek to do (think of Skinner's work, for example). However, there are two points at which its agenda might be said to be weak and where a consideration of the modernity debate as I have discussed it here could help.

First, such a task inevitably needs to develop an investigation into the kinds of political language that the dominant modes ignore, marginalize or, indeed, seek to refute. In these languages we might find many resources available to us which can help to express the realities of our changing political situations and in ways we find more helpful than current versions of liberalism, Marxism or other similar vocabularies that have dominated the twentieth century. This indeed, is what Toulmin, for example, found so useful in the language of the literary, humanistic (and we might add largely republican) Renaissance, before it became dominated by scientific and Cartesian terminologies and strategies.

In these contexts, then, it is not difficult to see how the concerns of participants in the modernity debate and the concerns of those political theorists and historians of political thought associated with the new history of political thought might intersect. Of course, there would be many differences and many disputes (especially methodologically); this after all is the 'home ground' of the new history of political thought. Yet the task is surely sufficiently broad to require – let alone allow – a multiplicity of approaches. Such a multiplicity might itself help to deepen and fill out our perceptions of the possible exclusions or hidden assumptions of our own political vocabularies, and in doing so, however much they might be in dispute with one another, such approaches would perform a vital part of the first task of political theory as Dunn conceived it.

Moreover, a perspective which emphasized modernity in the sense that we have discussed here, might have the additional benefit of directing attention to the ways in which particular languages and vocabularies became dominant or marginalized not just in terms of the intellectual trends of the age but in terms of the relation of those trends to wider socio-cultural forms. The absence of such a focus is, I think, a weakness of the 'new history of political thought', at least as practised by the Cambridge School, irrespective of many of the more serious methodological problems raised by some of their critics.[35] In the process of paying attention to such relations it might be, of course, that the focus of some of this work would have to change, but in the end it could only strengthen the understanding of the evolution of the political languages and ideologies that is its central focus and greatest triumph.

## *Liberal/communitarian – modern/postmodern*

We can see, then, at least two ways in which the understanding of the modernity debate offered here might be advantageous to the work of those political theorists, such as Skinner and Dunn, concerned primarily with questions in the history of political thought. However, in a sense this is perhaps not surprising. As I pointed out in the introductory chapter, studies in this area are in any case becoming more involved in questions to which the modernity debate is manifestly relevant.

What, however, of those debates in mainstream Anglo-American political theory that I discussed briefly in the opening chapter? Of course, it is true that a hard-and-fast definition of Anglo-American political theory is impossible. At times, ironically resembling the modernity debate, it too seems more like a mood, a cast of mind, than any more specific methodological and normative commitment. To illustrate what I want to argue here, however, I want to return to an example discussed in the first chapter. I suggested there that the debate that has most engaged the normative focus of Anglo-American political theory in the 1980s, the so-called 'liberal–communitarian' debate, has shown increasing signs of strain. Liberals like Rawls have stolen some of their communitarian critics' clothes, and 'communitarians' like Taylor and Walzer sometimes appear to be liberals of a sort.[36]

I also pointed out, however, citing the view of Will Kymlicka, that much of this debate has effectively centred on how we should understand moral argument considered 'as an appeal to our considered convictions', and I suggested that this provides an important clue to how what I called the epistemological and political halves of the debate (quoting Cohen and Arato) might be linked together. Those halves of the debate, it will be recalled, were seen as follows. The epistemological half revolved around whether it is possible to articulate a formal, universalistic conception of justice without presupposing a substantive, historically and culturally specific concept of the good. The political half consisted of a debate over whether the concept of freedom should be best seen in terms of individual rights or in terms of a community's shared norms.[37]

We are now in the position of being able to outline how the understanding of the modernity debate offered above might help in reflecting upon these questions and might, as a result, begin reorienting the debate. To begin with, a consideration of the argument of chapter 3 suggests that moral argument cannot just be about 'our considered convictions', though it will certainly be in part about them. As I suggested before, in part this begs the question of who 'we' are (I shall return to this in a moment), but consider also that in chapter 3 I suggested that we must needs pay attention to our *unconsidered* convictions, to our habitual, unreflective, almost 'unconscious' (if that is a term you like) convictions, if we are to have much hope of comprehending 'our' – political, ethical, social – circumstances. Often, indeed, it will be in these 'convictions' that the most important aspects of a way of living will be located. Thus, from the start, we must problematize our 'considered' convictions, ask just how considered they actually are and assess the possibility of alternative (perhaps currently unforeseen, or perhaps – as Clark might suggest – currently forgotten) views or convictions.

Moreover, this process, I suggested above, must of necessity go hand in hand with discussions about what it would be good or right to do or how what is being done is wrong, or – even – evil. An appeal to 'our considered convictions' in the case of the Eichmann example that I drew from Arendt earlier would be of little use because, if the argument I made was correct, the 'considered convictions' were 'nested', so to speak, inside a socio-cultural form that had made of them something quite monstrous. Moreover, who would the 'we' be in this case? Nazis? Germans? Western Europeans? All human beings?

This brings me on to a third point. An appeal to our convictions, considered or not, would, of course, require a way of determining between convictions when such convictions clashed. This point is, of course, similar to that made in connection with risk and trust above. We would need, in other words, a theory of judgement that could help us adjudicate between such convictions.

At the end of the last chapter, I looked briefly at the work of Bauman and Connolly (for example) on ethics and evaluation. I pointed out that, despite the many differences between us, particularly at the ontological level, their concern for ambivalence, ambiguity and the aporias of modern life are ones I would share. They give powerful reinforcement to the belief that something like a weak theory of prudence (in Dunn's terms) should be an important part of the conceptual armoury of modern human beings – and it is not accidental that he develops this argument in the context of an attack on the inadequacy of more conventional 'Anglo-American' accounts of reason and judgement. Without such a conception we could not properly discuss how to choose between 'our considered convictions'; and without an understanding of our time – of modernity, in other words, in all its complexity – we could not properly understand that about which political (which of course includes ethical) judgements have to be made.

A number of scholars are aware, of course, that the liberal–communitarian debate can benefit from a consideration of the modernity debate. Seyla Benhabib, for example, has pursued a powerful set of arguments designed to link communitarian and feminist critiques of liberalism to Habermasian themes about communicative rationality and the public sphere.[38] Jean Cohen and Andrew Arato's work on civil society pursues a similar trajectory. Meanwhile Kenneth Baynes has attempted to draw links between Kant and Rawls and Habermas. This interpenetration of 'Anglo-American' debates and thinkers who are participants in the modernity debate is indeed to be welcomed. However, my argument in this book has been to suggest that the integration of these hitherto relatively disparate activities would leave neither side unchanged. Considerations of how to understand modernity must themselves be rethought and rearticulated, and it is of course a version of this that I have attempted here. However, I do not suggest it is the only possible one: I hope simply that it might encourage others to improve on the above, all too brief remarks.

Let me close here, however, with just one argument derived from the above and which has, or so I hope, relevance for the 'liberal–communitarian debate'. One of the most important areas of this debate over the last few years has been the possibility of group rights or the rights of cultures or minorities. Critics of mainstream liberals (like Charles Taylor) have main-

tained that in its presently dominant form, rights-based liberalism is hostile to the idea or possibility of specific rights being
given to groups as such. This view has been rebutted by 'liberals' like Will Kymlicka, who have argued that on the contrary
it is only within a rights-based liberalism that such groups are
likely to be given any sort of rights.

On the view I have sketched here, however, we could argue
that focusing on rights (whether individual or group) is a blind
alley. Or that, at least, it is not really a question of who
(individuals *or* groups) possesses rights: it might be better seen
as a question of the duties we – both as individuals *and* as
groups – might owe to other selves, other elements of 'the web
on which we are all nodes' and of the duties they owe to us.
Modernity, we might say (paraphrasing Connolly) is a time
whose spatial (and political) categories are undergoing rapid
change (whatever this actually implies for contemporary institutions) and which therefore requires both a prudent realization
of the dangers likely to be created by precipitate actions, and
also an acceptance of new and different ways of conceiving of
the relations within and between human communities.

The understanding of modernity that I have attempted to
outline here reminds us, I suggest, that the real guarantee of
respect and dignity is not any given institutional or legal structure (though certainly such structures are necessary), but communities which allow time and space for the working out and
the working through of those plural and conflicting parts of our
natures that we will never eradicate; the affections, loyalites
and, of course, conflicts that are inevitable (and ineradicable) in
humans. In this context we might well suggest that discussions
of 'rights' are irrevocably contextual and that it is not the case
that there can ever be a decision about what rights people
should have (or whether they should be seen as 'individual
rights' or 'group' rights) in advance of specific situations or
circumstances.

More radically, however, I suggest that neither liberals nor
communitarians (whether liberal or otherwise) will be able to
sustain such communities without recognizing the requirements
of 'forgiveness' I discussed in the last chapter. It is a moot point
whether liberal-democratic societies as currently configured can

recognize such claims. If not, they either will have to configure them differently or – as I suspect is more likely – seek for our 'moral communities' in a different kind of society altogether.

## Towards a Political Theory for Modernity

To conclude the overall argument of this book, I want finally to look at the implications of the interpretation of the modernity debate offered herein for political theory and for politics more generally. In the process, I shall reintroduce the discussion about late/post/reflexive modernity that I began earlier in this chapter, and also take up some of the issues (of risk, trust and so on) that I have just looked at. First, however, I want to recap briefly.

The overall position I have been outlining can be briefly summarized as follows. The tasks of political theory can broadly be seen in terms of the three categories that John Dunn outlines. However, to properly perform these tasks it is necess–ary to consider rather more thoroughly than Dunn does, the parameters and meanings that might be ascribed to the term 'modernity'. In looking at this term, it is necessary to under–stand the wide variety of possible uses it has and the character of the debate to which it has given rise in modern social and political theory. In doing this, however, a range of different approaches to modernity (both 'modern' and 'postmodern') become identifiable, and a number of problems either specific to certain approaches or common to virtually all, become identified.

Among the most interesting and ambiguous problems, is the treatment of the question of nature and convention offered by both moderns and postmoderns. In working through this ques–tion, a rather different way of conceptualizing the modernity debate becomes apparent; one which helps us to reconsider both modernity itself and the tasks of political theory. This reconceptualization, however, is performed through an in–terpretation of the Platonic–Aristotelean idea of understanding, and of the practical philosophy that emerges from it. The frame–work also implies, however, that the understanding of 'the

Enlightenment' which underlies a good deal of the modernity debate must be heavily qualified or revised in such a way that we cannot any longer simply read 'modern' thinkers (say, Kant) or ancient thinkers (say, Plato) in ways which allow us to be 'for' or 'against' them in the rather simplistic sense that this usage implies.

The framework adopted in the book thus suggests that we must see politics and ethics as integrally connected with one another, and indeed with questions in metaphysics and even wider areas of the human sciences, and that we must also see politics as a much more broadly based phenomenon than modern political science (and a good deal of modern political theory) is willing to concede. If we do take this view seriously, we can return to questions such as those raised by historians of political thought and contemporary Anglo-American political theorists, and find that their concerns can be aided by an understanding of modernity rather, as many seem to have supposed, hindered or blocked by such terms or such concerns.

Even if all this is true, however, can we say that there are any more general conclusions to be drawn from what, after all, could easily be seen as a particularly academic set of concerns? Of course, I do not see in that term any reason for apology. However, I should also emphasize that there are a number of wider implications of this argument that take it beyond a narrowly theoretical agenda.

To illustrate this, let me return to one of the points I made in my introductory chapter. I pointed out there[39] that Anglo-American political theory had grown up (so to speak) accounting for politics in the territorial state. Indeed, more narrowly than that, it had largely been concerned with the character, institutions and problems of the liberal-democratic territorial state. Such a concern is, of course, a very important one. Such states are not only in their own terms very interesting; they also happen to be the seed bed and experimental home of many of the most highly prized ideas and practices of modern politics, ideas and practices that retain their importance beyond the (geographically) relatively narrow terrain of Western Europe and North America. The sorts of ideas I have in mind – democracy, human rights, constitutional government, the rule of law

and so on – are widely seen today as vitally important for most
political communities.[40] Of course political science more generally has always had a concern for wider topics, but normative
political theory in the West was largely concerned with topics
(justice, rights, equality, welfare, liberty) that were seen in the
context of the modern state.

Of late, however, an increasing number of Anglo-American
political theorists have recognized that such topics today have
an inevitably international, interstate dimension. Thus there has
been a marked increase in what we might call the political
theory of international relations.[41] Much of this work is extremely ingenious and it has rightly picked up the extent to
which contemporary politics in any given state or territorial
location is affected by and affects other states or locations.[42]

Yet I submit that this 'recognition' does not go anything like
far enough. Let me refer back to the discussion of globalization,
risk and trust that took place earlier in the chapter. Leaving to
one side the terminological issues,[43] one thing that might be
agreed upon is that such issues clearly indicate that for the first
time politics is, at least potentially, truly global in its reach and
reference. Of course, this does not mean, by itself, that any
specific claims (decline of the nation state, hyperreality, etc.)
associated with these issues are true; merely that in many
respects contemporary politics – of all sorts – is increasingly
and exponentially 'world politics', in the sense that the
possible levels of interaction and interpenetration are – at least
potentially – global.

However, if the argument that I made in chapter 3 is correct,
we must, in order to understand these phenomena, understand
the modernity debate in all its complexity (as mood as well as
socio-cultural form). That, inevitably, requires us to ask questions about the ethical and normative standards with which we
evaluate and interpret our current political dispositions and
therefore also of the legitimacy and character of the distinctions
to which they have given rise. I want now to take and to discuss
one example of such questioning and such scrambling: that
questioning of the disjunction between 'domestic' and 'international' politics.

I must be clear about what I mean here, because it could be easily misinterpreted. I am not suggesting that my argument requires us to imagine that there is no distinction between 'domestic' and 'international politics'. There quite clearly is. However, it *is* meant to suggest that this distinction is itself a creation (though not perhaps exactly an intended creation) of the political languages and dispositions and socio-cultural possibilities that modernity has created and sustained. Thus, in questioning these dispositions and in elaborating these socio-cultural possibilities, we question the validity of the distinction between 'domestic' and 'international' politics, even while we recognize its current force.[44]

However, on the argument I gave in chapter 3 we cannot stop at this point either. We have to recognize that our attempts to answer the questions about the relationship between reason and the good, will inevitably reach out to include this question also. Thus, there can be no difference, in this sense, between 'political theory' and 'international political theory', since in both cases the fundamental questions are the same. The tasks of political theory, given the character of modernity, must include a consideration of types and character of political associations, the way they are united, integrated or simply linked, the manner of that union, integration or linking, the ends at which such political associations should aim and how those ends might be themselves united, and indeed, whether they should be.

Indeed, I will go so far as to suggest that at least in a certain sense, as Clark's argument suggested earlier (though the point is not specific to Clark, a version of it having been made by Kant, for example[45]), the consideration of what we might call 'world order' will be prior to considerations of more local political concern, since it is *through* such orders that other aspects of the relationship between reason and the good can be understood and evaluated.[46]

This is especially significant if the discussions of trust and risk that are shared concerns between moderns such as Dunn, Giddens, Beck and Lash,[47] and postmoderns such as Bauman, Connolly and Walker, are borne in mind. I agree with all of them that the question of trust is, indeed, a central one for

political agency and legitimacy. Yet how can 'trust' be understood except in the context of a framework that places it as one
among a number of interlocking virtues (honesty, courage,
fidelity and so on) without which trust would be impossible?
Then again, how could any of these be made manifest in political terms unless we have confidence that the 'setting', the conditions of our societies, are such as to permit and sustain such
virtues? Thinkers such as MacIntyre are thus quite right to
stress 'the virtues', but quite wrong to suppose that the virtues
*must* oppose conceptions of justice that are more at home in the
modern world. Indeed, as Onora O'Neil has recognized, one of
the greatest tasks of contemporary moral philosophy (and, of
course, as I see it, one of the greatest tasks of contemporary
political theory) is to attempt to work out ways in which
modern conceptions of justice and 'older' conceptions of the
virtues can be integrated.[48] Without this link, the risks to which
contemporary societies are prone will continue to grow and the
chances of our evolving political forms in which 'trust' can be
instantiated will continue to decline. The future of that equation
is bleak indeed.

One of the most pressing tasks as a corollary of this is a need
that by now will have become painfully apparent: that is to say,
a much more adequate account of practical reason and judgement than currently exists. Any attentive reader (if there still are
any at this stage) will have noticed that I have emphasized the
need for such an account on a wearingly high number of occasions in this book. I must say at once that I do not pretend
that I can provide one here.[49] Such an account will not be an
account just of 'rationality' – though it certainly will be that as
well; rather, it will be an account of how we can put togther
conceptions of rationality and judgement and apply them in
ways that relate more adequately to the complex features of our
ethico-political situation as I have tried to outline them here. In
the absence of such an account, we can at least stress the need
for one and emphasize that any meaningful conception of the
tasks of political theory must include it as a goal.

Even without venturing such an account here, however, we
can suggest further ways in which this interpretation of 'modernity' can help to point political theory. Let me simply suggest

two. In the first place, one of the themes that has surfaced several times throughout this book is the importance of not remaining within (usually) dichotomous oppositions that often seem to dominate contemporary thinking (modern/postmodern, domestic/international, liberal/communitarian and so on). As we saw earlier, among the most important of such dichotomies is that between the universal and the particular. Negotiating that dichotomy, such that neither gives up its rightful place to the other, seems to me to be a central 'task' for contemporary political theory (it would, I think, fall under the third of Dunn's categories).

Of course, this is hardly an original point. Of late, a number of writers have chosen it as their main focus.[50] The argument I have sought to develop here, however, has the advantage that it has at its centre the assumption that such a dichotomy offers us a false, indeed, damaging, choice. To see human beings as 'natural' in the sense deployed above means to see them as both necessarily universal and irredeemably particular. Many moderns and postmoderns would be happy with this claim, of course. I hope, however, that the present argument has shown that in the manner in which the current debate is usually couched, such happiness would be ill judged.

A second theme which my current argument points toward is the centrality for political theory of the study of regimes (types of constitution and constitutional arrangement) and the inter-relationship such regimes might have with more generally particularist patterns of behaviour (habits, national or ethnic affections and loyalties, and so on). The importance of this theme was recognized by a good deal of political science in the early twentieth century – and was, of course, absolutely central to Aristotelean political science – but it largely disappeared after World War II, though, of late, there has been the beginnings of a welcome revival.[51]

In that my argument has emphasized the Platonic–Aristotelean tradition, it is perhaps not surprising that I say this. However, it is worth bearing in mind that on the reading of modernity that I have given above such a task will now be an inevitably global one, in that at least to some degree, the 'regimes' that shape and constrain practice are now transnational as well as local, regional or national. What that realization does to the analysis of regime type is just one of the interesting questions to arise, for political science more generally, from this reading of modernity.[52] In any event, such an emphasis would clearly push political theory and political science in a rather different direction from much of what passes by that name today.

## Conclusion

I have finally reached the end of what to many will no doubt have seemed a long and extremely winding road.

It will be more than apparent from this argument that the *political* theory that I think modernity requires is a very complex and multi-faceted one. It is, moreover, hardly one that can remain corralled within the boundaries of 'political theory' as it is most often taught, practised or expected to behave, just as it cannot remain corralled within the boundaries of the state, though neither should it ignore those boundaries and what they imply, or – worse – pretend they somehow do not exist.

However, I take comfort in the fact that, as I have insisted all along, such a conception is a very old one, as the quotation from Aristotle at the head of this chapter indicates. Of course, the trick is realizing how we can relate that old conception to those parts of our situation that are genuinely new (and as the interpretation of this chapter has, I hope, suggested, there are several of those), as well as to those parts that are more familiar.

In a sense, however, understanding modernity consists precisely in the juggling of old and new, ideas and practices, moods and socio-cultural forms, thinkers and issues. A political theorist must, therefore, of necessity be something of a jack of all trades. If this is borne in mind, it seems to me that the current diversity of political theory, so bemoaned by some, is in fact one of its greatest strengths. To try to fit political theory – or if it comes to that, political science in any of its guises – into any kind of conceptual or theoretical straitjacket is not simply a rude abuse of scholarly etiquette but a procedure that will have the direst consequences for our ability to comprehend the political in all its multifarious forms. Not the least of the lessons that the modernity debate can teach political theory is that conceptual, normative and epistemological disagreements of the very first order can by their very existence and interplay help us to understand more fully the centrality of diversity to the task of understanding the part and the whole, the rational and the good.

## Notes

1 Bauman, *Intimations of Postmodernity* (London: Routledge, 1992).
2 See David Lyon, *Postmodernity* (Buckingham: Open University Press, 1994).
3 Bauman, *Intimations of Postmodernity*, p. 187.
4 See, for the most famous example of its early use, Daniel Bell, *The Coming of Post Industrial Society* (New York: Basic Books, 1973).
5 In addition to Bell, for example, sociologists such as David Lyon, Bryan Turner and Barry Smart have written on it and, perhaps most famously, Lyotard picked up the theme in *La Condition postmoderne* (Paris: Minuit, 1979). For some other treatments see Bryan Turner, 'From PostIndustrial Society to Postmodern Politics', in John Gibbins (ed.), *Contemporary Political Culture* (London: Sage, 1989); Barry Smart, *Postmodernity* (London: Routledge, 1993); and David Lyon, 'From Postindustrialism to Information Society: A New Social Transformation?', *Sociology*, 20, 4 (1986), pp. 577–88. As far as the 'supporting hypotheses' are concerned, I mean to suggest here work, often quite independent, which in some sense lends support to at least some of the theses of post-industrialism. For example, Ronald Inglehart's well-known work on post-materialism to some extent suggests that the ideational base for traditional industrialism is withering. See Ronald Inglehart, *The Silent Revolution* (Princeton: Princeton University Press, 1977); Ronald Inglehart and Scott C. Flanagen, 'Value Change in Industrial Societies', in the *American Political Science Review*, 81, 4 (1987), pp. 1289–1319.
6 See especially David Harvey, *The Condition of Postmodernity* (Oxford: Blackwell, 1989), and Scott Lash and John Urry's two books *The End of Organized Capitalism* (Cambridge: Polity Press, 1987) and *Economies of Signs and Space* (London: Sage, 1994); and Stephen Crook, Jan Paluski and Malcom Waters, *Postmodernisation: Change in Advanced Society* (London: Sage, 1992). I shall return to Lash's position in more detail in the next section.
7 For discussions of these phenomena unconnected to the modernity debate as I have discussed it here, see e.g. Hoshana Uboff, *In the Age of the Smart Machine: The Future of Work and Power* (New York: Basic Books, 1988); Sherry Turkle, *Computers and the Human Spirit* (New York: Simon and

Schuster, 1984); and for sceptical views on the prospects for artificial intelligence, Hubert Dreyfus, *What Computers Can't Do: The Limits of Artificial Intelligence* (New York: Harper and Row, 1979; 2nd edn 1993), and John Searle, *The Rediscovery of the Mind* (Cambridge: MIT Press, 1993). See also the interesting discussion in James Rosenau, *Turbulence in World Politics* (Hemel Hempstead: Harvester, 1992).

8　Lyon, *Postmodernity*, pp. 38–43.

9　In *La Condition postmoderne*.

10　See Lyon, *Postmodernity*, p. 46; Smart, *Modern Conditions, Postmodern Controversies* (London: Routledge, 1992).

11　Mark Poster, *The Mode of Information: Poststructuralism and Social Context* (Cambridge: Polity Press, 1990), p. 14. Cited in Lyon, *Postmodernity*, p. 46.

12　One to whom I shall return, in that he is especially interesting about the tasks of political theory, is Stephen K. White. See his *Political Theory and Postmodernism* (Cambridge: Cambridge University Press, 1991).

13　For discussions of the above phenomena see especially Lash and Urry, *Economies of Signs and Space*; Harvey, *The Condition of Postmodernity*; Nigel Thrift, 'Muddling Through: World Orders and Globalisation', *Professional Geographer*, 44, pp. 3–7 (1992).

14　See, for example, Baudrillard's works cited in chapter 2. See also Gianni Vattimo, *The Transparent Society* (Cambridge: Polity Press, 1992), and, especially, Paul Virilio, *Bunker archéologie* (Paris: Centre Georges Pompidou, 1975), *L'insécurité du territoire* (Paris: Galilée, 1977), *Vitesse et politique* (Paris: Galilée, 1978), *Guerre et cinéma, logistique de la Perception* (Paris: Editions de l'Etoile, 1984), *L'inertie polaire* (Paris: Christian Bourgeois, 1990).

15　For a (very small) sample, see e.g. the science fiction novels William Gibson, *Neuromancer* (New York: Ace Books, 1984); Philip K. Dick, *The Simulacra* (New York: Ace Books, 1964); the films *Blade Runner* (actually based on a Philip Dick short story) and *Blue Velvet*; and on art see Roy Boyne, 'The Art of the Body in the Discourse of Postmodernity', in *Theory, Culture and Society*, 5, nos 2–3 (June 1988).

16　Bauman, *Intimations of Postmodernity*, pp. 187–8.

17　Ibid., 196–7.

18　Taken from ibid., 196–200.

19　See White, *Political Theory and Postmodernism*, pp. 10–12.

20　It is present, for example, in William Connolly's argument at the end of *Identity/Difference: Democratic Negotiations of Political Paradox* (Ithaca: Cornell University Press, 1991), and is a theme in R. B. J. Walker, *One World, Many Worlds* (London: Lynne Reiner, 1984), and (though it is not as significant) *Inside/Outside: International Relations as Political Theory* (Cambridge: Cambridge University Press, 1992).

21　See James Der Derian, *On Diplomacy: A Genealogy of Western Estrangement* (Oxford: Blackwell, 1987); *Anti-Diplomacy: Spies, Terror, Speed and War* (Oxford: Blackwell, 1992). I shall return to the writings of Der

Derian and other writers on international politics in a postmodern mood, such as Walker, a little later on.

22 As we saw in the last chapter this is the argument of soft-sceptical postmoderns such as Mouffe, Connolly and Honig.

23 One of the best general treatments of globalization in world politics is Roland Robertson, *Globalisation: Social Theory and Global Culture* (London: Sage, 1992).

24 It is probably fair to say, at this point, that there are a number of scholars from a variety of fields who would want to dispute this point in various ways. However, I think that the disputation will really take place over the implications of these developments, not the fact of them.

25 These scholars developed their particular views independently, of course. See, for their individual presentations, Ulrich Beck, *Risikogesellschaft: Auf dem Weg in eine andere Moderne* (Frankfurt: Suhrkamp, 1986); *Gegengifte: Die organisierte Unverantwortlichkeit* (Frankfurt Suhrkamp, 1988); *Die Erfindung des Politischen* (Frankfurt: Suhrkamp, 1993). Anthony Giddens, *The Consequences of Modernity* (Cambridge: Polity, 1990); *Modernity and Self Identity* (Cambridge: Polity, 1991). Scott Lash, *Sociology of Postmodernism* (London: Routledge, 1990), and, of course, Lash and Urry, *The End of Organised Capitalism* and *Economies of Signs and Space*. However, it is also important to note that recently Beck, Giddens and Lash have co-authored a book whose express intent is to display their common concerns (though they also debate with one another). See Beck, Giddens and Lash, *Reflexive Modernization: Politics, Tradition and Aesthetics in the Modern Social Order* (Cambridge: Polity Press, 1994).

26 See Beck, Giddens and Lash, *Reflexive Modernization*, p. vi.

27 Ibid., vii.

28 Of course, how we define 'Western' in this context is another question. For simplicity, I simply take it to refer to the history of European thought over the last six or seven hundred years, though implicated in that is of course a much larger story about Eurasian and North African thought over a much longer period.

29 Here, I mean to refer to those discussions of post-colonial life and thought that have been so brilliantly chronicled by (amongst others) Homi Bhabha, Bikhu Parekh and, perhaps above all, Edward Said. See, for good discussions of the theme, the special issue of *New Formations, Post-Colonial Insecurities*, 21 (winter 1993); Homi Bhabha (ed.), *Nation and Narration* (London: Routledge, 1988); Edward Said, *Culture and Imperialism* (London: Chatto and Windus, 1993); and Benita Parry, Keith Ansell-Pearson and Judith Squires (eds), *On Edward Said* (London: Lawrence and Wishart, 1995).

30 On the rebirth of theorizing about the state see, for a (small) sample, Peter B. Evans, Dietrich Rueschemeyer and Theda Skocpol (eds), *Bringing the State Back In* (Cambridge: Cambridge University Press, 1985); John Hall, *Coercion and Consent: Essays on the Modern State* (Cambridge: Polity

Press, 1994); David Held, *Political Theory and the Modern State* (Cambridge: Polity Press, 1989); Stephen D. Krasner, *Defending the National Interest: Raw Materials Investments and US Foreign Policy* (Princeton: Princeton University Press, 1978).

For the Walzer quotation, see his *Thick and Thin: Moral Argument at Home and Abroad* (Notre Dame: University of Notre Dame Press, 1994), esp. ch. 4.

31 John Dunn, *Interpreting Political Responsibility* (Cambridge: Cambridge University Press, 1990), p. 193.

32 Skinner emphasizes this in his chapter in Mouffe (ed.), *Dimensions of Radical Democracy* (London: Verso, 1992), esp. pp. 222–3.

33 Dunn, *Rethinking Modern Political Theory* (Cambridge: Cambridge University Press, 1986).

34 An appeal which, incidentally, echoes the sorts of concerns that we have seen in Connolly, Mouffe and Honig, pointing up again the connections between some 'moderns' (as I think Bellamy would want to describe himself in this context) and some postmoderns.

35 For an argument related (though not identical to this, see e.g. John Keane, 'More Theses on the Philosophy of History', in James Tully (ed.), *Meaning and Context: Quentin Skinner and His Critics* (Cambridge: Polity Press, 1988).

36 Rawls has been accused (or commended, depending on the point of view) of adopting quasi-communitarian arguments by a number of scholars, whose tone has sometimes bordered on the hysterical. For a more balanced discussion of the changes in Rawls' outlook since the publication of *A Theory of Justice,* see Chandran Kukathas and Philip Pettit, *Rawls: A Theory of Justice and Its Critics* (Cambridge: Polity Press, 1990). For the liberal (though certainly not *procedurally* liberal) sympathies of Walzer and Taylor, see e.g. Charles Taylor and Amy Guttman (eds), *Multiculturalism and the Politics of Recognition* (Princeton: Princeton University Press, 1992): see the essays by Taylor and Walzer. Also see Charles Taylor, 'Cross Purposes: The Liberal–Communitarian Debate', in Nancy Rosenblum (ed.), *Liberalism and the Moral Life* (Cambridge: Harvard University Press, 1989).

37 See J. Cohen and A. Arato, *Civil Society and Political Theory* (Cambridge: MIT Press, 1992), p. 8.

38 See e.g. Seyla Benhabib, *Situating the Self: Gender, Community and Postmodernism in Contemporary Ethics* (Cambridge: Polity Press, 1992).

39 See above pp. 2–9, 60–7.

40 It should not be assumed, of course, that there would be *no* challenge to this. There clearly would. Equally, there would be a very wide variety of likely definitions or manifestations of these ideas and practices. However, that these ideas are widely seen as important beyond their original home is, I think, no longer in doubt, though the reasons and implications most certainly are. For discussions that emphasize both points see e.g. John Dunn (ed.), *Democracy: The Unfinished Journey* (Oxford:

Oxford University Press, 1992); R. J. Vincent, *Human Rights and International Relations* (Cambridge: Cambridge University Press, 1986); Hedley Bull and Adam Watson (eds), *The Expansion of International Society* (Oxford: Clarendon Press, 1984).

41 To give just a very short list of some of the more prominent Anglo-American political theorists to write on these topics, see Michael Walzer, *Just and Unjust Wars* (Harmondsworth: Penguin, 1977; 2nd edn 1992); Charles Beitz, *Political Theory and International Relations* (Princeton: Princeton University Press, 1979); Brian Barry, *Liberty and Justice: Essays in Political Theory, vol. 2* (Oxford: Clarendon Press, 1991) (see the essays, 'Can States be Moral?', 'Humanity and Justice in Global Perspective', 'Justice as Reciprocity' and 'The Ethics of Resource Depletion'); Onora O'Neill, 'Transnational Justice', in David Held (ed.), *Political Theory Today* (Cambridge: Polity Press, 1991); John Rawls, 'On the Law of Peoples', in Susan Hurley and Michael Shute (eds), *Human Rights* (Oxford: Oxford University Press, 1994).

42 I should add, I think, that the interest in 'international ethics' (as it is often called among Anglo-American political theorists) has been met by an increasing interest in normative questions by scholars interested in international relations. Of course, such an interest was prominent in some of the most influential and important scholars of international relations in the twentieth century (such as Hans Morgenthau), and the fact that international relations scholars have only just rediscovered it is no cause for congratulation on their part. However, that having been said, much very interesting work is being done by these scholars – including a good deal that goes considerably further along the road I recommend than most Anglo-American political theorists have so far been prepared to travel. I shall come back to this in a moment. For excellent discussions of the rebirth of interest in ethical questions from the 'international relations side', as it were (not, as we shall see, a distinction I really accept), see Chris Brown, *International Relations Theory: New Normative Approaches* (Hemel Hempstead: Harvester, 1992); Terry Nardin, *Law, Morality and the Relations of States* (Princeton: Princeton University Press, 1983); Terry Nardin and David Mapel (eds), *Traditions of International Ethics* (Cambridge: Cambridge University Press, 1992); and Steve Smith, 'The Forty Year Detour: The Resurgence of Normative Theory in International Relations', in *Millennium: Journal of International Studies* 21, no. 3 (winter 1992).

43 i.e. whether or not such issues are indicative of late or post- or reflexive 'modernity'.

44 This is a point that will be familiar to some, in that it is close to arguments made by Connolly in *Identity/Difference* and has been discussed in differing ways by international relations scholars influenced on the one hand by Habermasian arguments and on the other by postmodern ones. As an example of the former, see Mark Hoffman, 'Critical Theory and the Interparadigm Debate', *Millennium: Journal of International Studies*, 16,

no. 3 (winter 1987); Andrew Linklater, *Men and Citizens in the Theory of International Relations* (London: Macmillan, 1982; 2nd edn, 1990). As an example of the latter see Walker, *Inside/Outside: International Relations as Political Theory*. While my own interpretation of the question is rather different from both, we all end up in more or less the same place, and I am happy to acknowledge the stimulus I have received both from their writings and their conversation.

45  I am referring of course to the celebrated passage in *Zum Ewigen Freiden*, where Kant refers to the problem of international right as being in a certain sense prior to that of domestic right.

46  This, therefore, is the theme of my next book, *Duties Beyond Orders* (London: Routledge, 1995, forthcoming).

47  These concerns have been picked up by some others. See e.g. Gwyn Prins, *Notes Towards a Definition of Global Security* (Cambridge: Global Security Programme, 1994); Philip Allot, *Eunomia* (Oxford: Clarendon Press, 1992); Ken Booth, 'Security in Anarchy: Utopian Realism in Theory and Practice', *International Affairs*, 67, no. 3 (July 1991).

48  See Onora O'Neill, *Justice and the Virtues* (Cambridge: Cambridge University Press, forthcoming). See also, for a different view, though one close in other respects to both my argument here and those of MacIntyre, Rosen and Habermas, *A Community of Character: Towards a Constructive Christian Social Ethic* (Indiana: University of Notre Dame Press, 1981).

49  Needless to say, I hope to do so in the not too distant future. A preliminary account can be found in N. J. Rengger, 'Thucydides, Injustice and Judging the Good Regime', in *Polis: the Journal of the Society of Greek Political Thought*, 14, no. 1 (spring 1996), forthcoming; Rengger, 'The Cave of Knowledge: Practical Reason and the Public Sphere in Republic 514a–540c', in Maurizio Passerein D'Entreves and Ursula Vogel (eds), *The Public/Private Debate in Modern Political Theory* (forthcoming); Rengger, 'Political Judgement and the Good in Platonic–Aristotelean Thought', paper to the Political Thought Conference, Durham, July 1995.

50  See among a number of interesting recent discussions, Tzvetan Todorov, *On Human Diversity: Nationalism, Racism and Exoticism in French Thought* (Cambridge: Harvard University Press, 1993). It is also a central aspect of Michael Walzer and Charles Taylor's work, of course, and it is becoming increasingly central to questions of international political theory.

51  See e.g. Stephen L. Elkin and Karol Edward Soltan (eds), *A New Constitutionalism: Designing Political Institutions for a Good Society* (Chicago: University of Chicago Press, 1993). It has also, of course, been a concern of the students and allies of Leo Strauss. See e.g. Harvey C. Mansfield, *Taming the Prince: The Ambivalence of Modern Executive Power* (Baltimore: Johns Hopkins University Press, 1989). While I do not always agree with the way in which they have done it (and certainly not with the conclusions they appear to have reached), they should be applauded for having emphasized this perspective when others allowed it to fall away;

charmed, no doubt, by the siren voices of behaviouralism and other seducers.

52 I am trying to elaborate this in some current work; see 'Regime and Regimes in Political Theory and World Politics', paper to the Seminar in World Politics and Security at the University of Southern California, April 1995.

# SELECT BIBLIOGRAPHY

In what follows I have listed only those books and articles that I have found most useful in developing my argument. Other books, on which I have drawn for particular sections of the argument, are, of course, mentioned in the notes at the relevant points in individual chapters. Where, as for example with Plato and Aristotle, I have discussed classical authors, I have listed the copy of the text I have used for purposes of translation as well as those extant English translations that I consulted. Translations in the text are usually my own, except where otherwise noted. For works that are widely cited in their English versions (for example, Lyotard's *La Condition postmoderne*) I have quoted from the translations, adapting them only occasionally.

Adorno, Theodor and Horkheimer, Max, *Dialektik der Aufklarung* (Frankfurt: Suhrkamp Verlag, 1986 [1947]).

Adorno, Theodor, *Negativ Dialektik* (Frankfurt: Suhrkamp Verlag, 1966).

Adorno, Theodor, *Zur Metaphysik der Erkenntnistheorie* (Frankfurt: Suhrkamp Verlag, 1971).

Apel, Karl-Otto, *Diskurs und Verantwortung* (Frankfurt: Suhrkamp Verlag, 1988).

Arendt, Hannah, *Eichmann in Jerusalem: A Report on the Banality of Evil* (New York: The Viking Press, 1965).

Arendt, Hannah, *Lectures on Kant's Political Philosophy*, ed. Ronald Beiner (Chicago: University of Chicago Press, 1982).

Arendt, Hannah, *The Human Condition* (Chicago: University of Chicago Press, 1958).

Arendt, Hannah, *The Life of the Mind* (New York: Harcourt Brace Janovitch, 1978), 2 vols.

Arendt, Hannah, *The Origins of Totalitarianism* (New York: Harcourt Brace, 1966 [1951]).

Aristotle, *Nicomachean Ethics*, Greek text in the version edited by Franciscus Susemihl (Leipzig: B. G. Teubner, 1903). Trans. J. A. K. Thomson (Harmondsworth: Penguin, 1953).

Aristotle, *The Politics*, Greek text in the version edited by Alois Dreizehnter, *Studies in Testimonia Antiqua* VII (Munich: Wilhelm Fink Verlag, 1970). Trans. Carnes Lord (Chicago: University of Chicago Press, 1984) and trans. Ernest Barker (Oxford: Clarendon Press, 1968).

Barry, Brian, *Democracy and Power: Essays in Political Theory 1* (Oxford: Clarendon Press, 1991).

Barry, Brian, *Liberty and Justice: Essays in Political Theory 2* (Oxford: Clarendon Press, 1991).

Baudrillard, Jean, *Les Stratégies fatales* (Paris: Bernard Grasset, 1983).

Bauman, Zygmunt, *Modernity and the Holocaust* (Cambridge: Polity Press, 1989).

Bauman, Zygmunt, *Intimations of Postmodernity* (London: Routledge, 1992).

Bauman, Zygmunt, *Postmodern Ethics* (Oxford: Blackwell, 1993).

Baynes, Kenneth, *The Normative Grounds of Social Criticism: Kant, Rawls, Habermas* (New York: State University of New York Press, 1992).

Beck, Ulrich, *Die Erfindung des Politischen* (Frankfurt: Suhrkamp Verlag, 1993).

Beck, Ulrich, Giddens, Anthony and Lash, Scott, *Reflexive Modernization: Politics, Tradition and Aesthetics in the Modern Social Order* (Cambridge: Polity Press, 1994).

Beck, Ulrich, *Risikogesellschaft: Auf dem Weg in eine andere Moderne* (Frankfurt: Suhrkamp Verlag, 1986).

Bell, Daniel, *The Coming of Post Industrial Society* (New York: Basic Books, 1973).

Bellamy, Richard, *Liberalism and Modern Society* (Cambridge: Polity Press, 1992).

Benhabib, Seyla, *Situating the Self: Gender, Community and Postmodernism in Contemporary Ethics* (Cambridge: Polity Press, 1992).

Benhabib, Seyla and Dallmayr, Fred (eds), *The Communicative Ethics Controversy* (Cambridge: MIT Press, 1980).

Bennington, Geoffery, *Legislations: The Politics of Deconstruction* (London: Verso, 1994).

Berman, Marshal, *All that is Solid Melts into Air* (New York: Basic Books, 1982).

Bernstein, Richard (ed.), *Habermas and Modernity* (Cambridge: Polity Press, 1985).

Bernstein, Richard, *Philosophical Profiles* (Cambridge: Polity Press, 1986).

Bernstein, Richard, *The New Constellation: The Ethical-Political Horizons of Modernity and Postmodernity* (Cambridge: Polity Press, 1991).

Bloom, Allan, *The Closing of The American Mind* (Harmondsworth: Penguin, 1987).

Bloom, Allan, *Giants and Dwarfs: Essays 1960–90* (New York: Simon and Schuster, 1990).

Blumenberg, Hans, *Die Legitimät der Neuzeit (erweiterte und uberarbeitete neuausgabe)* (Frankfurt: Suhrkamp Verlag, 1966). Trans. Robert M. Wallace, *The Legitimacy of the Modern Age* (Cambridge: MIT Press, 1983).

Boyne, Roy and Rattansi, Ali (eds), *Postmodernism and Society* (London: Macmillan, 1990).

Bronner, Stephen Eric, *Of Critical Theory and Its Theorists* (Oxford: Blackwell, 1994).

Brown, Chris, *International Relations Theory: New Normative Approaches* (Hemel Hempstead: Harvester, 1992).

Brunner, Otto, Conze, Werner and Koselleck, Reinhart, (eds), *Geschichtliche Grundbegriffe: Historisches lexikon zur politische-sozialen Sprache in Deutschland* (Stuttgart: Klett-Cotta, 1972).

Burnyeat, Miles, 'Sphinx Without a Riddle', in the *New York Review of Books*, 32 (20 May 1985), 30–6.

Calhoun, Craig (ed.), *Habermas on the Public Sphere* (Cambridge: MIT Press, 1989).

Camic, C., 'The Matter of Habit', in the *American Journal of Sociology*, 91 (1986), 1039–87.

Canovan, Margaret, *Hannah Arendt* (Cambridge: Cambridge University Press, 1993).

Caputo, John, *Against Ethics* (Indiana: Indiana University Press, 1992).

Cassirer, Ernst, *Die Philosophie der Aufklärung* (Tübingen: JCB Mohr, 1932).

Clark, Stephen R. L., *Civil Peace and Sacred Order* (Oxford: Clarendon Press, 1989).

Clark, Stephen R. L., *A Parliament of Souls* (Oxford: Clarendon Press, 1990).

Clark, Stephen R. L., *God's World and the Great Awakening* (Oxford: Clarendon Press, 1991).

Cohen, Jean and Arato, Andrew, *Civil Society and Political Theory* (Cambridge: MIT Press, 1992).

Coleman, Janet, *Ancient and Medieval Memories* (Cambridge: Cambridge University Press, 1992).

Connolly, William E., *Political Theory and Modernity* (Oxford: Blackwell, 1984).

Connolly, William E., *Identity/Difference: Democratic Negotiations of Political Paradox* (Ithaca: Cornell University Press, 1992).

Connolly, William E., 'The Post-Nietzschean Ethics of Michel Foucault', in *Political Theory*, 21, no. 3 (1993), pp. 365–90.

Connolly, William E., *The Augustinian Imperative* (London: Sage, 1993).

Crook, Stephen, Paluski, Jan and Waters, Malcom, *Postmodernisation: Change in Advanced Society* (London: Sage, 1992).

Dallmayr, Fred, *Lifeworld, Modernity and Critique: Paths Between Heidegger and the Frankfurt School* (Cambridge: Polity Press, 1991).

D'Entreves, Maurizio Passerein, *The Political Philosophy of Hannah Arendt* (London: Routledge, 1993).

Der Derian, James, *On Diplomacy: A Genealogy of Western Estrangement* (Oxford: Blackwell, 1987).

Der Derian, James and Shapiro, Michael (eds), *International/Intertextual Relations: Postmodern Readings of World Politics* (Lexington, Mass.: Lexington Books, 1989).

Der Derian, James, *Anti-Diplomacy: Spies, Terror, Speed and War* (Oxford: Blackwell, 1992).

Derrida, Jacques, *De la grammatologie* (Paris: Minuit, 1967).

Diels, H. and Kranz, W., *Die Fragmente der Vorsokratiker*, 6th edn (Berlin: Suhrkamp Verlag, 1952).

Drury, Shadia, *The Political Ideas of Leo Strauss* (London: Macmillan, 1988).

Dunn, *Political Obligation in its Historical Context* (Cambridge: Cambridge University Press, 1980).

Dunn, John, *Rethinking Modern Political Theory* (Cambridge: Cambridge University Press, 1985).

Dunn, John (ed.), *The Economic Limits to Modern Politics* (Cambridge: Cambridge University Press, 1990).

Dunn, John, *Interpreting Political Responsibility* (Cambridge: Cambridge University Press, 1990).

Dunn, John, *Western Political Theory in the Face of the Future* (Cambridge: Cambridge University Press, 1979; 2nd edn, 1993).

Emberly, Peter and Cooper, Barry (eds), *Faith and Political Philosophy: The Correspondence between Leo Strauss and Eric Voeglin 1934–64* (Pennsylvania: Pennsylvania University Press, 1993).

Evans, Peter B., Ruschemeyer, Dietrich and Skocpol, Theda (eds), *Bringing the State Back In* (Cambridge: Cambridge University Press, 1985).

Farias, Victor, *Heidegger et le nazisme* (Paris: Legraffe, 1988).

Ferry, Luc, *Philosophie politique 1. Le droit: la nouvelle querelle des Anciens et des Modernes* (Paris: Presses Universitaires de France, 1984). Trans. Franklin Philp, *Political Philosophy 1. Rights: The New Quarrel Between the Ancients and the Moderns* (Chicago: University of Chicago Press, 1990).

Findlay, John, *The Written and Unwritten Doctrines of Plato* (London: Routledge and Kegan Paul, 1974).

Fish, Stanley, *Doing What Comes Naturally* (Oxford: Oxford University Press, 1989).

Foucault, Michel, *The Order of Things* (London: Tavistock, 1970).

Foucault, Michel, *Power/Knowledge* (New York: Pantheon, 1980).

Foucault, Michel, *The Foucault Reader*, ed. Paul Rabinow (Harmondsworth: Penguin, 1984).

Gadamer, Hans-Georg, *Dialogue and Dialectic: Eight Hermeneutical Studies on Plato*, trans. P. Christopher Smith (New Haven: Yale University Press, 1980).

Gadamer, Hans-Georg, *Reason in the Age of Science*, trans. Frederick G. Lawrence (Cambridge: MIT Press, 1981).

Gadamer, Hans-Georg, *The Idea of the Good in Platonic-Aristotelean Philosophy*, trans. P. Christopher Smith (New Haven: Yale University Press, 1986).

Gadamer, Hans-Georg, *Plato's Dialectical Ethics* (New Haven: Yale University Press, 1989).

Gaiser, Kurt, 'Plato's Enigmatic Lecture on the Good', *Phronesis*, 25 (1980), 5–37.

Gay, Peter, *The Enlightenment: An Interpretation*, 2 vols (New York: Wildwood House, 1970).

Geuss, Raymond, *The Idea of a Critical Theory* (Cambridge: Cambridge University Press, 1978).

Giddens, Anthony, *The Consequences of Modernity* (Cambridge: Polity Press, 1990).

Griswold, Charles (ed.), *Platonic Writings, Platonic Readings* (London: Routledge, 1988).

Habermas, Jürgen, *Strukturwandel der Öffentlichkeit: Untersuchungen zu einer Kategorie der bürgerlichen Gesellschaft* (Berlin: Luchterhand, 1962).

Habermas, Jürgen, *Knowledge and Human Interests* (Boston: Beacon Press, 1971).

Habermas, Jürgen, *Der philosophische Diskurs der Moderne: Zwölf Vorlesungen* (Frankfurt: Suhrkamp Verlag, 1985).

Habermas, Jürgen, *Erlauterungen zur Diskursethik* (Frankfurt: Suhrkamp Verlag, 1988).

Habermas, Jürgen, *Theorie des kommunikativen Handelns* (Frankfurt: Suhrkamp Verlag, 1981), 2 vols. Trans. Thomas McCarthy, *The Theory of Communicative Action*, 2 vols (Cambridge: Polity Press, 1989).

Habermas, Jürgen, *Faktizität und Geltung* (Frankfurt: Suhrkamp Verlag, 1992).

Hansen, Philip, *Arendt: Politics, History, Citizenship* (Cambridge: Polity Press, 1993).

Harvey, David, *The Condition of Postmodernity* (Oxford: Blackwell, 1989).

Heidegger, Martin, *Vorträge und Aufsätze* (Pfullingen: Neske, 1967).

Held, David, *Introduction to Critical Theory: Horkheimer to Habermas* (Cambridge: Polity Press, 1980).

Held, David (ed.), *Political Theory Today* (Cambridge: Polity Press, 1991).

Holmes, Stephen, *The Anatomy of Anti-Liberalism* (Cambridge: Harvard University Press, 1993).

Honig, Bonnie, *Political Theory and the Displacement of Politics* (Ithaca: Cornell University Press, 1993).

Huyssens, A., 'Mapping the Postmodern', in *New German Critique*, 33 (1984), 50–2.

Jameson, Fredric, *Postmodernism, or, The Cultural Logic of Late Capitalism* (London: Verso, 1991).

Jencks, Charles, *What is Postmodernism?* (London: Academy Editions, 1986).

Joas, Hans and Honneth, Axel, *Soziales Handeln und menschliche Natur* (Frankfurt: Campus Verlag GmbH, 1980).

Kennington, Richard, 'Strauss' Natural Right and History', in *The Review of Metaphysics*, 25 (1974).

Kramer, Hans Joachim, *Plato and The Foundations of Metaphysics*, trans. John Caton (New York: State University of New York Press, 1990).

Kymlicka, Will, *Contemporary Political Philosophy: An Introduction* (Oxford: Oxford University Press, 1990).

Lash, Scott, *Sociology of Postmodernism* (London: Routledge, 1990).

Lash, Scott and Urry, John, *The End of Organised Capitalism* (Madison: University of Wisconsin Press, 1987).

Lash, Scott and Urry, John, *Economies of Signs and Space* (London: Sage, 1994).

Lipovetsky, Gilles, *Le Crépuscule du devoir* (Paris: Gallimard, 1992).

Löwith, Karl, *Meaning in History* (Chicago: University of Chicago Press, 1949).

Lyon, David, *Postmodernity* (Buckingham: Open University Press, 1994).

Lyotard, Jean-François, *La Condition postmoderne* (Paris: Minuit, 1979). Trans. Geoffery Bennington, *The Postmodern Condition: A Report on Knowledge* (Manchester: Manchester University Press, 1984).

Lyotard, Jean-François, *Driftworks* (New York: Semiotext(e), 1982).

Lyotard, Jean-François, *Le Postmoderne expliqué aux enfants* (Paris: Galilée, 1986).

Lyotard, Jean-François, and Thébaud, J.-L., *Au Juste* (Paris: Christian Bourgeois, 1979).

MacIntyre, Alisdair, *After Virtue* (London: Duckworth, 1981; 2nd edn, 1987).

MacIntyre, Alisdair, *Whose Justice? Which Rationality?* (London: Duckworth, 1988).

MacIntyre, Alisdair, *Three Rival Versions of Moral Inquiry* (London: Duckworth, 1990).

Masters, Roger, *The Nature of Politics* (New Haven: Yale University Press, 1989).

McCarthy, Thomas, *Ideals and Illusions: On Reconstruction and Deconstruction in Contemporary Critical Theory* (Cambridge: MIT Press, 1993).

Mendus, Susan and Horton, John, *After MacIntyre: Critical Perspectives on the Work of Alisdair MacIntyre* (Cambridge: Polity Press, 1994).

Mestrovic, Stjepan, *The Barbarian Temperament: Towards a Postmodern Critical Theory* (London: Routledge, 1993).

Milbank, John, *Theology and Social Theory: Beyond Secular Reason* (Oxford: Blackwell, 1992).

Miller, David, 'The Resurgence of Political Theory', in *Political Studies*, 38, no. 3 (Sept. 1990).

Morchen, Hermann, *Adorno und Heidegger: Untersuchung einer philosophischen kommunikationsverweigerung* (Stuttgart: Klett-Cotta, 1981).

Mouffe, Chantal, *Rethinking the Political* (London: Verso, 1992).

Mouffe, Chantal (ed.), *Dimensions of Radical Democracy* (London: Verso, 1992).

Mulhall, Stephen and Swift, Adam, *Liberals and Communitarians* (Oxford: Blackwell, 1992).

O'Neill, Onora, 'Transnational Justice', in D. Held (ed.), *Political Theory Today* (Cambridge: Polity, 1991).

Pippen, Robert B., 'The Modern World of Leo Strauss', in *Political Theory*, 20, no. 3 (Aug. 1992), 448–72.

Plato, *The Gorgias*, Greek text in E. R. Dodds edn for Oxford University Press, 1959. Trans. Walter Hamilton (Harmondsworth: Penguin, 1960).

Plato, *The Laws*, trans. Thomas Pangle (New York: Basic Books, 1980).

Plato, *The Republic*. Greek text in vol. IV of the Oxford Classical texts Plato series, ed. J. Burnet (Oxford: Clarendon Press, 1962). Trans. Allan Bloom (New York: Basic Books, 1968; 2nd edn, 1989).

Pocock, J. G. A., *Politics, Language and Time* (Chicago: University of Chicago Press, 1971).

Poster, Mark, *The Mode of Information: Poststructuralism and Social Context* (Cambridge: Polity Press, 1990).

Poster, Mark (ed.), *Jean Baudrillard: Selected Writings* (Cambridge: Polity Press, 1988).

Press, Gerald A. (ed.), *Plato's Dialogues: New Studies and Interpretations* (Maryland: Rowan and Littlefield, 1993).

Rawls, John, *A Theory of Justice* (Oxford: Oxford University Press, 1972).

Rengger, N. J., *Reason, Scepticism and Politics: Theory and Practice in the Enlightenment's Politics* (unpublished Ph.D. dissertation, University of Durham, 1987).

Rengger, N. J., 'No Time Like The Present: Postmodernism and Political Theory', in *Political Studies*, 40, no. 3 (Sept. 1992).

Rengger, N. J., 'Thucydides, Injustice and Judging the Good Regime', *Polis: Journal of the Society for Greek Political Thought*, 14, no. 1, spring 1996.

Rengger, N. J., *Duties Beyond Orders* (London: Routledge, 1996).

Robertson, Roland, *Globalisation: Social Theory and Global Culture* (London: Sage, 1992).

Rorty, Richard, *Philosophy and the Mirror of Nature* (Oxford: Blackwell, 1980).

Rorty, Richard, *The Consequences of Pragmatism* (Minneapolis: University of Minnesota Press, 1982).

Rorty, Richard, *Contingency, Irony and Solidarity* (Cambridge: Cambridge University Press, 1989).

Rorty, Richard, *Objectivity, Truth and Relativism: Collected Philosophical Papers 1* (Cambridge: Cambridge University Press, 1991).

Rorty, Richard, *Essays on Heidegger and Others: Collected Philosophical Papers 2* (Cambridge: Cambridge University Press, 1991).

Rorty, Richard, 'Human Rights, Rationality and Sentimentality', in Stephen Shute and Susan Hurley (eds), *On Human Rights* (New York: Basic Books, 1993).

Rosen, Stanley, *Plato's Sophist: The Drama of Original and Image* (New Haven: Yale University Press, 1983).

Rosen, Stanley, *Hermeneutics as Politics* (Oxford: Oxford University Press, 1987).

Rosen, Stanley, *The Ancients and the Moderns: Rethinking Modernity* (New Haven: Yale University Press, 1989).

Rosen, Stanley, *The Question of Being: A Reversal of Heidegger* (New Haven: Yale University Press, 1992).

Rosenau, Pauline, *Postmodernism and the Social Sciences: Insights, Inroads and Intrusions* (Princeton: Princeton University Press, 1991).

Rosenblum, Nancy (ed.), *Liberalism and the Moral Life* (Cambridge: Harvard University Press, 1989).

Ryan, Michael, 'Postmodern Politics', in *Theory, Culture and Society*, 5, nos 2–3 (June 1988).

Said, Edward, *Culture and Imperialism* (London: Chatto and Windus, 1993).

Shklar, Judith, *Ordinary Vices* (Cambridge: Harvard University Press, 1986).

Shklar, Judith, *Faces of Injustice* (New Haven: Yale University Press, 1990).

Sinclair, T. A., *A History of Greek Political Thought* (London: Routledge and Kegan Paul, 1951).

Skinner, Quentin, *The Foundations of Modern Political Thought*, 2 vols (Cambridge: Cambridge University Press, 1978).

Smart, Barry, *Modern Conditions, Postmodern Controversies* (London: Routledge, 1992).

Smart, Barry, *Postmodernity* (London: Routledge, 1993).

Smith, Bruce James, *Politics and Remembrance: Republican Themes in Machiavelli, Burke and Tocqueville* (Princeton: Princeton University Press, 1985).

Squires, Judith (ed.), *Principled Positions: Postmodernism and the Rediscovery of Value* (London: Lawrence and Wishart, 1993).

Stearns, William and Chaloupka, William (eds), *Jean Baudrillard: The Disappearence of Art and Politics* (London: Macmillan, 1992).

Strauss, Leo, *Natural Right and History* (Chicago: University of Chicago Press, 1950).

Strauss, Leo, *Persecution and the Art of Writing* (Glencoe, Ill.: The Free Press, 1952).

Strauss, Leo, *What is Political Philosophy?* (Chicago: University of Chicago Press, 1959).

Strauss, Leo, *The City and Man* (Chicago: Chicago University Press, 1963).

Strauss, Leo, *Political Philosophy: Six Essays by Leo Strauss*, ed. Hilail Gildin (New York: Bobbs-Merill, 1975).

Strauss, Leo, *Studies in Platonic Political Philosophy* (Chicago: University of Chicago Press, 1983).

Strauss, Leo, *Liberalism, Ancient and Modern* (Ithaca: Cornell University Press, 1989 [1968]).

Strauss, Leo, *The Rebirth of Classical Political Rationalism*, ed. Thomas Pangle (Chicago: University of Chicago Press, 1989).

Strauss, Leo, *On Tyranny: Including the Strauss–Kojève Correspondence*, eds Victor Gourevitch and Michael S. Roth (New York: The Free Press, 1991).

Taylor, Charles, *Philosophy and the Human Sciences* (Cambridge: Cambridge University Press, 1985).

Taylor, Charles, *Sources of the Self* (Cambridge: Cambridge University Press, 1989).

Taylor, Charles and Guttman, Amy (eds), *Multi-Culturalism and the Politics of Recognition* (Princeton: Princeton University Press, 1992).

Toulmin, Stephen, *Cosmopolis: The Hidden Agenda of Modernity* (Chicago: University of Chicago Press, 1990).

Tully, James (ed.), *Meaning and Context: Quentin Skinner and his Critics* (Cambridge: Polity Press, 1989).

Vattimo, Gianni, *The Transparent Society* (Cambridge: Polity Press, 1992).

Virilio, Paul, *Bunker archéologie* (Paris: Centre Georges Pompidou, 1975).

Virilio, Paul, *L'insécurité du térritoire* (Paris: Galilée, 1977).

Virilio, Paul, *Vitesse et politique* (Paris: Galilée, 1978).

Virilio, Paul, *L'inertie polaire* (Paris: Christian Bourgeois, 1990).

Walker, R. B. J., *Inside/Outside: International Relations as Political Theory* (Cambridge: Cambridge University Press, 1992).

Waller, W. T., 'The Concept of Habit in Economic Analysis', *Journal of Economic Issues*, 22 (1988), 113–26.

Walzer, Michael, *Spheres of Justice* (Oxford: Blackwell, 1983).

Warnke, Georgia, *Gadamer: Hermeneutics, Tradition and Reason* (Cambridge: Polity Press, 1987).

White, Stephen K., *Political Theory and Postmodernism* (Cambridge: Cambridge University Press, 1991).

Wiggershaus, Rolf, *The Frankfurt School: Its History, Theories and Political Significance* (Cambridge: Polity Press, 1993 [German edn, 1986]).

Wolin, Sheldon, *Politics and Vision: Continuity and Change in Western Political Thought* (London: George Allen and Unwin, 1966).

# INDEX

Ackerman, Bruce, liberal
  neutrality 5
Adorno, Theodor
  Habermas's criticism of 100
  two senses of modernity 43
advocacy, modernity debate
  109, 111–12, 115
Anglo-American political theory
  Dunn's analysis 14–15,
    18–20, 24–5, 27–8, 29,
    213
  equality a core value of 30
  fall and rise of 2–9, 69–70,
    221–2
  liberal–communitarian
    debate: ontological and
    advocacy levels 5, 6;
    rebirth of political theory
    and 4–8, 29–30; tasks of
    political theory 216–20
  Toulmin and MacIntyre's
    modernity for, implications
    of 54–5
Arato, Andrew, liberal–
  communitarian debate 4–5,
    7, 216–17, 218
Arendt, Hannah
  evil 177–8, 217
  memory 152
Aristotle

habits 148–51, 155, 156
  naturalism 136, 137, 145
  or Nietzsche, MacIntyre's
    Enlightenment project 46
  political science 133
Ashley, Richard
  postmodern scepticism 88
  poststructuralism 85
Augustine
  evil of suffering 88–9
  first overcoming of
    Gnosticism 58

Barry, Brian, rebirth of political
  theory 3, 9–10
Baudrillard, Jean 86, 87–8, 111
  globalization 208
  hyperreality 87, 166
Bauman, Zygmunt, postmodern
  soft-scepticism 179–82,
    183, 200, 203, 204–5,
    217–18
Baynes, Kenneth, liberal–
  communitarian debate 218
Beck, Ulrich
  the complex world 21
  reflexive modernization
    206–7
Bellamy, Richard, liberalism 6,
    26–8, 210, 211–12

Benhabib, Seyla, liberal–
communitarian debate 218
Benjamin, Walter, two senses of
modernity 43
Bennington, Geoffrey, 'debates'
77
Berman, Marshall, modernism
93
Bernstein, Richard
ethico-political philosophy
44, 103–4, 107, 134–5,
137, 144, 172–3
on MacIntyre and the
Enlightenment 155–6
modernity as mood 41, 43–4
Bhabha, Homi 88
Bloom, Allan
critique of Rawls 27–8
on Strauss's esotericism 143
Blumenberg, Hans, modernity
55–60
evil and Evil 74 n. 51, 112,
176
Strauss's ideas, integration of
64–7
Bohman, James, rational choice
147
Booth, Ken, utopian realism and
prudence 19, 21

Cambridge School
modernity debate and 214–15
new history of political
thought 10–11
Toulmin and MacIntyre's
modernity and 55
see also Dunn, John; Skinner,
Quentin
Cassirer, Ernst, reason 160
Christianity
Löwith's views on
eschatological schemes of

56, 57
second overcoming of
Gnosticism 57–60
city, relationship with
philosophy 138–9, 142,
172
Clark, Stephen R. L., nature and
political theory 163–73,
223
classical thought, ethico-
political philosophy and
130–1
Bernstein's arguments 44,
107, 134–5
divine madness 162–3,
169–73
habits 148–51, 171
naturalism 135–7
Strauss's arguments 132–4,
136–44, 169–70, 172
Cohen, Jean, liberal–
communitarian debate 4–5,
7, 216–17, 218
communitarianism see liberal–
communitarian debate
conditionality, in two senses of
modernity 111–12, 115
Connolly, William
on Blumenberg's view of
modernity 55
evil 88–9, 112, 176
on Foucault 101
globalization 208
postmodern soft-scepticism
88–9, 179, 181, 182, 183,
217–18
senses of modernity 40–1, 42
contractarianism, Locke and
Dunn 17–18
convention, nature and see
nature, ethico-political
philosophy

cosmopolis, in Toulmin's
'hidden agenda' of
modernity 51–2
critical theory
postmodern, Mestrovic
157–61
two senses of modernity 43

democratic liberalism 6, 211,
212
Der Derian, James, postmodern
soft-scepticism 88, 205
Descartes, René, Toulmin's
'hidden agenda' of
modernity and 49, 52
desire, habit and 158, 161
divine madness, political theory
162–73
Dunn, John, tasks of political
theory 13–28, 29, 69–70,
210, 211–15
Durkheim, Emile, Mestrovic's
analysis of cultural habits
157, 158
Dworkin, R., liberal neutrality 5

Eichmann, K. Adolf, 'evil'
explored 177–8, 217
emotivism 46
Enlightenment
Clark's liberal modernist
dogmas and 164
MacIntyre's Enlightenment
project 45–8, 108, 155–6
Mestrovic's hostility to
158–61
postmodern rejection of 82,
83, 90, 92: Habermas's
reassertion of rationality
94–7, 108; modern/
postmodern positions
summarized 103, 104–5,

106–7; Rorty's position 92,
93; Taylor's defence
97–102
role in modernity debate
108–10, 113–15, 174–5,
221
Strauss's analysis of classical
and modern science and
134, 138–9
Epicureanism, postmodern
version 91–3, 166
equality, in Anglo-American
political theory 30
esotericism, of Strauss 139–40,
141, 143
ethical liberalism
in liberal–communitarian
debate 6
need for modernity theory
and 26, 211
ethico-political philosophy 44,
103–7, 115, 129–84
evil and suffering 88–9
nature/convention:
clarification 131–7; divine
madness and political
theory 162–73; habits and
political theory 145–62,
171; reinterpretation
137–45
relation to modernity debate
173–84, 220–6
rights-based liberalism and
219–20
ethics
Foucault's thinking 85–6
MacIntyre and the
Enlightenment project 46–8
rebirth of political theory and
3–4, 29–30
evil
suffering and 88–9

two senses of 74 n. 51,
112–13, 114, 176–9, 217
expressivism, Taylor 99–101

fascism
'evil' in national socialism
177–8, 217
Strauss's third wave of
modernity and 64
fear, liberalism of 5
Fish, Stanley 81
postmodern 'Epicurean' 91
Foucault, Michel, postmodern
scepticism 85–6, 101–2,
104, 107
Frankfurt School, two senses of
modernity 43
freedom, in liberal–
communitarian debate 4–5,
216–17
Freud, Sigmund, Mestrovic's
analysis of cultural habits
157, 158

Gadamer, Hans-Georg
habits 152
Plato and Aristotle 149–50,
172
Gay, Peter, Enlightenment 109
Giddens, Anthony
modernity 41, 42
reflexive modernization 206–7
utopian realism 19, 21
globalization 202–3, 204, 206,
208–9, 222–4
Gnosticism, second overcoming
of 57–60
good
in liberal–communitarian
debate 4, 5, 216–17: ethical
liberalism 6
teaching or development of

virtue 148, 149–51, 171
*see also* ethico-political
philosophy
good life, MacIntyre's
conception of virtue and
153–6
group rights 218–20

Habermas, Jürgen
ethics and politics 104, 105–6
reassertion of rationality
94–7, 108, 110–11
social integration 96–7
Taylor's critique of 100–1
habits 145–62, 171
classical philosophy 148–51
material conditions 151–2
natural conditions of politics
157–62
or practices 153–6
temporality 152–3
Hampsher-Monk, Iain, history
of political thought 11
Hansen, Philip, on Arendt 177
Harvey, David, postmodernity
42–3
Hegel, G. W. F.
Enlightenment legacy 110
Strauss's second wave of
modernity and 62–3
Heidegger, Martin
Löwith and Strauss and 56
national socialism of 84
Heraclitus, nature 135
history of political thought
9–13
habits 152–3
implications of modernity
debate for 214–15
Toulmin and MacIntyre's
modernity, implications of
54–5

*see also* Dunn, John
Hobbes, Thomas, pre-modern political philosophy rejected 61, 65–6
Holmes, Stephen, illegitimacy of modernity 54
Homer, nature 135
Honig, Bonnie
liberal–communitarian debate 8
postmodern soft-scepticism 88, 89–90
Hume, David, reason 160
Hurley, Susan, natural reason 162–3
Huyssens, A., postmodernism described 80
hyperreality 87, 166

information technology 202, 203, 205, 206
instrumentalism
Dunn's 'modern prudence' and 19
Habermas's critique of 96–7
Taylor 98–102, 106
international relations, political theory 222–4
Irwin, Terence, naturalists 135

Jay, Martin, on Habermas's defence of modernism 95–6
Judaism, Löwith's views on eschatological schemes of 56, 57

Kant, Immanuel
classicism of 130
displacement of politics in thought of 89–90
Eichmann's reference to 177
Enlightenment legacy 110

Strauss's second wave of modernity and 62–3
Kymlicka, Will
Anglo-American political theory 29, 30
liberal–communitarian debate 7, 216

language
history of political thought and 11, 214–15
Leibniz's ideas on 51
Lash, Scott
reflexive modernization 206–7
socio-economic change and political theory 67–8
late modernity 205, 206–7
Leibniz, Gottfried Wilhelm von, language 51
liberal democracy
liberal–communitarian debate 6
Strauss's ideas on pre-modern thought 64
liberal modernism, Clark's dogmas of 163–70, 171
liberal–communitarian debate
ontological and advocacy levels 5, 6, 109–10
rebirth of political theory and 4–8, 29–30
tasks of political theory 216–20
liberalism
evolution of 6
problems of 26–8, 210, 211
rights-based 218–20
Lipovetsky, Giles, Bauman's criticism of 180
literary criticism, postmodernist 81, 91

Locke, John, Dunn's
  interpretations 16–18, 23,
  210
Löwith, Karl
  Blumenberg's critique of 57
  illegitimacy of modernity 56
Lyon, David
  postmodernity 200
  progress 202
Lyotard, Jean-François
  Enlightenment role 108
  postmodern mood 81, 82, 86,
  87
  progress 202
  Rorty's differences with 92–3

Machiavelli, pre-modern
  political philosophy rejected
  61, 64
MacIntyre, Alisdair 45
  communitarianism of 5
  'Enlightenment project' 45–8,
  108, 155–6
  habits or practices 153–6,
  161
  Toulmin's modernity,
  comparison with 52–5, 59
  virtue 153–6, 224
Man, Paul de 84
Marxism, rebirth of Anglo-
  American political theory
  and 8
Masters, Roger, nature 145
material conditions, habits and
  political theory 151–2
McCarthy, Thomas, Habermas's
  ethics and politics 105
McMylor, Peter, practices 153,
  155
memory, importance to politics
  152–3
Mestrovic, Stjepan, habits 146,

147, 157–62
minority rights 218–19
modernity, need for a theory of
  26–31
modernity debate
  defenders of modern mood
  93–102: Habermas 94–7;
  Taylor 97–102
  Enlightenment role in
  108–10, 113–15, 174–5
  ethico-political philosophy
  173–84
  evil and Evil 112–13
  implications for political
  theory 220–6
  nature issue, ethics and
  politics 102, 103–7, 114,
  220–1
  postmodern moods and
  political theory 79–93
  rationality 102, 103, 114
  temporality 102–3, 114, 115
  two senses of modernity
  39–70, 107: *see also* mood,
  modernity as; socio-cultural
  form, modernity
mood, modernity as 39–42,
  43–4
  Blumenberg 55–60, 64–7
  Enlightenment core values
  114–15
  MacIntyre 45–8, 52–5, 59
  socio-cultural form of
  modernity and 67–9, 107,
  110–12, 115, 151–2,
  175–9
  Strauss 55–6, 60–7
  Toulmin 48–55, 59
morality *see* ethico-political
  philosophy; ethics
Mouffe, Chantal, postmodern
  soft-scepticism 88, 93

Mullhall, Stephen, liberal–
    communitarian debate 4
musicians, postmodernist 81

national socialism, evil
    explored 177–8, 217
nature
  Blumenberg and Strauss
      integrated 65–7
  ethico-political philosophy
      103–7, 114, 115, 129–84:
      divine madness and political
      theory 162–73; habits and
      political theory 145–62,
      171; nature/convention
      clarified 131–7; nature/
      convention reinterpreted
      137–45; relation to
      modernity debate 173–84,
      220–6
  evil 88–9, 112–13, 114
  implications for modernity
      debate 209
  Strauss's waves of modernity
      and 61–4
  Taylor's instrumentalism and
      99–102
new history of political thought
    10–13
  language and 215
  *see also* Dunn, John
Nietzsche, Friedrich Wilhelm
  Enlightenment legacy 110
  Habermas's criticism of 95
  Honig's reading of 90
  influence on Strauss 63–4,
      140, 141–2
  MacIntyre's Enlightenment
      project 46
nihilism
  Baudrillard 87–8
  Honig's reading of Kant and

Nietzsche 90
  in positivistic social science
      97
*nomos*, ethics and politics 44,
    104–5, 107, 135, 144

Oakeshott, Michael, habits 152
ontological divisions, modernity
    debate 109–10, 111–12,
    115

philosophical paganism 170–1,
    172–3
*physis*, ethics and politics 107,
    135
Plato
  defence of philosophy 138
  dialogic interpretation 142–3
  habits 148–51
  modernism of 130
  naturalism 136, 141, 144,
      145, 162
Pocock, J. G. A., historical
    stories 152
political science, implications of
    science for 133
political theory
  contextualization of 9–13
  ethico-political imperative
      129–30, 220–6
  of international relations
      222–4
  natural conditions: divine
      madness 162–73; habits
      145–62, 171
  postmodern moods and, in
      the modernity debate
      79–93
  postmodernities 199–210
  tasks of 13–28, 29, 69–70,
      210–20: language and
      history 214–15; liberal–

communitarian and
modern–postmodern debate
216–20; risk and prudence
16, 18–19, 20–5, 26, 210,
211–14, 218
*see also* Anglo-American
political theory
Porter, Roy, Enlightenment 108
positivistic social science
habits 147
instrumental reason in 96–7
post-industrialism 201–3
Poster, Mark
hyperreality 87
post-industrialism and
postmodernity 202
postmodern critical theory,
Mestrovic 157–61
postmodern mood
defenders of modern mood
93–102: Habermas 94–7;
Taylor 97–102
ethics and politics 103–7,
114, 179–83
as historical condition 43
as mood within modernity
200–1
nature/convention: Clark's
liberal modernist dogmas
and 165, 166–9, 171;
ethics and politics 103–7,
114; habits 147–8;
implications for modernity
debate 220–1
postmodern soft-scepticism
*see under names*
political theory and 79–93:
postmodern epicureanism
91–3; postmodern sceptics
83–91
rationality 103, 114
as a return to pre-Cartesian

moderns 53
temporality 102–3, 114
use of term in modernity
debate 78–9
postmodernity 199–210
definition of 199–201
elements of 201–6
or late modernity 206–7
putting modernity in question
207–10
poststructuralism
Ashley on 85
inclusion in postmodernism
81
practices, or habits 153–6
Press, Gerald, classical
interpretation 136
prudence 16, 18–19, 20–5, 26,
210, 211–14, 218

rationality *see* reason
Rawls, John 2
Bloom's critique 27–8
Dunn's critique 14–15, 18
liberal–communitarian debate
4, 5, 216: displacement of
politics 8; ethical liberalism
6; reflective equilibrium 7
realism
Bellamy's liberalism 26–7
notions of prudence and 19,
21
reason
Dunn's 'modern prudence' 19
Enlightenment project 47–8
Habermas's reassertion of
rationality 94–7
liberal modernist dogmas and
164–70
modern and postmodern
defences 103, 114
natural laws and: Strauss's

waves of modernity 62–3;
*see also* ethico-political
philosophy
tasks of political theory and
70
Taylor's instrumentalism
98–102, 106
in Toulmin's 'hidden agenda'
of modernity 49–52
reflective equilibrium, liberal–
communitarian debate 7
reflexive modernization 206–7
relativism
postmodern sceptics and 84,
166–7
two senses of modernity 68
religion
classical/modern philosophy
138–9
Löwith's views on
eschatological schemes 56,
57
second overcoming of
Gnosticism 57–60
rights-based liberalism 218–20
risk
implications for modernity
222–4
in reflexively modern culture
207
in tasks of political theory
211–14
*see also* prudence
Rorty, Richard
influence on Bellamy 26
political and ethical
distinctions 104–5
postmodernism of 81, 82:
'Epicurean' 91–3, 166;
Habermas's criticism 97
Rosen, Stanley, classical models
130, 138–42, 143, 144,

161, 172
Rosenau, Pauline
affirmative postmodernism 90
Baudrillard's scepticism 87
Rousseau, Jean-Jacques, second
wave of modernity 62
Ryan, Michael, postmodernism
80–1

Sandel, Michael, liberal–
communitarian debate 4, 5,
7, 8
Schopenhauer, Arthur, habits
and desire 157, 158
self-assertion, as defining feature
of modernity 60, 65, 66
self-preservation, Blumenberg's
ideas on 58–9, 65–6
self-understanding, modern
identity 97–102, 107
Shapiro, Michael, postmodern
soft-scepticism 88
Shklar, Judith, liberalism of fear
5
Simmel, Georg, cultural habits
157, 158
Sinclair, nature 135
Skinner, Quentin
history of political thought
10, 11–13; Tully's analysis
12–13, 25
Locke's influence 23
Smart, Barry, post-industrialism
and postmodernity 202
social theory
John Dunn's critique of
15–16, 18–19
liberal–communitarian debate
6, 8, 26
socio-cultural form, modernity
39–43
and modernity as mood 67–9,

107, 110–12, 115, 151–2,
175–9
reflexive modernization 208
risk and prudence and
211–13
Toulmin's linkage of mood
and 49–51
Socrates
habits 148
naturalism 136
*sophistai* 135, 149–50
Spengler, Oswald, critique of
modernity 61
Squires, Judith, postmodernism
90–1
*Stimmung*, modernity as mood
41, 44
Strauss, Leo 55–6, 60–4
classical science and 132–4,
136–44, 161, 169–70, 172
Enlightenment and 134,
138–9
integration of Blumenberg's
ideas 64–7
Swift, Adam, liberal–
communitarian debate 4
system integration, Habermas
96

Taylor, Charles
core of Anglo-American
political theory 30
ethics and politics 106–7
on Foucault's truth 85
liberal–communitarian debate
216: ontological and
advocacy levels 5, 6,
109–10
self-understanding 97–102,
107
technical reason *see*
instrumentalism

temporality
Blumenberg and Strauss's
analyses 56–65, 67
Connolly's conception of
40–1
Enlightenment complexity and
174–5
Giddens' conception of 41
habits and political theory
152–3
MacIntyre and Toulmin's
analyses 45–6, 48–52, 53
modernity as historically
generated condition 43
moderns and postmoderns
102–3, 114, 115
theory-centred philosophy 49
Toulmin, Stephen 45, 48–52
MacIntyre's modernity
compared 52–5, 59
scientific phase 49–52, 133
tradition
late modernity 206–7
notions of 154–5
trust and trustworthiness
implications for modernity
207–9, 222–4
prudence and 18, 19, 21–4
truth
Foucault's position on 85
hyperreality and 87
science not value free 169–70
Tully, James, history of political
thought 12–13, 25

Unger, Roberto, prudence
21–2
Urry, John
reflexive modernization
206–7
socio-economic change and
political theory 68

utopian realism, notions of
prudence and 19, 21

Veblen, Thorstein, habits 147,
157
virtue
MacIntyre's conception of
153–6, 224
teaching or development of
148, 149–51, 171
trust and 224

Walker, Rob, postmodern soft-
scepticism 88
Wallace, Robert M., second

overcoming of Gnosticism
57, 60
Walzer, Michael, liberal–
communitarian debate 5, 7,
216
West, Cornell, postmodern
'Epicurean' 91
White, Stephen, postmodernity
205

Yack, Bernard, total revolution
92

Zolo, Danilo, influence on
Bellamy 26